Bar and Beverage Management

ManageFirst
PROGRAM®

NATIONAL
RESTAURANT
ASSOCIATION®

PEARSON

Boston   Columbus   Indianapolis   New York   San Francisco   Upper Saddle River

Amsterdam   Cape Town   Dubai   London   Madrid   Milan   Munich   Paris   Montréal   Toronto

Delhi   Mexico City   São Paulo   Sydney   Hong Kong   Seoul   Singapore   Taipei   Tokyo

Pearson

Editorial Director: Vernon R. Anthony
Executive Acquisitions Editor: Alli Gentile
NRA Product Development: Randall Towns and
Todd Schlender
Senior Managing Editor: JoEllen Gohr
Associate Managing Editor: Alexandrina B. Wolf
Senior Operations Supervisor: Pat Tonneman
Senior Operations Specialist: Deidra Skahill
Cover photo: Steve Cukrov

Cover design: Karen Steinberg, Element LLC
Director of Marketing: David Gesell
Senior Marketing Manager: Thomas Hayward
Marketing Coordinator: Les Roberts
Full-Service Project Management: Barbara Hawk and
Kevin J. Gray, Element LLC
Text and Cover Printer/Binder: LSC Communications
/Harrisonburg
Text Font: Minion Pro, Myriad Pro Semicondensed

Photography Credits

Front matter: i Steve Cukrov/Cutcaster; vii (left) Suhendri Utet/Dreamstime; (right) Meryll/Dreamstime;
viii (top) Mtr/Dreamstime; (bottom) Stratum/Dreamstime; ix (bottom left) Aprescindere/Dreamstime;
xiii, 20, 162, 251 Giovanni Reda/Courtesy of Spike TV; xv (bottom left) Petar Neychev/Dreamstime;
24, 75, 97, 125, 187, 237, 269 Nikada/istockphoto; 109 Annamarie Boley/Element LLC

All other photographs owned or acquired by the National Restaurant Association Educational Foundation, NRAEF

9 2022

ISBN-10:   0-13-272573-8
ISBN-13: 978-0-13-272573-6

ISBN-10:   0-13-274173-3
ISBN-13: 978-0-13-274173-6

Contents in Brief

Contents

HB 06.17.2022 1347

About the National Restaurant Association and the National Restaurant Association Educational Foundation

Founded in 1919, the National Restaurant Association (NRA) is the leading business association for the restaurant and foodservice industry, which comprises 960,000 restaurant and foodservice outlets and a workforce of nearly 13 million employees. We represent the industry in Washington, DC, and advocate on its behalf. We operate the industry's largest trade show (NRA Show, restaurant.org/show); leading food safety training and certification program (ServSafe, servsafe.com); unique career-building high school program (the NRAEF's *ProStart*, prostart.restaurant.org); as well as the *Kids LiveWell* program (restaurant.org/kidslivewell) promoting healthful kids' menu options. For more information, visit www.restaurant.org and find us on Twitter *@WeRRestaurants*, *Facebook*, and *YouTube*.

With the first job experience of one in four U.S. adults occurring in a restaurant or foodservice operation, the industry is uniquely attractive among American industries for entry-level jobs, personal development and growth, employee and manager career paths, and ownership and wealth creation. That is why the National Restaurant Association Educational Foundation (nraef.org), the philanthropic foundation of the NRA, furthers the education of tomorrow's restaurant and foodservice industry professionals and plays a key role in promoting job and career opportunities in the industry by allocating millions of dollars a year toward industry scholarships and educational programs. The NRA works to ensure the most qualified and passionate people enter the industry so that we can better meet the needs of our members and the patrons and clients they serve.

What Is the ManageFirst Program?

The ManageFirst Program is a management training certificate program that exemplifies our commitment to developing materials by the industry, for the industry. The program's

most powerful strength is that it is based on a set of competencies defined by the restaurant and foodservice industry as critical for success. The program teaches the skills truly valued by industry professionals.

ManageFirst Program Components

The NRAEF ManageFirst Program includes a set of books, exams, instructor resources, certificates, a new credential, and support activities and services. By participating in the program, you are demonstrating your commitment to becoming a highly qualified professional either preparing to begin or to advance your career in the restaurant, hospitality, and foodservice industry.

These books cover the range of topics listed in the chart above. You will find the essential content for the topic as defined by industry, as well as learning activities, assessments, case studies, suggested field projects, professional profiles, and testimonials. The exam can be administered either online or in a paper-and-pencil format (see inside front cover for a listing of ISBNs), and it will be proctored. Upon successfully passing the exam, you will be furnished with a customized certificate by the NRAEF. The certificate is a lasting recognition of your accomplishment and a signal to the industry that you have mastered the competencies covered within the particular topic.

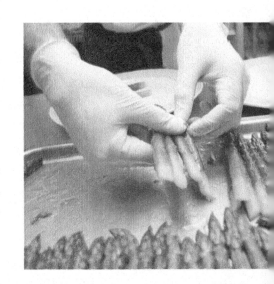

To earn the NRAEF's new credential, you will be required to pass four core exams and one foundation exam (to be chosen from the remaining program topics) and to document your work experience in the restaurant and foodservice industry. Earning the NRAEF credential is a significant accomplishment.

We applaud you as you either begin or advance your career in the restaurant, hospitality, and foodservice industry. Visit www.nraef.org to learn about additional career-building resources offered by the NRAEF, including scholarships for college students enrolled in relevant industry programs.

MANAGEFIRST PROGRAM ORDERING INFORMATION

Review copies or support materials

FACULTY FIELD SERVICES
Tel: 800.526.0485

Domestic orders and inquiries

PEARSON CUSTOMER SERVICE
Tel: 800.922.0579
http://www.pearsonhighered.com/

International orders and inquiries

U.S. EXPORT SALES OFFICE
Pearson Education International Customer Service Group
200 Old Tappan Road
Old Tappan, NJ 07675 USA
Tel: 201.767.5021
Fax: 201.767.5625

For corporate, government, and special sales (consultants, corporations, training centers, VARs, and corporate resellers) orders and inquiries

PEARSON CORPORATE SALES
Tel: 317.428.3411
Fax: 317.428.3343
Email: managefirst@prenhall.com

For additional information regarding other Pearson publications, instructor and student support materials, locating your sales representative, and much more, please visit *www.pearsonhighered.com/managefirst*.

Acknowledgements

The National Restaurant Association Educational Foundation is grateful for the significant contributions made to this book by the following individuals.

Mike Amos
Perkins & Marie Callender's Inc.

Steve Belt
Monical's Pizza

Heather Kane Haberer
Carrols Restaurant Group

Erika Hoover
Monical's Pizza Corp.

Jared Kulka
Red Robin Gourmet Burgers

Tony C. Merritt
Carrols Restaurant Group

H. George Neil
Buffalo Wild Wings

Marci Noguiera
Sodexo—Education Division

Ryan Nowicki
Dave & Busters

Penny Ann Lord Prichard
Wake Tech/NC Community College

Michael Santos
Micatrotto Restaurant Group

Heather Thitoff
Cameron Mitchell Restaurants

Features of the ManageFirst Books

We have designed the ManageFirst Books to enhance your ability to learn and retain important information that is critical to this restaurant and foodservice industry function. Here are the key features you will find within this book.

BEGINNING EACH BOOK

Real Manager

This is your opportunity to meet a professional who is currently working in the field associated with the book's topic. This person's story will help you gain insight into the responsibilities related to his or her position, as well as the training and educational history linked to it. You will also see the daily and cumulative impact this position has on an operation, and receive advice from a person who has successfully met the challenges of being a manager.

BEGINNING EACH CHAPTER

Inside This Chapter

Chapter content is organized under these major headings.

Learning Objectives

Learning objectives identify what you should be able to do after completing each chapter. These objectives are linked to the required tasks a manager must be able to perform in relation to the function discussed in the book.

Case Study

Each chapter begins with a brief story about the kind of situations that a manager may encounter in the course of his or her work. The story is followed by one or two questions to prompt student discussions about the topics contained within the chapter.

Key Terms

These terms are important for thorough understanding of the chapter's content. They are highlighted throughout the chapter, where they are explicitly defined or their meaning is made clear within the paragraphs in which they appear.

THROUGHOUT EACH CHAPTER

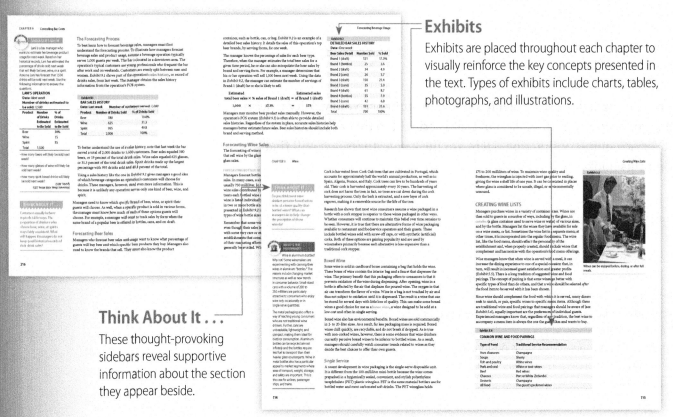

Exhibits

Exhibits are placed throughout each chapter to visually reinforce the key concepts presented in the text. Types of exhibits include charts, tables, photographs, and illustrations.

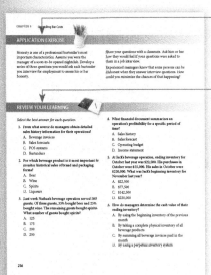

Think About It . . .

These thought-provoking sidebars reveal supportive information about the section they appear beside.

AT THE END OF EACH CHAPTER

Application Exercises and Review Your Learning

These multiple-choice or open- or close-ended questions or problems are designed to test your knowledge of the concepts presented in the chapter. These questions have been aligned with the objectives and should provide you with an opportunity to practice or apply the content that supports these objectives. If you have difficulty answering the Review Your Learning questions, you should review the content further.

AT THE END OF THE BOOK

Field Project

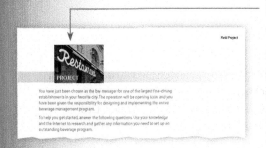

This real-world project gives you the valuable opportunity to apply many of the concepts you will learn in a competency guide. You will interact with industry practitioners, enhance your knowledge, and research, apply, analyze, evaluate, and report on your findings. It will provide you with an in-depth "reality check" of the policies and practices of this management function.

REAL MANAGER

Jon Taffer

Host and co-executive producer,
Bar Rescue on SPIKE TV

Chair, *Taffer Dynamics, Inc.*

Philosophy: It's all about the guest. I own the term Reaction Management™ and that expression sums up all that I believe. The chef in the kitchen is *not* preparing an entrée; he or she is, in fact, preparing a guest reaction. When that plate hits the table, one of two things will happen . . .

1. The guest *reacts*—sits up, looks at his or her and the other plates, thereby reacting to them, or

2. Nothing happens. The guest does *not* react. If nothing happens, that restaurant or bar will be "stuck."

Remember, the entrée is in fact the vehicle, not the product. The product is the reaction. Some managers are pleased with an entrée. I will redesign that plate a hundred times until the guest sits up and reacts. That is who I am. I live to create employee and guest reactions.

MY BACKGROUND

I grew up in Great Neck, Long Island, New York. My family has a two-generation background in consumer marketing. Both my grandfather and uncle were well-respected direct marketing and communication experts who helped develop that industry by working with famous established and emerging brands. I had a two-year stop at University of Denver after high school and then, like many others, I migrated to Southern California to chase my dreams.

I've always assumed the lead—even back at summer camp when I was 10 years old. I started a company running errands for the counselors. I had six to eight friends working for me, and I split the hourly fee with them. While they did the work, I counted the quarters. I believe people are born leaders; I don't believe they become them.

Here's my original and absolute view: No one ever said the Pied Piper was a good musician—but peopled followed. Leaders do not always lead from knowledge or experience; most lead with heart, and then use experience to make things happen.

MY CAREER PATH

My career path was anything but direct. I was a musician (a drummer), playing with bands in the Los Angeles club circuit. We played at clubs like the Whisky a Go Go, The Roxy, The Troubadour, and the Starwood. Thirty years later, all of these venues are still going strong, except for the Starwood.

To make a living while trying to "make my mark" in the music business, I took a job at Doug Weston's Troubadour as a doorman. The "Troub" is a famous club that has launched some of contemporary music's

most talented performers. In my case, though, I fell in love with the club business and really got into making the place better. Maybe because of my energy, commitment, or just my sheer enthusiasm, I became the manager of the Troubadour in a surprisingly short time.

I learned many things at the Troub that have helped me to this day—mostly about the power of controls and the environment. First of all, the club had no controls. Employees ate, drank, and gave the place away without a second thought. I saw this legendary venue regarded as one of the best in the world—but it never made money. As manager, I ran the place with cash from a safe day to day, hoping I had money to buy the necessary products and pay the people to open up. Fixing the Troubadour meant managing a staff that had never been managed before. Learning how to do that with a rock and roll staff—without a mutiny and with keeping everyone motivated—was a powerful lesson in management. As a result, I learned how to say no and take control as a young rookie, in a totally unmanaged venue, with no previous training. The result gave me confidence that I could accomplish things I never thought I could by sheer will and desire.

Next, I learned the power of environment or ambience. As a musician and manager of a music venue, I saw the importance of energy and entertainment. I believe that this is the single most important lesson I have acquired. For example, you can see how the same 10 songs, played in a different order, provide a completely different experience. Feeling the impact of pace or tempo, content, music mix, and other factors had a strong impact on me. As a result, I have the only federal patent ever issued for "managing music to achieve a desired ambience in hospitality properties." Music identity, pace, and content all impact sales—not only in bars, but in virtually *every* type of hospitality property, including quick-service restaurants, casual dining, fine-dining, and hotels. Who wants to go to a restaurant or bar that's "uncool"? And not enough operators get that.

Remember: **This business is all about people. To be successful, you have to love looking each guest and employee in the eye every day. Great operators and great managers connect!**

When I left the Troubador, I went to Barney's Beanery as lead bartender/night manager. This place was the opposite of the Troubadour. Barney's owner was *all* about controls. He used tight inventory management and controls systems. Looking back, I realize that I never chose my career. I just loved each step I took . . . and so I kept going.

I'm a self-trained man. In my specific work, I like to keep my thoughts and processes original, not contaminated by the "predeterminations of others." I know this is a unique perspective, but it has worked for me. I have been everything from mixologist, to kitchen manager, to restaurant general

manager, to hotel general manager, to resort food and beverage director, to VP of operations, to owner—but I love the bar business. Making people smile is a nice legacy.

Here's how I feel: The second public building built in America was a bar (pub). Our first distiller was George Washington, and one of our first vineyards was grown by Thomas Jefferson. Our independence was first discussed in a bar, as was the bill of rights. Bars were the center of our early communities and, to this day, provide locations where business deals, candidacies, and marriages are discussed. Bars are in the center of the "American fiber," and I want to keep the focus on that.

Something I always think about: **First and foremost, sensitivity to all environmental aspects of the guest experience is critical. As I said earlier, I love creating guest reactions. Over the past 30 years, my quest for creating the best guest reactions has led me to become a bit of a scientist. Based on my experiences, I believe we can purposefully effect a huge impact on the sales and profitability of a business by embracing the concept of guest reactions.**

MY ADVICE TO YOU

Over the years, I've learned much that I still use every day. One thing I teach regularly is the real meaning of operating standards. Standards are measurements of performance that are: Qualifiable (what you do); Quantifiable (when you do it); Verifiable (I'll make sure you do it).

The other point that really hit home with me was when a senior hotel executive once said, "You look, but you don't see." I was depressed for days over that, and then I began to train my eye to see. Now I see things that many others miss.

Remember: **Real, sustained success in this business comes from a genuine and sincere desire to create great guest experiences. Financial modeling, décor, product specs, HR selection, and training are all foundations from which to build the experience. If any of them steal from the guest experience, they rob you of potential. No experience, no business. Invest in your guest!**

1

Alcoholic Beverages

CHAPTER LEARNING OBJECTIVES

After completing this chapter, you should be able to:

- Explain the chemical makeup of beverage alcohol.
- Explain the physiological effects of drinking alcohol.
- Describe the history of alcoholic beverage consumption in the United States from its founding through the present.
- Identify the current consumer trends affecting the consumption and marketing of alcoholic beverages.
- Identify the different types of establishments serving alcoholic beverages.

KEY TERMS

alcoholic beverage, p. 4

beer, p. 5

blood alcohol content (BAC), p. 6

blue laws, p. 11

distillation, p. 5

dry (wine), p. 15

fermentation, p. 5

intoxication, p. 7

lager, p. 13

legally impaired, p. 7

liqueur, p. 16

liquor, p. 5

mixed drink, p. 16

oenology, p. 15

Prohibition, p. 10

proof, p. 15

spirits, p. 5

straight (drink), p. 16

sweet (wine), p. 15

wine, p. 5

wine list, p. 15

CASE STUDY

"I don't know," Jack says. "I think maybe just beer and wine would be enough."

"I understand what you're saying, but it won't cost that much more to add liquor," replies Jana. "And I think it would be really good for business."

Jack and Jana are talking about the soon-to-be-opened Mainsail Restaurant. Jana was the owner of the Mainsail and she had hired Jack to be the restaurant's manager. They are discussing applying to their state's regulatory agency for a license to sell alcoholic beverages. From prior discussions with that agency, Jana knows her new operation would qualify for the license of her choice.

Jack feels that a beverage license permitting the Mainsail to sell only beer and wine would be enough to satisfy the great majority of the new establishment's customers. Jana feels the addition of liquor products to the beer and wine they had already agreed to sell could expand their customer base and might make the operation even more profitable.

"Well," says Jack, "I guess adding the liquor could attract more customers, but what about the extra effort that goes along with that. Do you think it will be worth it?"

1. Why do you think it will be important for Jack and Jana to understand what their target customers like to drink before, during, and after their meals prior to making this important decision?

2. Why do you think serving alcoholic beverage products generally makes a restaurant more attractive to potential guests than similar restaurants that do not serve these popular beverages?

Exhibit 1.1

AN OVERVIEW OF ALCOHOLIC BEVERAGES

The history of alcoholic beverages is a long one. An alcoholic beverage is defined as any drinkable liquid that contains ethyl alcohol (*Exhibit 1.1*). It is unknown when the first alcoholic beverage was created. However, evidence suggests the first liquids fermented to create an alcoholic beverage were produced between 10,000 and 5000 B.C.

Today, managers know that the sale and responsible service of alcoholic beverages can play a large role in satisfying their customers. It also can help make and keep operations profitable. The effective management of bars and restaurants and the alcoholic beverages served in them is an essential management skill. This book presents important information about the way professional managers purchase, store, and responsibly serve alcoholic beverages to guests.

There is no question that the popularity of alcoholic beverages means many customers enjoy drinking them with meals and in other settings. It is also important to recognize, however, that no restaurant or foodservice business or manager has a "right" to serve alcohol. Rather, it is a privilege that is carefully regulated by law, and one that should not be taken lightly. To begin the study of alcoholic beverages and the professional management of them, it is important to know about three things:

- The history of alcoholic beverages
- The chemistry of alcohol
- The physiological effects of alcohol

The History of Alcoholic Beverages

Alcoholic beverages have been used throughout all of history. From the earliest times to the present, alcohol has played an important role in the lives of individuals and in society.

Alcoholic beverages played a key role in the health and diet of ancient civilizations. The medicinal value of alcoholic beverages has long been recognized by many societies. In the days before clean water was readily available to large numbers of people, alcoholic beverages provided a safe thirst quencher. The way they are produced and their resulting chemical makeup mean many alcoholic beverages contain few disease-causing bacteria. Because beer and wine were not associated with the diseases caused by drinking contaminated water, they became an accepted part of everyday meals. They were particularly important for travelers, who had to be especially cautious about contracting strange diseases.

Alcoholic beverages also have been an important source of nutrients and calories for large numbers of people. In ancient Egypt, the phrase "bread and beer" stood for all food and was also a common greeting. Many alcoholic beverages contain high levels of protein, fat, and carbohydrates. This fact helps explain the frequent lack of nutritional deficiencies in some populations whose diets are generally poor, but who consume moderate amounts of alcoholic beverages.

Whether for religious, health, or nutritional purposes, or for the simple reason of enjoyment, alcoholic beverages have been consumed in a variety of ways:

- Warm
- Chilled
- Pure (by itself)
- Flavored
- Mixed with water
- Mixed with other beverages

Regardless of how it is served, it is the unique chemical composition of the alcohol in each of these combinations that makes these beverages so popular with so many people.

The Chemistry of Alcohol

Alcohol is a colorless liquid created by fermenting a liquid containing sugar. Fermentation is a chemical reaction that splits a molecule of sugar into equal parts of ethyl alcohol and carbon dioxide. This chemical reaction is caused by yeast. The yeast may occur naturally or be introduced into the process by a beverage maker. After fermentation, the carbon dioxide escapes into the air and the ethyl alcohol remains in the liquid. The result is an alcoholic beverage.

Remember that an alcoholic beverage is any drinkable liquid that contains ethyl alcohol. Government regulations set minimum and maximum amounts of alcohol for various types of alcoholic beverages. Generally speaking, alcoholic beverages can contain as little as 2 percent ethyl alcohol or as much as 80 percent.

One way to classify alcoholic beverages is by identifying them as wine, beer, or a spirit. Wine is the term used for an alcoholic beverage produced from fermented fruit and especially grapes. Beer is fermented from cereals and malts and is usually flavored with hops. Spirits are made by distillation. Distilling is the process of removing water from a liquid that contains alcohol. Spirits are sometimes referred to as "hard liquor" or liquor because of the greater percentage of alcohol these concentrated beverages contain.

KEEPING IT SAFE

Liquids containing 40 percent alcohol will catch on fire if heated to about 79°F (26°C) and then an ignition source such as a spark or flame is applied to it. This is called the "flash point" of the beverage. The flash point of pure alcohol is 62.9°F (17.17°C), which is less than the average room temperature in a restaurant or foodservice operation. Alcoholic beverages with lower concentrations of alcohol, such as wine, can also be set aflame if they are heated sufficiently and then ignited.

Managers take advantage of this flammable property of alcohol when they create flavorful flambéed dishes. But all beverage managers need to recognize the danger in handling highly flammable alcoholic beverages. Safety in bars is important for employees and customers; managers must ensure that all their employees understand the fire risks associated with storing and serving alcoholic beverages.

In the United States, some states vary the legal requirements of beverage operations based on whether the facility sells beer; beer and wine; or beer, wine, and spirits. In most cases, local governments regulate the sale of spirits to a greater degree than wine or beer. This makes sense because the alcohol content of spirits is generally many times higher than that of wine and beers. Managers must be familiar with these regulations; while the greatest numbers of people enjoy alcoholic beverages in moderation, some abuse it by consuming too much.

In moderation, alcohol has a tranquilizing effect. It relaxes, stimulates the appetite, and provides a sense of well-being or happiness. In large quantities, it can become an addictive and even deadly toxin. It is because of their physiological effects that the service of alcoholic beverages is so tightly regulated and their responsible sale is so critically important to managers.

The Physiological Effects of Alcohol

Managers, bartenders, servers, and other key personnel must know how alcohol affects customers. The three basic processes that take place when alcohol enters the body are absorption, distribution, and elimination. First, alcohol is absorbed into the bloodstream. A small percentage is absorbed in the mouth and stomach, but most of the alcohol is absorbed in the small intestine.

If the stomach is full of food, the absorption process is slowed down since the food must be digested before it goes to the small intestine, and the alcohol does not act on the system as quickly. The type of food consumed also affects the absorption rate. Fatty food such as cheese, nuts, and fried food take longer to digest than high-carbohydrate food such as pasta, breads, and fruit. Once alcohol is absorbed into the bloodstream, it is distributed to the different body organs in a ratio based on the amount of water each organ contains. The brain, which has a high water content, receives a high percentage of the alcohol.

Once alcohol is absorbed into the bloodstream, for legal purposes it is measured in its percentage of blood alcohol content (BAC). BAC is the amount of alcohol contained in the blood of a drinker. A BAC of 0.10 means 1 gram of alcohol per 1,000 grams of blood. While the effect of alcohol varies widely by individual, the impact of different BAC levels has been well studied and generalizations about their effect can be stated:

0.02–0.03 BAC: No loss of coordination, slight euphoria and loss of shyness. Depressant effects not apparent.

0.04–0.06 BAC: Feeling of well-being, relaxation, lower inhibitions, sensation of warmth. Some minor impairment of reasoning and memory.

0.07–0.09 BAC: Slight impairment of balance, speech, vision, reaction time, and hearing. Judgment and self-control are reduced, and caution, reason, and memory are impaired. A BAC of 0.08 means the drinker is legally impaired; it is illegal in all states to operate a motor vehicle at this level.

0.10–0.125 BAC: Significant impairment of motor coordination and loss of good judgment. Speech may be slurred; balance, vision, reaction time, and hearing will be impaired.

0.13–0.19 BAC: Gross motor impairment and lack of physical control. Blurred vision. Judgment and perception are severely impaired.

0.20–0.25 BAC: Feeling dazed, confused, or otherwise disoriented. May need help to stand or walk. Blackouts are likely, so drinkers may not remember what has happened. All mental, physical, and sensory functions are severely impaired.

0.30 BAC and above: Drinkers may pass out suddenly and be difficult to awaken. Coma and even death is possible due to respiratory failure.

Intoxication, also known as drunkenness or inebriation, is the physiological state that occurs when a person has a high level of alcohol in his or her blood. The only way to reverse intoxication is to eliminate alcohol from the bloodstream. Alcohol is eliminated from the body by the liver. The liver breaks down and eliminates alcohol at a constant rate of about one drink per hour (*Exhibit 1.2*).

Exhibit 1.2

1 Drink =   or   or   or

5 ounces of wine
(Domestic wine at 12% alcohol)

12 ounces of beer
(American lager at 4–5% alcohol)

1½ ounces of 80-proof liquor

1 ounce of 100-proof liquor

Several factors can affect the BAC of individual guests:

- **Drinking rate and amount consumed:**
  - The liver can remove alcohol from the body at the rate of only one drink per hour. Drinking more than this will result in a buildup of alcohol in the bloodstream, raising BAC.
  - Alcohol can affect guests long after they have stopped drinking, because alcohol will continue to enter their bloodstreams through absorption.
- **Drink strength:** The more alcohol a drink contains, the more that will end up in the bloodstream. This will raise BAC.
- **Body size:** A small person will have a higher BAC than a large person, all other factors being the same. That is because small people have less blood in their bodies to dilute the alcohol.
- **Body fat:** A person with a large percentage of body fat will have a higher BAC than a lean person, all other factors being the same.
  - Body fat does not absorb alcohol. This forces it to remain in the bloodstream until broken down by the liver.
  - Alcohol will pass through muscle in a lean person more quickly and spread throughout the body.
- **Gender:** A woman will have a higher BAC than a man, all other factors being the same (see *Exhibit 1.3*). That is because women are different from men in several ways:
  - Women have a higher percentage of body fat.
  - Women have a smaller amount of a stomach enzyme that helps break down alcohol.
  - Women are typically smaller than men, and so have less blood in their bodies.
- **Age:** An older person will have a higher BAC than a younger guest, all other factors being the same.
  - Body fat typically increases with age.
  - Enzyme action tends to slow as a person gets older.
- **Emotional state:** An emotional guest will have a higher BAC than a guest who is calm, all other factors being the same.
  - When a person is stressed, angry, or afraid, the body diverts blood to the muscles and away from the stomach and small intestine. This reduced blood flow slows the absorption of alcohol into the bloodstream. The guest will not feel the effects of the alcohol and may continue to drink. As the guest begins to calm down and blood flow returns to the stomach, he or she may experience a sudden increase in BAC.

Exhibit 1.3

Men and women usually absorb alcohol at different rates due to their gender and average size.

- **Medications:** Drinking alcohol while taking medications or using illegal drugs can intensify the effects of alcohol or cause dangerous interactions.

- **Food:** A guest who has not eaten will have a higher BAC than a guest who has eaten, all other factors being the same. Food keeps alcohol in the stomach for a longer period of time. This slows the rate at which alcohol reaches the small intestine.

- **Carbonation:** A guest who is drinking a carbonated drink will have a higher BAC than a guest whose drink is not carbonated, all other factors being the same. Carbonation may speed the rate at which alcohol passes through the stomach. This causes a person to reach a higher BAC at a faster rate.

Clearly, it is not in the best interest of management to allow the BAC of customers to get so high that it could result in danger to the customer or to others. Contrary to popular opinion, fresh air, black coffee, and concoctions featuring raw eggs do not affect BAC. The only thing that will reduce the BAC of a drinker is time. For that reason, care and ensuring the safe serving of alcohol is one of a food and beverage manager's most important responsibilities.

ALCOHOLIC BEVERAGE PRODUCTION AND SERVICE IN THE UNITED STATES

Alcoholic beverages are very popular in the United States. To best understand the consumption habits and the laws related to responsible beverage service, managers must first understand the country's history of alcoholic beverage production and consumption in three key time periods:

- Pre-Prohibition
- Prohibition
- Post-Prohibition

Pre-Prohibition

Prior to departing for the New World, the Puritans loaded more beer than water onto the *Mayflower*. In fact, beverages served at the first Thanksgiving included beer, wine, and spirits. The early colonists made alcoholic beverages from carrots, tomatoes, celery, squash, and corn. While alcoholic beverages were popular and widely consumed, the laws of most American colonies required towns to license and monitor the people who were allowed to sell wine and spirits.

Manager's Memo

Those managers whose establishments sell alcoholic beverages have a special responsibility to ensure they do not knowingly sell alcoholic beverages to guests who may cause a danger to themselves or to others.

All states have drunk driving laws that limit how much alcohol can be consumed before it is illegal to drive a motor vehicle. Currently the BAC limits for driving are 0.08 percent, but managers should continually monitor these limits as the limits can change.

Punishments for drunk driving violations include fines, loss of driver's license, and even imprisonment. Many states have similar laws related to the operation of boats, bicycles, and even in-line skates!

Alcoholic beverages and their service were an important part of community life in the colonies. Religious services and court sessions were often held in a town's major tavern. In fact, Thomas Jefferson wrote the first draft of the Declaration of Independence in a tavern in Philadelphia.

As is true today, taxes levied on the production and sale of alcohol were an important part of financing local, state, and federal government activities. While the overconsumption of alcohol was frowned upon in the early years of the country, the moderate use of alcohol was well accepted in most communities.

Prohibition

Beginning in the early 1800s, the temperance movement in the United States began to discourage, and then to seek an outright ban on, the production and consumption of all alcoholic beverages. While some communities already tightly controlled or prohibited the sale of alcohol at that time, members of the temperance movement opposed the consumption of alcohol for a variety of reasons, and they wanted the entire country to become "dry" (without the presence of alcoholic beverages).

The temperance movement was successful in its goals and in 1917, the U.S. Senate proposed the Eighteenth Amendment to the U.S. Constitution. Section 1 of the amendment stated:

> *After one year from the ratification of this article the manufacture, sale, or transportation of intoxicating liquors within, the importation thereof into, or the exportation thereof from the United States and all territory subject to the jurisdiction thereof for beverage purposes is hereby prohibited.*

Because the Eighteenth Amendment prohibited beverage alcohol, the period in which it was in effect in the United States is called Prohibition. Having been approved by 36 states, the Eighteenth Amendment was ratified in January 1919 and went into effect one year later.

It is important to understand that during Prohibition, alcoholic drinks were illegal in the United States, but Canada, Mexico, and the Caribbean maintained flourishing liquor industries. It is also true that although it was not legal to make and sell alcohol in the United States, many groups and individuals still did so.

It is generally recognized that Prohibition was successful in reducing the amount of liquor consumed; however, it also stimulated a large amount of crime, and in many cases, violence. For a variety of reasons, including that thousands of citizens were killed, blinded, or paralyzed as a result of drinking contaminated, unregulated alcohol, Prohibition became increasingly unpopular with the citizens of the United States following the Great Depression that began in 1929.

Post-Prohibition

In 1932, Franklin D. Roosevelt campaigned for president on the promise to repeal Prohibition. Calling on the "wet" rather than "dry" voter to support him, Roosevelt promoted the idea that repeal would bring in new tax revenues. He won the presidency in a landslide, getting 57 percent of the popular vote and carrying all but six states. "What America needs now is a drink," he told the nation in 1933.

Despite the repeal, the use of alcoholic beverages was not quickly re-accepted in American society. The Twenty-First Amendment specifically allowed individual states, counties, and towns to control the sale and usage of alcoholic beverages. It gave each state the right to restrict or even ban the purchase or sale of alcohol. As a result, varieties of state and local alcohol-related laws still exist throughout the United States today.

Every state restricts the sale of alcoholic beverages to those under the age of 21. Most states also have increasingly strict laws against drinking and driving. In addition, the U.S. courts have consistently held that those individuals and groups that sell alcoholic beverages can be held liable for the actions of those they serve. Thus, if a guest who is intoxicated is served additional drinks by an establishment, that establishment can be held liable, or legally responsible, for the resulting actions of the guest.

While the conditions in which alcoholic beverages can be sold varies widely, in nearly all cases those granted permission to sell alcohol will be required to adhere to specific regulations:

- **Hours of sales:** Local communities can prohibit the sale of alcohol before or after a specified time of day. Some communities also have "blue laws" that restrict or prohibit the sale of alcohol on Sundays.

- **Age restrictions:** Local communities set the ages of guests who may buy alcohol, and determine if those guests must be served only in operations that also sell food.

- **Location of sales:** In some states, establishments that serve alcohol are prohibited from operating in close proximity to a school or a church.

- **Records:** Establishments that sell alcohol must keep detailed records of the amount of alcohol purchased and sold.

- **Advertising:** Most states have regulations restricting the types of promotions and advertising that are permitted.

Most states are very careful when authorizing licenses to distribute and sell alcohol. They are also aggressive in revoking the licenses of operations that do not follow the rules for selling alcohol. While the choices of both beverages and serving locations for consumers are greater than ever, the moral and legal responsibilities of establishments that serve those who drink are also greater.

Manager's Memo

When repealing Prohibition, the U.S. federal government explicitly gave states the right to regulate the manufacture and sale of alcoholic beverages within their state borders. For that reasons, in most states decisions regarding the issuance of liquor licenses is primarily made at the state government level.

In some states, the decision has been made to allow counties, cities, and towns to exercise some control over alcoholic beverage sales within their legal jurisdictions. Examples include rules allowing diners to bring in their own wines for consumption with meals and taking unfinished bottles of wine home with them after meals. Because rules can vary, managers must ensure they know and follow all of the state and local rules that may affect the service of alcoholic beverages at the locations they manage.

Exhibit 1.4

Illinois Liquor Control Commission

To be sold or served ALCOHOLIC BEVERAGES on these premises, your birthday must be on or before today's date in

1991

Be prepared to show PROOF OF AGE.

For bar and restaurant managers, the good news is that demand for alcoholic products will remain high. The beverage business is competitive, and for that reason, only those managers who consistently operate in a professional manner will be able to survive. In today's marketplace, the emphasis on beverage profitability will come from serving ever-greater numbers of customers responsibly, not by serving greater quantities of beverages to a single individual.

Current Trends in Alcohol Service

The legal age for buying and possessing alcohol has been 21 years in every state since shortly after the passage of the National Minimum Drinking Age Act in 1984. That law provided federal highway funds only to states that maintain a minimum drinking age of 21 (*Exhibit 1.4*). According to the Gallup poll, the percentage of Americans of legal age who say they drink alcohol has remained fairly steady at approximately 65 percent since the 1950s. The specific beverage products that are the favorites among this market change over time as do the methods beverage managers use to market and promote the sale of alcoholic beverages.

An example here may be helpful. From the late 1970s to the mid-1980s, a product called the "wine cooler" was very popular. Essentially, it was not a new product. For centuries, wine drinkers have mixed water and flavorings in wine to enhance its taste. To understand the decline of the wine cooler market, it is important to first know that their lower alcohol content caused them to be taxed at a rate lower than that of wine. Also, because much of the wine flavor in a wine cooler was obscured by the fruit and sugar, the wine used in wine coolers tended to be low grade. As a result, wine coolers were inexpensive to make and sell.

The wine cooler found a ready acceptance, primarily among female drinkers looking for a refreshing alternative to beers and traditional wines. Backed by multimillion-dollar ad campaigns, the wine cooler market virtually exploded.

In 1991, the U.S. Congress significantly raised the federal excise tax on wine coolers. Immediately, most manufacturers dropped wine from their "coolers" and substituted it with less costly malt to create flavored "malt" beverages. Today, the wine cooler is rarely found on the mass market, while flavored malt beverages have gained in popularity.

The lesson to be learned from wine coolers is twofold. First, consumers' taste in alcoholic beverage products can change. Second, legislation related to alcoholic beverages is ongoing and managers must be aware of changes in the laws.

TRENDS IN PRODUCT POPULARITY

Just as managers want to serve the food items their guests want to buy, managers serving alcoholic beverages want to provide the beverages their guests prefer. One way to better understand the drinking habits of Americans, and specifically what customers drink, is to examine their preferences within the three major alcoholic beverage categories:

- Beer
- Wine
- Spirits

BEER Beer is the third most frequently ordered beverage served in bar, restaurant, and foodservice operations, exceeded in popularity only by soft drinks and coffee. Beer is easily the most popular alcoholic beverage sold in the United States, followed by wine and then spirits.

Chapter 4 describes the various types of beer sold in bar, restaurant, and foodservice operations. The alcohol content of the most popular beers sold in the United States varies based on their style and how they are made, but in general ranges from 3 to 6 percent. The most popular beer type in the United States, and in the world, is lager, a beer with an approximately 4 to 5 percent alcohol content.

Lager refers to the type of beer originally brewed in Central Europe. The name "lager" comes from the German word *lagern* for "to store." Brewers in Germany stored their beers in cool cellars and caves during the warm summer months to help preserve it; thus they were called lager or stored beers. The most popular type of lager beer is referred to as a "pale" lager because of its light, pale color.

Lager beers, as well as all other beer styles, are sold to bar, restaurant, and foodservice operators in cans, bottles, and kegs. One very important type of pale lager is commonly referred to as "light" (often spelled "lite") beer because of its reduced alcohol content and resulting lower level of calories per serving. Today, the number one selling beer in the United States is a light, pale lager. Beer drinkers who wish to reduce their alcohol consumption or their calorie intake often choose light beers.

Exhibit 1.5

Despite their popularity with the general public, light beers, and even lager beers in general, are often criticized for being less flavorful than full-strength beers. These types of beer are thought to taste "watered-down" and are widely avoided by beer connoisseurs, who tend to prefer more flavorful brews (*Exhibit 1.5*).

Bar, restaurant, and foodservice operators, of course, seek to offer beers that suit the tastes of a variety of customers, thus they most often serve a variety of types of beers. Many operators also

THINK ABOUT IT . . .

The best-selling beers in the United States are often not among those preferred by individuals who consider themselves "serious" beer drinkers. What strategies might a manager use to promote a broad spectrum of beer products?

produce their own beers on-site (brewpubs) or purchase them from microbreweries or small regional brewers. The last several decades have seen tremendous growth in micro- and regional breweries, often dubbed craft breweries. However, the vast majority of beer sales in the U.S. foodservice industry consists of pale lager beers produced by national and international brewing companies.

Beer is popular when consumed on its own or with a variety of well-liked food such as pizza, burgers, sausages, and Mexican-style cuisines. Increasingly, the more flavorful beers are being paired with dishes or used as an ingredient. Managers serving beer can do so by selling it in bottles, cans, glasses, or pitchers. Because of its low cost and long shelf life, beer is among a manager's most profitable beverage items.

Because consumer preferences in beer products change over time, managers should stay informed about the most popular beer styles and brands. Information of this type is often available from an operator's beer supplier and from other food industry sources that can be accessed via the Internet.

WINE Wine is second only to beer as the most popular alcoholic beverage served in restaurant and foodservice operations. Chapter 5 details the various types of wines consumed by today's wine drinkers.

Wine is any alcoholic beverage made from fermented fruit juice, but the term is most often used to describe beverages made from fermented grapes (*Exhibit 1.6*). The natural chemical makeup of grapes allows fermentation to occur without the addition of extra sugar, acid, or other ingredients. Fermenting crushed grapes using various types of yeast produces grape wine. The yeast consumes the sugars in the grapes and converts them into alcohol during the fermentation process. Different varieties of grapes and different strains of yeasts produce different types of wine.

Wines made from other fruit (e.g., apples or berries) are commonly named after the fruit from which they are produced—for instance, apple wine or elderberry wine. However, these wines are not as popular as the wine made from grapes. Some wines are made by fermenting grains, such as sake made from rice rather than fruit. These products resemble beer or spirits more than grape wine.

Interestingly, despite the fact that wine has been produced for thousands of years, it was not until the early 1860s that anyone knew the process that converted grape juice to wine. Louis Pasteur, a French chemist and microbiologist, was the first to prove that fermentation was the process by which wine was produced. His work advanced the ability of winemakers worldwide to replace guesswork with proven wine-making techniques that resulted in improved, and more consistent, wine quality.

Exhibit 1.6

Today, high-quality wines are produced in many areas of the world. The unique characteristics of these various growing regions, as well as the grapes and methods used to produce the wines, permit managers to offer their guests a wide variety of wine products at a wide range of competitive prices. Managers sell wines in bottles of various sizes and by the glass. Wines are popular when consumed by themselves as well as when they are consumed with meals and desserts.

Oenology is the science and study of all aspects of wine and winemaking. Many managers spend a great deal of time learning about the wines their customers will like best and the specific food that pairs with specific wines. The most important thing to know about wines, however, is that they are produced to be enjoyed by wine drinkers. As a result, the "best" wine for any customer is the one that he or she enjoys drinking most.

Because very popular wines range from sweet (those with a high sugar content) to dry (those with a low sugar content), it is important that managers help their guests know as much as possible about the wines they offer for sale and the taste characteristics of those wines. Managers do this by creating informative wine lists, or wine menus, that inform customers about the wines the customers will be buying.

SPIRITS Chapter 6 outlines the many different spirit products popular with today's customers. In the United States, spirits (*Exhibit 1.7*) are often referred to as "hard liquor" to indicate they contain more alcohol than beer and wine (softer alcoholic beverage products).

Spirits are produced by distillation. The essence of distillation is the fact that alcohol vaporizes (becomes a gas) at a lower temperature than water. The boiling point of water at sea level is 212°F (100°C), at which point it vaporizes and becomes steam. The boiling point of ethyl alcohol is 173°F (78.3°C). As a result, if heat is added to a liquid containing alcohol and the temperature of the liquid is kept below the boiling point of water, the alcohol can be separated from the original liquid. If, at the same time, a method is used to capture the alcohol vapor and not let it escape into the air, it is possible to re-condense those vapors back into liquid form. The result is an alcohol with a high level of purity. This alcohol can be cooled and then added back to water or a variety of flavored beverages to make a spirit with alcohol content higher than beer or wine.

Exhibit 1.7

A spirit is a distilled alcoholic beverage that contains at least 20 percent alcohol. The percentage of alcohol in a beverage is also referred to as its proof. The proof of an alcoholic beverage is two

Manager's Memo

Managers must monitor drinking trends carefully, and the recent popularity of combining highly caffeinated beverages with alcoholic beverages is one such trend.

Combining caffeine (a stimulant substance) with alcohol (a depressant) can cause different mechanisms to occur in the brain. The brain becomes more alert due to the caffeine and, as a result, users of highly caffeinated alcoholic drinks can become *less* aware of how intoxicated they actually are. The caffeine causes the drinkers to feel that they have not consumed much alcohol, yet in reality they are consuming much more alcohol than they are used to. For that reason, in 2008, two of the major U.S. breweries discontinued the inclusion of caffeinated ingredients in their beer products.

Responsible managers monitor and respond to changes in consumer preferences, but they must always do so with an understanding of their special responsibilities as sellers of alcohol.

times its alcohol content. Thus, for example, a spirit containing 50 percent alcohol would be classified as 100 proof:

$$50\% \text{ alcohol} \times 2 = 100 \text{ proof}$$

Whereas vodka, a colorless, odorless spirit is currently the most popular type served in the United States, there are many other popular spirits:

- Flavored vodka
- Gin
- Rum
- Whiskey/Whisky
- Tequila
- Brandy (made from grapes)
- Fruit brandy (made from other fruit and also referred to as schnapps)

Distilled spirits are often called liquors and those that are bottled with added sugar and added flavorings are known as liqueurs. Because most drinkers ignore the fine distinction between liquors and liqueurs, in common usage all alcoholic beverages that are not beer or wine are referred to as spirits. Spirits are popular when consumed by themselves as well as before, during, or after meals.

In some cases a spirit may be consumed by itself, which is referred to as being served straight. They may be served chilled, over ice, or at room temperature. In other cases a spirit may be combined with one or more other beverages to produce a mixed drink. Like beer and wine, however, the popularity of specific spirits and mixed drinks can change as consumer tastes change. Managers must stay up-to-date with these changing preferences. Additionally, some spirits are more popular at specific times of the year or even days, than they are at other times—for example, rum-based eggnogs during December holidays, whiskey-based Irish coffees on St. Patrick's Day, and whiskey-based mint juleps on the day of the Kentucky Derby.

Because spirits contain higher levels of alcohol, managers must use caution in serving spirits. In most states, special licenses are required to sell spirits. As a result, managers whose operations sell spirits must manage their sales extra carefully and serve them responsibly.

Marketing Alcoholic Beverages

What brings customers to a specific beverage establishment? Most *do not* come primarily to drink. They could drink more easily and certainly less expensively at home. Other important needs and wants are met when customers socialize in various settings. These needs and wants include relaxation, entertainment, conversation, a good mix of food and drink, and a setting that is frequented by the same customers on a regular basis (the informal social club).

Alcoholic beverage customers have a variety of expectations:

- Quality beverage products
- Good portion sizes
- Fair prices
- Professional, courteous service
- Special, personalized attention
- An appealing atmosphere
- Comfort
- A convenient location
- Safety in entering and leaving the location

Although all customers share some of the same beverage service needs, it is essential to realize that there are also major differences among guests. Certain customers quickly feel out of place in a setting that does not suit them. Customers differ in age, lifestyle, socioeconomic level, and social standing. The phrase "not my crowd" is probably used in reference to bars, restaurants, and clubs more frequently than to many other places or situations.

Successful beverage operations define the types of customers they want to attract. Once this decision has been made, everything connected with a particular operation (featured products, types of food, furnishings, lighting, music, entertainment, and the like) is geared to appeal to the targeted groups. Businesses that have failed are often those that have tried to provide something for everyone and ended up appealing to no one.

ALCOHOLIC BEVERAGES IN BARS, RESTAURANTS, AND FOODSERVICE ESTABLISHMENTS

Beverage service today is available to the public in a number of ways ranging from the basic to the elaborate. It can range from the serving of a drink by itself to complete alcoholic beverage service along with food, entertainment, and even lodging. Among the establishments that sell alcoholic beverages are neighborhood bars, diners, restaurants, hotels, nightclubs, wine bars, breweries, sports complexes, and specialty clubs.

Although at first glance these might appear to be quite different from one another, they are, in many respects, similar. Because they are all in the business of selling alcohol, their methods of purchasing, inventory control, and accounting are comparable. Also, they are all required to meet specific

RESTAURANT TECHNOLOGY

Advanced software programs now allow customers in beverage facilities to use handheld devices to play interactive TV-based games. Players compete against each other and against players in other beverage facilities across the country.

In most games, players are posed a question about sports, art, literature, pop culture, and more. They are then given a fixed amount of time to choose their answers. Those choosing the largest number of correct answers in the shortest period of time score the most points. The points earned by each player are displayed for all players to see.

The games are entertaining and help a beverage operation attract customers by giving guests the chance to be active and to have fun when they visit a beverage operation.

local, state, and federal beverage regulations. There are basically three types of operations that serve alcoholic beverages:

- Beverage only
- Beverage and food
- Beverage and entertainment/activity

Beverage Only

The beverage-only operation has been in existence in the United States for a little more than a hundred years. Actually, in these facilities, snacks such as pretzels, chips, and nuts are often served, but beverage service is clearly most important. Beverage-only bars are often neighborhood gathering places. Some are frequented by businesspeople who work nearby, although sometimes travelers may drop in when they are in the area.

Décor can be anything from comfortably casual to upscale. Entertainment, when provided, may consist of television, live music, recorded music, a pool table, video games, or interactive customer activities such as karaoke or specialized TV programming. In some cases, an outdoor setting may be an attractive customer draw. In all cases, however, the facility must appeal to its customers' needs and wants. Some of these may be price, location, and friendly service.

Beverage-only bars usually have a predictable traffic flow. Because they deal only in beverages, these are the easiest beverage service operations to manage. However, the number of these establishments is declining, since many owners have found that beverage and entertainment/activity combinations are more profitable.

Even boutique wineries and breweries have found that consumers want to "do" something as they enjoy their beverages. The neighborhood bar that provides "socializing" as an activity will continue to do well. For all other locations, it is probably true that alcohol alone will not be enough to sustain a profitable business.

There are a variety of beverage-only operations:

- Neighborhood bars
- Taverns
- Hotel bars
- Airport and bus terminal bars
- Bar/package stores
- Breweries
- Wineries

Beverage and Food

Beverage and food operations are the predominant type of beverage operation in the United States and a major industry in the world today. Restaurants and other foodservice operations with wine, beer, and liquor service, and bars that serve light meals are examples of this type of service. There is great variation in the comparative importance of beverage service and food service, with the operational profit typically coming from both food and beverage sales.

It is important to remember that the profit made from the sale of alcoholic beverages is generally much higher than that of food. It often makes good business sense to add alcoholic beverages to the service of providing food whenever possible. While it is impossible to state the "appropriate" profit levels for alcoholic beverages, profits are generally two to five times greater for beverage products than for food products. It is highly likely that the profit in the pitcher of beer exceeds that of its accompanying pizza by a great deal, even though it may be sold for half of the price of the pizza. And because many alcoholic beverages were created to be enjoyed with food, it is only natural for professional food and beverage managers to seek out and promote these combinations.

A major responsibility of the beverage manager, especially one who works in the beverage and food area, is to monitor consumer taste trends and to respond *when appropriate*. Obviously, a microbrewery that serves food does not stop making burgers and beer and start making wine and cheese just because a new variety or style of wine becomes popular. Similarly, the local sandwich shop serving Chicago-style hotdogs should pay more attention to the introduction of a new "ice" beer than would a French restaurant serving traditional recipes from the famous French cooking book *Le Guide Culinaire*.

There is no question that people's taste in alcoholic beverages change over time. The real question for the manager is, "What changes are occurring in the tastes of the customers I hope to attract to my establishment?"

Many types of beverage and food operations are popular in the United States:

- Quick-service restaurants (QSRs)
- Fast-casual restaurants
- Casual restaurants
- Fine-dining restaurants
- Self-service restaurants and cafeterias
- Airport bars
- Sports complexes
- Grocery stores
- Brewpubs
- Banquet halls
- Country clubs

MANAGER'S MATH

OPEN FOR BUSINESS

Amanda is the manager of the Golden Harvest fine-dining restaurant. Each month, Amanda monitors the amount of food and beverage sales in her operation. Use a chart like the one that follows to calculate her sales results from last month.

Time Period	Food Sales	Beverage Sales	Total Sales
Last month	$185,000	$65,000	
Sales percentage			100 %

1. What were Amanda's total food and beverage sales last month?
2. What percentage of total sales last month was contributed by the sale of food?
3. What percentage of total sales last month was contributed by the sale of beverages?

(Answers: Total sales, $250,000; food sales percentage, 74%; beverage sales percentage, 26%)

19

INVEST IN THE GUEST

Many operators have stories about how the four walls of a restaurant or foodservice operation or bar are the most important marketing tools we have—in fact, more important than any marketing vehicle. I wanted to test this premise, so I began reducing marketing and promotional expense and reinvesting those dollars into "experiences"—entertainment, events, contests, tastings, and so on. Over six months, I increased guest frequency by over two visits a month and increased revenue by over 24 percent. Rather than radio relationships, I had guest relationships. This changed the way I viewed marketing and its relationship with our guest experience. Invest in your guest, not in media.

Beverage and Entertainment/Activity

Beverage and entertainment/activity operations exist because most people want to "do" something while they consume their favorite alcoholic beverage. As discussed earlier, eating is one of those favorite activities. The beverage and entertainment/activity segment of the beverage business, however, offers even more.

There is enormous variety in the types of entertainment and activities that accompany beverage service, ranging from dartboards and pool tables to elaborate stage shows in nightclubs and cabarets. Dance clubs provide recorded music while their customers enjoy dancing. Piano bars and small clubs provide quiet, intimate places to enjoy music and conversation. There are high-tech clubs where the entertainment comes from giant video screens and computerized games. The atmosphere and the quality of the entertainment help determine success in these establishments, but quality beverage products, excellent service, and cleanliness are also extremely important.

Successful beverage/entertainment operations provide entertainment that meets the current interests and needs of their customers. Just as in beverage preferences, consumer preferences in activities change over time. Current interests of consumers may change, but effective managers know that some factors in the successful operation of these facilities do not.

Successful beverage/entertainment operations typically have a good ratio of male to female customers and employ a friendly service staff. Pricing is fair both for the operation and the customer. Responsible drinking, not mass consumption, is reflected throughout the operation. The quality of entertainment or activity is in keeping with consumer expectations. Success in this beverage segment often depends on the ability to keep up with and capitalize on the latest trends. In fact, smaller clubs offering a specific type of entertainment—such as a piano bar, jazz, comedy, or a local band—are often the most stable type of beverage/entertainment operations because they meet an unchanging need of their customers.

There is a variety of beverage and entertainment/activity operations in the United States:

- Comedy clubs
- Entertainment clubs
- Sports complexes
- Nightclubs
- Country clubs
- Dance clubs
- Music clubs
- Bowling alleys

SUMMARY

1. **Explain the chemical makeup of beverage alcohol.**

   Alcohol is a colorless liquid that is created by fermentation. Fermentation is the chemical reaction that splits a molecule of sugar into equal parts of ethyl alcohol and carbon dioxide. The fermentation process is caused by yeast that may occur naturally in the liquid or may be added to the liquid by an alcoholic beverage maker. After fermentation, the carbon dioxide escapes into the air and the ethyl alcohol remains in the liquid. The result is an alcoholic beverage. The major types of alcoholic beverages are beer, wine, and spirits.

2. **Explain the physiological effects of drinking alcohol.**

   When it is consumed, alcohol is absorbed into the blood of the drinker. The absorption takes place in the mouth, stomach, and small intestine and the alcohol is then distributed throughout the body. The amount of alcohol built up in a drinker's bloodstream is measured by blood alcohol content (BAC). Increasing BAC levels have a direct effect on a drinker's motor skills, judgment, and emotional state. An individual's actual BAC will be affected by a variety of factors including body size, gender, age, emotional state, and amount of food consumed. Alcohol is eliminated from the body by the liver at the rate of approximately one standard-sized drink per hour.

3. **Describe the history of alcoholic beverage consumption in the United States from its founding through the present.**

   In the United States, the manufacture and sale of alcoholic beverages can be viewed during three significant time periods: pre-Prohibition, Prohibition, and post-Prohibition. In the pre-Prohibition period, taverns selling alcohol were an important part of community and political life. Prohibition was the time period from 1920 to 1932. During this period, the manufacture and sale of alcoholic beverages was illegal. After Prohibition ended, each state and local community was allowed to regulate the sale of alcoholic beverages. As a result, the current laws related to the sale of alcohol vary widely, and managers must know the beverage sales-related laws in effect in the area in which they operate their businesses.

4. **Identify the current consumer trends affecting the consumption and marketing of alcoholic beverages.**

   Lager beers, and specifically light lager beers, are currently the most popular types of beer sold in the United States. Those who consider themselves to be more serious beer drinkers often prefer more flavorful beers. Beer is sold in the United States in bottles, cans, by the glass, and by the pitcher. Wines sold in restaurant and foodservice operations range from sweet (high sugar content) to dry (low sugar content) and come from many different wine-growing regions. The detailed information guests need to know about the wines they are buying is included in an operation's wine list. Spirits are beverages with higher concentrations of alcohol and may be consumed by themselves (straight) or mixed with other spirits, beverages (such as soft drinks), juices, or flavorings to produce mixed drinks. The higher potency levels of spirits means that their sale must be very carefully managed.

5. **Identify the different types of establishments serving alcoholic beverages.**

There are basically three types of operations that serve alcoholic beverages: beverage only, beverage and food, and beverage and entertainment/activity. Beverage-only establishments sell little if any food. Examples include many small bars and taverns. Beverage and food operations include restaurants and other foodservice operations that sell meals. Beverage and entertainment/ activity facilities sell alcoholic beverages and may offer their patrons a choice of things to do and eat while they are drinking. These types of establishments include bowling alleys, golf courses, amusement parks, comedy clubs, nightclubs, and music clubs.

APPLICATION EXERCISE

Consider the three main types of operations serving alcohol identified in this chapter:

- Beverage only
- Beverage and food
- Beverage and entertainment/activity

1. What is the name of a popular beverage-only operation in your area? How would you describe the operation? What types of beverages are most popular at this establishment? What personal characteristics do you think describe this operation's target customer?

2. What is the name of a popular beverage and food operation in your area? How would you describe the operation? What types of beverages are most popular at this establishment? What personal characteristics do you think describe this operation's target customer?

3. What is the name of a popular beverage and entertainment/activity operation in your area? How would you describe the operation? What types of beverages are most popular at this establishment? What personal characteristics do you think describe this operation's target customer?

REVIEW YOUR LEARNING

Select the best answer for each question.

1. What two products result from the fermentation of a liquid containing sugar?
   A. Yeast and ethyl alcohol
   B. Carbon dioxide and yeast
   C. Sucrose and carbon dioxide
   D. Ethyl alcohol and carbon dioxide

2. What ingredient is needed to begin the fermentation process in a liquid containing sugar?
   A. Malt
   B. Yeast
   C. Ethyl alcohol
   D. Carbon dioxide

3. During what time period was the manufacture and sale of alcoholic beverages prohibited in the United States?
   A. Early 1800s
   B. Late 1800s
   C. Early 1900s
   D. Late 1900s

4. At what BAC level is it illegal to operate a motor vehicle?
   A. 0.04
   B. 0.06
   C. 0.08
   D. 0.10

5. At what approximate rate is alcohol eliminated from the body?
   A. 0.5 drink per hour
   B. 1.0 drink per hour
   C. 1.5 drinks per hour
   D. 2.0 drinks per hour

6. What human organ eliminates alcohol from the body?
   A. Kidney
   B. Skin
   C. Liver
   D. Stomach

7. Approximately what percentage of Americans who are of legal age drink alcoholic beverages?
   A. 25%
   B. 45%
   C. 65%
   D. 85%

8. What alcoholic beverage is the most popular in the United States?
   A. Wine
   B. Beer
   C. Spirits
   D. Liquor

9. What is the most popular spirit consumed in the United States?
   A. Gin
   B. Rum
   C. Vodka
   D. Whiskey

10. What is an example of a beverage and entertainment/activity operation?
    A. Tavern
    B. Winery
    C. Brewpub
    D. Sports complex

FIELD PROJECT

Every state has the right to regulate the sale of alcoholic beverages within its borders. Research the regulations that apply to the restaurants and foodservice operations serving alcohol in the locale in which you are now living and then answer the following questions:

1. What is the name of the governmental agency responsible for regulating alcoholic beverage sales?

2. What is the address and phone number of the governmental agency responsible for regulating alcoholic beverage sales?

3. What are the forms or classifications of liquor licenses available to restaurant or foodservice operators in your area if they wish to serve the following:

   - Beer only

   - Beer and wine

   - Beer, wine, and spirits

4. Find the answers to the following questions:

   - Are guests allowed to bring in their own bottles of wine and be assessed a service charge by the establishment?

   - If a guest does not finish a bottle of wine ordered with dinner, may the guest take home the remainder of the bottle?

   - Are there special rules for Sunday or holiday sales of alcohol?

   - What is the amount of sales tax applicable to alcoholic beverage sales?

   - What, if any, are the legal limits on alcohol levels for each type of beverage: beer, wine, and spirits?

5. Complete a chart like the following one that indicates the permitted times for serving alcoholic beverages in your area.

Day of Week	Start Alcohol Sales	End Alcohol Sales
Monday		
Tuesday		
Wednesday		
Thursday		
Friday		
Saturday		
Sunday		

2

The Legal Aspects of Alcoholic Beverage Service

CHAPTER LEARNING OBJECTIVES

After completing this chapter, you should be able to:

- Explain why the ability to serve alcohol is a privilege, not a right.

- Explain the concept of *duty of care* as it relates to the serving of alcohol.

- Explain the concept of *standard of care* as it relates to the serving of alcohol.

- Identify the three major governmental entities responsible for regulating the sale of alcoholic beverages and explain each entity's role.

- Describe the concept of *legal liability* as it relates to the sale of alcoholic beverages.

- Explain the concept of *third-party liability* as it relates to the sale of alcoholic beverages.

KEY TERMS

actual damages, p. 44

civil lawsuit, p. 43

criminal proceeding, p. 43

defendant, p. 43

depressant, p. 28

dram shop legislation, p. 45

drug, p. 28

duty of care, p. 29

foodborne illness, p. 31

foreseeable (harm), p. 29

gross negligence, p. 43

guest, p. 33

liable, p. 43

licensee, p. 38

liquor license, p. 38

negligent, p. 29

plaintiff, p. 43

public accommodation, p. 34

public space, p. 30

punitive damages, p. 44

reasonable care, p. 29

standard of care, p. 33

third-party liability, p. 46

CASE STUDY

"Don't mind him," said Veronica, the manager at a local bar. "He's harmless."

"He" was a regular customer at the bar. Veronica was talking to Hillary, one of the bar's servers. He had seated himself in Hillary's section. That had been two hours ago, and he had been served two drinks. This was the second time that Hillary had approached Veronica about his behavior.

"I know him," said Hillary. "And usually he's not all that bad. But like I told you earlier . . . tonight he just keeps, well . . . saying things."

"Saying what kinds of things?" asked Veronica.

"Like how cute I am . . . and how he only comes in here because of me," replied Hillary. "It's kinda creepy."

"He's just kidding around," said Veronica. "Just ignore his comments."

"I have been," replied Hillary, "but he just asked me for my cell number. That's scary. I don't want to go back to his table."

1. Is Veronica's advice to "just ignore" the customer the appropriate response to Hillary's genuine concerns about this customer? Why or why not?

2. How important do you think it is that Veronica takes the steps necessary to protect her employees from this guest's inappropriate behavior?

SERVING ALCOHOL IS A PRIVILEGE

The alcoholic beverage industry is one of the country's most highly regulated. Federal, state, and local regulations directly affect many aspects of alcohol sales:

- Where a business selling alcoholic beverages can be located
- What specific beverage products may be sold (*e.g.,* beer; beer and wine; or beer, wine, and spirits)
- Who may be served an alcoholic beverage
- Who may serve alcoholic beverages
- How many guests may be permitted in the operation at one time
- The days and hours in which alcohol may be served
- From whom a seller must purchase alcohol that will be resold
- Records of purchases and sales that must be maintained
- Allowable beverage marketing and pricing strategies

Clearly, the sale of alcoholic beverages is regulated much more closely than the sale of food. To better understand why alcoholic beverage sales are tightly controlled, recognize that alcohol is a drug. A drug is any substance that, when absorbed into the body, alters normal bodily function. Using that definition, ethyl alcohol (alcohol) is one of the most commonly used drugs in the world.

Alcohol is a drug that is classified as a depressant:

- It decreases the body's activities.
- It acts as a tranquilizer.
- It has been used for centuries as a medicine (for example, as an anesthetic or to relieve pain).
- Its misuse can cause coma or even death.

Communities across the globe tightly regulate the dispensing of most depressants. Alcohol is no exception. In cases of stronger depressants such as tranquilizers, only pharmacists are licensed to dispense them. Pharmacists must go to school to earn the right to distribute these drugs, as well as other types of powerful drugs. The right to dispense alcoholic beverages also is very carefully granted by society. This right is granted only to those who will be responsible with alcohol service.

No manager has an inherent "right" to sell alcohol. Rather, the privilege is given to those who appreciate their responsibilities and agree to continually live up to them. Only those who have proven themselves responsible to serve alcohol are granted and allowed to retain the right to sell it. In the United States, it is illegal to sell alcohol in a state without the state's consent. Doing so can lead to fines and imprisonment.

BEVERAGE MANAGERS' RESPONSIBILITIES WHEN SERVING ALCOHOL

Those individuals responsible for the management of a food and beverage facility owe a duty of care to all those who enter their operations. A duty of care is a legal concept that requires managers to use reasonable care when performing any act that could potentially harm others. Reasonable care is the degree of caution and concern for the safety of others that an ordinarily reasonable, prudent, and rational person would use in the circumstances. Using reasonable care is a subjective test of determining if a manager is negligent, meaning he or she did not exercise reasonable care.

Some duties of care are rather straightforward. For example, a restaurateur has a duty of care to provide food that is safe to eat. Similarly, a beverage manager must take reasonable care to provide only beverages that are safe to drink. Failure to do so would be a failure to have met this important duty of care.

It is essential for managers in the U.S. restaurant and foodservice industry to understand that there are no duties of care enforced at the federal government level. Each of the 50 U.S. states is a separate legal entity, so each is free to define the duties of care that will be recognized within its borders. As a result, the duties of care required of beverage managers vary from state to state.

Despite the lack of uniformity of law, in most states a duty of care will be recognized when the potential harm to another is foreseeable, meaning it is able to be reasonably anticipated or predicted. To illustrate, assume a manager knew that a small plumbing leak in the women's restroom of a popular beverage operation caused water to form puddles on the floor. Assume further that the manager knew the water could not easily be seen by guests and that it made the restroom floor very slippery. If the manager did not take steps to repair the leak promptly, or to warn his or her guests of the potential danger to them of slipping and falling, that manager would have failed to exercise reasonable care. The manager knew of the problem, would have been able to readily foresee the danger it presented, and yet did not take the steps needed to protect the safety of the operation's guests.

Exhibit 2.1

In a similar manner, assume a manager believed a guest had consumed enough alcohol to make the guest intoxicated (*Exhibit 2.1*). If the manager continued to allow alcohol service to this guest, that manager would have failed to exercise reasonable care in the service of alcohol because an intoxicated guest can easily get hurt or could hurt others.

However, operations managers are not required to ensure that their guests will always be safe. The actions of guests themselves, as well as the unanticipated acts of others not under the control of the manager, can all result in harm to guests. Because of variation in the types of facilities operated and the variation in state laws, it is not feasible to list every possible duty of care applicable to those managers serving alcoholic beverages. For most managers serving alcohol, however, the following duties of care will apply.

Duty to Provide a Safe Facility

A safe facility is one that does not put people's personal protection at risk. In this case, the *facility* is defined as the entire restaurant or foodservice operation. It includes entrance drives and parking areas, reception areas, dining and drinking areas, restrooms, and all other public space. Public space is any area in the facility to which guests are routinely permitted access.

For managers selling alcoholic beverages, the duty to provide a safe facility means well-lit parking areas, and parking lots and sidewalks that are free from potholes or broken concrete that could cause trips or falls. Inside, the facility should provide adequate lighting and safe seating, and be operated in a way that does not permit allowable guest capacity to be exceeded.

Duty to Provide a Secure Facility

A secure facility is one that does not put people's property at risk. Property examples include vehicles in parking lots and personal valuables such as jewelry, cash, and credit or debit cards. Experienced managers know that guests who do not feel secure will avoid frequenting facilities that make them feel that way.

Managers may discover that their facilities are not secure as evidenced, for example, by multiple vehicle break-ins occurring in the facility's parking lot. In such a case these managers have, due to the concept of foreseeability, a duty of care to warn their guests about these potential dangers. For that reason, the initial prevention of such security-related incidents is very important.

Duty to Warn of Unsafe Conditions

When managers know or should have known about a hidden or not readily obvious condition that could pose a safety or security threat to customers, those managers have a duty to warn their guests about the unsafe condition. Perhaps one of the most visual examples of restaurant and foodservice operators fulfilling this duty of care is the bright yellow "Wet Floor" signs used to identify freshly mopped floor areas. In this example the sign not only warns of wet floors that could cause guests to slip and fall, they are also a very visual reminder to guests and employees alike of management's concern for guest safety.

KEEPING IT SAFE

In most states, the local fire department or department of public safety issues occupancy permits. These permits identify a facility as safe to operate and designate the building's maximum number of allowable occupants.

In some cases, a beverage facility can be so popular with customers that the number of guests seeking admission is greater than the occupancy limit. In such cases, managers must restrict entry.

Managers who willfully permit occupancy levels to exceed those allowed by the occupancy permit put themselves in danger. If problems result from the overcrowding, the manager's behavior will undoubtedly be seen as being negligent. If the manager cannot prove he or she provided reasonable care, the responsibility for injuries resulting from overcrowding will likely fall on the business and, in some states, on the manager personally!

Note that managers do not have a duty to protect customers from, or warn them about, a dangerous condition that is open and obvious. For example, in a climate that routinely receives large amounts of snow, a beverage facility manager would not be required to warn guests that snow-covered parking areas may be slippery. The same manager would, under the duty of care related to facility, be held responsible for ensuring that the operation's sidewalks were snow and ice free within a reasonable time if the walks became snow covered and slippery and posed a threat to guests.

Duty to Hire Qualified Staff

This duty must be satisfied to protect managers and owners against charges of being negligent in their hiring practices. To illustrate the importance of this duty of care, assume that a state has implemented legislation requiring servers of alcohol be at least 18 years of age. The state believes that those under 18 years old are not mature enough to make good decisions about who should and should not be served alcohol.

Assume further that, in the same state, a manager hired a 16-year-old to serve alcohol. Subsequently the server sold too much alcohol to a guest. This guest then injured himself and others while driving intoxicated. If it could be proven that the manager did not exercise reasonable care in confirming the age of the server, the operation could be found guilty of negligent hiring.

Duty to Train Staff Appropriately

After hiring employees, managers have a duty of care to train them to do their assigned jobs properly. For example, managers cannot assume that a newly hired employee will know how to properly clean equipment, glassware, dishware, or serving utensils in a specific beverage operation. It is reasonable, however, to assume that the manager will train the employee in how to do that job before assigning it. Failure to do so could lead to customers contracting a foodborne illness.

A foodborne illness is one resulting from the consumption of contaminated food, pathogenic (disease-causing) bacteria, viruses, or parasites that contaminate food. Improperly cleaned equipment, glassware, dishware, or serving utensils, for example, can be the cause of a foodborne illness. Managers have a duty of care to train employees in the techniques required to minimize occurrences of foodborne illnesses. Not providing proper training would be a failure to address this duty of care.

THINK ABOUT IT . . .

Consider the duties of care for which professional managers are responsible. Which of these do you think would be most challenging for managers to achieve? Why?

Exhibit 2.2

In a similar manner, managers have a responsibility to ensure bartenders and servers are trained in a number of key areas related to the responsible service of alcohol:

- Proper drink production
- Drink service
- Refusal of drink service

Preparing drinks properly incudes controlling the amount of alcohol in each drink (*Exhibit 2.2*). Training for proper drink service includes monitoring each guest's drink consumption. Finally, all those who serve alcohol should be properly trained in management's approved method for refusing service to guests when doing so is appropriate.

Duty to Terminate Staff If Appropriate

This duty must be satisfied to protect managers against charges of negligent employee retention. To illustrate the importance of this duty, assume that a manager provided training to all bartenders employed in her operation. As part of the training, the bartenders were taught to carefully measure the amount of alcohol included in each drink served. A single bartender, however, consistently chooses to ignore portion control procedures. As a result, he does not control the amount of alcohol served in each drink.

The manager knows that because the amount of alcohol per drink is not consistent, it will be impossible to monitor the rate at which guests are drinking. The manager spends a reasonable amount of time devoted to retraining, but the bartender refuses to control the amount of alcohol served in each drink. The manager has a duty of care to terminate this employee. Not doing so would be wrong. Serving unknown and uncontrolled amounts of alcohol to guests puts them and others at great risk.

Exhibit 2.3

Duty to Serve Wholesome Products

Just as restaurant and foodservice managers must serve only food that is safe to eat, beverage managers must serve only products that are safe to drink. This duty of care is shared with those who supply beverages to a bar, restaurant, or foodservice operation. It also includes the techniques and methods managers use to prepare and serve quality beverage products.

Duty to Serve Alcohol Safely

Managers must ensure that alcohol is served safely to consumers (see *Exhibit 2.3*). Because of its extreme importance, this duty of care will be examined in detail in the remaining portions of this chapter and in chapter 3.

RECOGNIZED STANDARDS OF CARE

In fulfilling their duties of care, managers must exercise a standard of care appropriate to the given situation. Appropriate standards of care are the reasonably accepted levels of performance that qualified managers use in fulfilling their duties of care. An appropriate standard of care is determined, in part, on the level of care a guest should reasonably expect and an operation should reasonably supply.

In some cases, the question of what constitutes a reasonable standard of care is not clear-cut. To illustrate, most restaurant and foodservice industry experts would advise managers to regularly inspect the seating in their operations to ensure the chairs and stools provided to guests are safe. Regular inspection would be part of the standard of care appropriate for ensuring safe seating. The question of how *frequently* the seating should be inspected is subject to some level of interpretation. Most managers would agree that an hourly or daily inspection of chairs would not be necessary. Alternatively, most industry professionals would agree that an inspection only once a year would be insufficient.

In this example, there is no question that managers have a duty of care to provide safe seating. The standard of care appropriate for meeting that duty, however, is subject to honest differences of opinion. Many legal disputes in the industry are centered on the question of what an appropriate standard of care was or should be. In general, individual managers are required to apply the same standards of care as any other reasonable manager would apply in a similar situation. Recall that "reasonable care" is the degree of caution and concern for the safety of others that an ordinarily prudent and rational person would use in a specific situation. Managers are required to use reasonable care in many key areas of their operations but must pay special attention to the needs of their guests and their employees.

For Guests

Restaurant and foodservice operators have specific duties of care and standards of care related to their guests. The law views the standards of care related to those who enter a business somewhat differently based on the characteristics and the intent of the person entering. For example, assume that a thief enters an establishment in the middle of the night. The thief trips and falls down a small flight of stairs leading from one area of the business to another. In this case, it would be very difficult for the thief to claim that the operator had a duty of care to provide sufficient lighting that could have prevented the fall.

Now assume that a guest of the operation tripped and fell on the same small flight of stairs during normal business hours. A guest is a customer who seeks to lawfully obtain food or beverages from a restaurant or foodservice business. It is important to recognize that a person can be a guest even if he or she is not

OPEN FOR BUSINESS

RESTAURANT TECHNOLOGY

Optical character recognition (OCR) is the process of converting data from scanned documents. In the past, electronic scanning technology was limited primarily to magnetic strip and bar-code reading. Increasingly, however, OCR technology is applied in identification systems such as those used in bars to confirm guests' ages.

Using OCR technology to scan or read state-issued driver's licenses or other documents can be an important management tool in identifying false IDs and in combating underage drinking. Look for more advances in electronic scanning technology, including photo scanning, that has the potential to provide even more powerful tools for managers.

the person actually making a purchase or paying the bill for ordered items. In the previous example, the questions of whether reasonable lighting levels had been provided and whether more light would have prevented the accident would be subject to objective examination. This example shows why it is important to understand who is, and who is not, legally considered to be a guest in a restaurant or foodservice establishment.

Pubs, taverns, bars, restaurants, and other beverage and foodservice establishments are considered public accommodation businesses. A **public accommodation** is one that provides eating, sleeping, or entertainment services to the general public. These businesses historically have been required to admit all guests who wanted to be served. It is illegal to deny service to any guest on the basis of their race, color, religion, or national origin. It is also a violation of the law to admit any type of customer and to then segregate them (for example, by restricting their seating only to predesignated sections of the business) based on those same characteristics. In addition, many towns and cities prohibit discriminatory practices even in privately owned and operated facilities such as country clubs and private city clubs.

More recently, new laws require managers in bar, restaurant, and foodservice operations to use reasonable care in determining who is to be served. While managers may not illegally discriminate against guests they can, and in some cases must, refuse to admit or serve guests in special situations. All of the situations involve preventing harm to others:

- Managers may refuse to serve alcohol to underage customers (*Exhibit 2.4*).
- Managers may refuse to serve alcohol to visibly intoxicated guests.

Exhibit 2.4

- Managers may refuse to serve guests if they cannot demonstrate the ability to pay for items as they are purchased.

- Managers may refuse to serve those with highly contagious diseases.

- Managers may refuse to serve guests with an item prohibited by law such as concealed guns or knives.

- Managers may refuse to serve anyone who poses a real threat to other guests or employees by his or her actions or words.

- Managers may refuse to allow entrance to guests with animals, except approved guide or assistance animals used by individuals with disabilities.

- Managers may refuse to allow entrance if doing so would cause the building's maximum number of allowable occupants or guests to be exceeded.

Note that managers are not permitted to "pick and choose" the guests affected when they exercise their right to refuse service. For example, assume an operation enforces a policy that requires that guests demonstrate the ability to pay prior to ordering beverages. That same policy must apply to all of the operation's guests, not merely to preselected groups of guests.

In addition, as operators of public accommodations, managers have a legal obligation to ensure their facilities meet all applicable local building codes. The facilities must also comply with access requirements mandated by Title III of the Americans with Disabilities Act (ADA). Title III requires public accommodations to provide access to people with disabilities on a basis that is equal to that of the general public. Title III makes specific requirements of businesses:

- Remove barriers that prevent making their facilities usable by people with mobility impairments. Examples include providing parking spaces for people who are disabled, wheelchair ramps or lifts, and accessible restroom facilities.

- Provide auxiliary hearing and visual aids. Examples include menus produced in Braille or large print. Menus in Braille are not required, however, if servers are trained to read the menu to customers with sight impairments.

- Modify any operating policies that could be considered to discriminate against people with disabilities. These can include policies such as requiring guests to prove their age by showing a driver's license prior to serving them alcohol. The reason is that some individuals who are disabled may not be permitted to drive and thus would not have the required license but would likely have other forms of identification.

Violations of laws related to the nondiscriminatory service of guests can result in civil or criminal penalties. They also can include losing the privilege of selling alcoholic beverages and damage to a company's reputation.

For Employees

Those employees who serve alcohol sometimes face special challenges that managers must recognize. Bartenders and alcoholic beverage servers should be qualified when hired and be well trained. However, alcohol affects different people differently. Even the best training cannot completely protect these employees from this fact. In some cases, customers who drink can behave in inappropriate or illegal ways. This behavior can cause potential legal problems for beverage operators who do not immediately take steps to stop the behavior.

To illustrate how this can happen and what managers should do about it, consider the case of Jana, who waits tables at a full-service operation. This establishment features char-grilled burgers and other sandwiches designed around a Caribbean beach theme. The establishment requires its male and female staff to wear khaki shorts, sandals, and brightly colored floral shirts while on duty.

In this scenario, Ron, a customer, develops a crush on Jana. He begins dropping by the establishment whenever Jana is there. Ron often calls Jana "Honey" and "Babe." He frequently tells her she looks terrific in her shorts. He repeatedly asks her to go out with him. Ron's comments and advances are all unwelcomed by Jana, but become bolder and more frequent the more drinks he consumes.

Jana tells Sonya, her boss, about Ron's behavior. Sonya provids no support to Jana. "It's not that big a deal," says Sonya. "He's harmless. And it's not good for our business to offend the customers." Ron continues to get more aggressive over several months. Jana becomes increasingly uncomfortable, and Sonya continues to ignore the situation.

One night, after a few drinks, Ron grabs Jana and tries to kiss her. Jana bursts into tears and runs from the establishment. The next day, Sonya receives a notice from Jana's lawyer. Jana is suing the establishment for sexual harassment. Sonya is shocked because no one on the staff has touched Jana, and the uniform she is required to wear is the same for male and female employees.

In this case, however, the court rules that the establishment has a legal obligation to protect its employees from being harassed by customers. The judge especially criticizes Sonya for failing to protect Jana. The establishment settles the lawsuit, but only after spending several thousand dollars on a defense attorney and court-imposed costs.

Employees should, of course, be polite and respectful to customers. However, they are not required to tolerate unwelcome sexual advances, flirtation, and verbal abuse, or to risk physical injury. Determining when a customer's behavior crosses the line into unlawful harassment is often a judgment call. Experienced managers know it is always best to err on the side of protecting employees.

Note that alcohol cannot be sold or supplied to a disorderly guest. A disorderly customer does not need to be intoxicated to be refused service. The person could be sober or under the influence of another substance. There are outward signs of disorderly conduct that should cause managers to refuse alcohol service to guests:

- Aggressive

- Violent

- Disruptive

- Argumentative

- Noisy

- Affecting the comfort or enjoyment level of others

Experienced establishment managers know it is good business to treat their guests well. But they also know it is good business to treat their employees well and to demand that their customers do the same.

REGULATIONS RELATED TO ALCOHOLIC BEVERAGE SERVICE

There are an extremely large number of laws related to the manufacture, sale, and service of alcoholic beverages. Recall that the Twenty-First Amendment specifically gave individual states the right to regulate the sale of alcohol within their borders. The federal government also imposes a number of restrictions and requirements on the sale of alcoholic beverages that managers must know and understand. Finally, local communities have been allowed the right to regulate the sale of alcoholic beverages within their own jurisdictions and many do so in a variety of ways. As a result, managers must understand the role of the federal, state, and local governmental entities that impact what these managers can and cannot do as they legally market and serve alcoholic beverages in their individual locations.

Federal Regulations

Nearly all restaurant, foodservice, and beverage operations and other businesses must comply with a variety of federal regulations such as the Americans with Disabilities Act (ADA), federal wage and hour laws, and employment-related regulations such as those issued by the Equal Employment Opportunity Commission (EEOC). The need to comply with these federal laws in beverage service operations is something all managers should recognize.

Legislative action at the federal level also can have a direct impact on state and local beverage laws and on local beverage operations. For instance, federal highway improvement funds were granted only to those states that established 21 years of age as the legal age for purchasing alcohol. This is one example of the direct influence the federal government can have on state liquor laws.

Two federal agencies also deal with the service of alcoholic beverages: the Alcohol and Tobacco Tax and Trade Bureau (TTB) and the Bureau of Alcohol, Tobacco, Firearms and Explosives (ATF). The mission of the TTB is to collect alcohol, tobacco, firearms, and ammunition taxes and to ensure that these products are manufactured and sold in accordance with applicable labeling, advertising, and marketing laws. It is this agency that is responsible for ensuring the alcoholic beverage products purchased by managers are wholesome and safe to drink. It is also the role of this agency to ensure that only beverage products that have been properly taxed are allowed to be sold. The TTB is a division of the federal government's Department of Treasury.

The ATF is under the Department of Justice and enforces federal laws and regulations relating to alcohol, tobacco, firearms, explosives, and arson in cooperation with other federal, state, local, and international law enforcement agencies. The ATF plays a variety of critical alcohol sales-related roles:

- Disrupting and eliminating criminal and terrorist organizations by identifying, investigating, and arresting offenders who traffic in contraband or illegal liquor

- Working to seize and deny further access to assets and funds used by criminal enterprises and terrorist organizations

- Preventing encroachment of the legitimate alcohol and tobacco industries by organizations trafficking in counterfeit or contraband cigarettes and illegal liquor

- Assisting local, state, and other federal law enforcement and tax agencies to thoroughly investigate the interstate trafficking of contraband cigarettes and liquor

State Regulations

In all states, those who sell alcohol are required to apply for and obtain a liquor license or liquor permit to do so. A liquor license is a document issued by a state that allows for the sale and service of alcoholic beverages. The entity holding the license is known as the licensee. Each state has an alcohol beverage commission (ABC), which grants licenses and regulates the sale of alcohol.

At the local level, some cities or counties may also have a local alcohol control board that works with the state agency to grant licenses and enforce the law. Although different types of liquor licenses exist based on the state issuing them, licenses can be divided into two general categories:

- Licenses for on-premises consumption (required for bars, restaurants, taverns, and clubs that serve alcohol)
- Licenses for off-premises consumption (required for liquor stores, grocery stores, and other markets that sell alcohol)

Most managers operate with on-premise licenses. These licenses may be issued to allow for the sale of various classifications of alcoholic beverage products:

- Beer only
- Beer and wine
- Beer, wine, and spirits

In most states, liquor licenses are issued for a period of one year, at the end of which the establishment must apply for a license renewal. Once an establishment has been granted a liquor license, it must operate according to all of the rules and regulations established by the state and any local governmental agencies authorized to control or monitor alcoholic beverage sales.

State laws addressing the sale of alcoholic beverages vary greatly. In most cases, they address permitted hours of sales. They also require that records of several types must be maintained:

- Beverages purchased (how much and from whom)
- Beverages sold
- Taxes collected
- Taxes paid

Exhibit 2.5

In most states, the ABC is permitted to conduct random audits to ensure compliance with its requirements.

There are other additional areas of control common in states. These include regulations that control dancing and other forms of entertainment, minimum-age requirements for those working in operations selling liquor, insurance coverage mandates, and the types of promotions and advertising that are permissible. Some, but not all, states have enacted legislation in the following areas:

- **Happy hours:** Some states outlaw reduced price or multiple drink alcohol sales practices and promotions (*Exhibit 2.5*).

- **Mandatory alcohol assessment and treatment:** Mandatory alcohol assessment and treatment laws mandate that convicted driving under the influence (DUI) and driving while intoxicated (DWI) offenders undergo an assessment of alcohol abuse problems and participate in a required treatment program.

- **Mandatory jail second offense:** These statutes mandate that individuals who have been convicted of a second offense of drunk driving receive a jail term as part of their punishment.

- **Open container laws:** These laws prohibit the possession of any open alcoholic beverage container in the passenger area of a motor vehicle.

- **Selling alcohol to youth:** Usually enforced by the state's alcohol beverage commission (ABC), these laws empower the ABC to revoke the license of any business that knowingly sells alcohol to an underage individual.

- **Youth attempt at purchase:** These statutes make it illegal for a person younger than 21 years of age to attempt to purchase alcohol.

- **Zero tolerance:** Laws that makes it illegal for drivers under the age of 21 to operate a motor vehicle with a blood alcohol level of .02 or more. All 50 states have zero tolerance laws.

- **Keg registration:** A requirement for beer kegs and other large beer containers to be tagged with identification tags and for the purchaser's name, address, and location where the keg is to be used to be recorded to track the source, if minors are served. There are 25 states with keg registration.

- **Mandatory server training:** States with these laws require establishments that serve or sell alcohol to train their employees to detect and not serve those who are underage or already impaired.

States are cautious about granting licenses to sell liquor. They will revoke the license of operations that fail to follow the state's laws regarding alcohol sales. Operators can lose their liquor licenses for a variety of reasons:

- Allowing frequent incidents of fighting or disorderly conduct
- Allowing the sale or use of drugs or narcotics
- Failing to pay collected liquor sales taxes
- Allowing prostitution or illegal adult entertainment
- Failing to maintain required records
- Selling alcohol to minors

The sale of alcohol to minors is a violation of law that all state ABCs take very seriously. In all states, representatives from the ABC can conduct unannounced inspections of any operation in which alcohol is served. That agency also can intentionally send minors into an establishment to determine if the operator will serve them.

Local Ordinances

State governments are the primary entities responsible for regulating the sale of alcohol. However, many states give local communities tremendous leeway in establishing their own local restrictions. Perhaps no state better illustrates the impact of local options on the sale of alcohol than does Mississippi.

Mississippi implemented statewide alcohol prohibition in 1907, over a dozen years before the rest of the country. It was the very first state to ratify the Eighteenth Amendment to create national Prohibition. Following national rejection of Prohibition through its repeal in 1933, the state maintained its own statewide prohibition for another 30-plus years. After that, it specifically "reaffirmed Prohibition" when it decided to permit local options regarding alcohol.

Today, less than half of the counties in Mississippi are "dry," but these counties retain their own prohibitions against the production, advertising, sale, distribution, or transportation of alcoholic beverages within their boundaries. Mississippi is an example of the importance to managers of knowing precisely what local law does and does not allow in the selling of alcoholic beverages. It should be noted that Mississippi, like most areas in the country, is relaxing, not increasing, its laws prohibiting the sale of alcohol. Again, the lesson for managers is clear: They must know current local laws and carefully follow any changes in them.

In addition to the types of local ordinances outlined previously, food and fire safety codes are typically the local regulations of most concern to many managers. Local health department inspectors inspect all establishments selling food and beverages. They want to know how the establishment stores alcoholic beverages, washes its glassware, and maintains and stores juices, fruit garnishes, ice cream, and other items used to prepare alcoholic beverages.

Some highly publicized nightclub fires that caused deaths in the early 2000s have made many community regulators increasingly concerned about fire safety in businesses serving alcohol. Local building codes related to construction materials, available building exits, and maximum occupancies may be enforced by police, fire, building department personnel, and zoning officials responsible for regulating business locations.

THINK ABOUT IT . . .

Increasing numbers of local communities are relaxing their laws against the selling of alcoholic beverages.

What factors do you think are most responsible for the changing attitudes about drinking in the United States?

Exhibit 2.6 summarizes the identities and roles of several important federal, state, and local governmental entities whose work directly affects those operating licensed beverage establishments.

Exhibit 2.6

GOVERNMENTAL ENTITIES AFFECTING LICENSED BEVERAGE OPERATORS

Jurisdiction	Agency or Entity	Purpose
Federal	Internal Revenue Service (IRS)	Monitors collection of taxes (e.g., employee withholding tax) and payment of taxes (e.g., federal income tax)
	Occupational Safety and Health Administration (OSHA)	Ensures, as far as possible, the safe and healthful working conditions of all employees
	Equal Employment Opportunity Commission (EEOC)	Enforces laws against discrimination in employment
	Department of Justice (DOJ)	Responsible for the enforcement of immigration laws and employment verification requirements as well as the Americans with Disabilities Act (ADA)
	Alcohol and Tobacco Tax and Trade Bureau (TTB)	Enforces federal law related to the making and selling of alcohol
	Department of Labor (DOL)	Enforces federal laws related to employee rights, including minimum wages, overtime wage payments, pensions, family medical leave, and unionization
State	Alcohol Beverage Commission (ABC)	Monitors alcoholic beverage sales, hours of operation, licensing, and reporting of sales for tax purposes, as well as administering any revocation of licenses
	Treasury or controller	Responsible for collecting state-imposed taxes as well as administering any state-sanctioned lottery or gaming activities
	Public health department	Responsible for the standards, inspection, and licensing of facilities that serve food and beverages
Local	Health and sanitation	Responsible for the local inspection and licensing of food facilities and ensuring compliance with any state- or municipality-imposed health and sanitation codes
	Building or zoning	Regulates land use, issues permits for building and renovation projects, and regulates parking requirements
	Fire department	Conducts facility inspections to ensure emergency lighting and sprinklers are installed and operating properly, and establishes and enforces limits on the maximum number of guests that can be legally served
	Local law enforcement (police and sheriff's departments)	Enforces laws related to underage drinking and illegal parking and responds to reported guest disturbances

UNDERSTANDING LEGAL LIABILITY

A lawsuit is a legal action brought in a court of law. In a lawsuit, the plaintiff is the party that claims to have suffered a loss as the result of something the defendant did. The defendant in a lawsuit is required to respond to the charge of the plaintiff. If the plaintiff is successful in proving a claim, the court will render a judgment in favor of the plaintiff. If the plaintiff is not successful, the lawsuit will be dismissed.

When the plaintiff is an individual or company, the lawsuit is considered a civil lawsuit. If the plaintiff is a governmental entity and the allegation is that a law has been broken by the defendant, the lawsuit is considered a criminal action or criminal proceeding. If, in a criminal proceeding, the defendant is found to be guilty of the plaintiff's charge, the court will issue a fine or impose other penalties that can include imprisonment, or both.

From the perspective of a manager, understand that in most cases a civil lawsuit is filed when the plaintiff feels the defendant did something he or she should not have done, or failed to do something he or she was required to do. A manager or company who has not used reasonable care in a specific situation that required a duty of care will, in many lawsuits, be declared legally negligent. That manager may be found potentially liable, or legally responsible, for the consequences of what he or she did or failed to do.

Negligence can be proven if four conditions are met:

1. A legal duty of care can be shown to exist (for example, the duty to provide a safe facility or to serve alcohol safely).
2. The operator failed to provide the reasonable standard of care needed to fulfill the duty.
3. The operator's failure to use reasonable care was the direct cause of any resulting harm or damage.
4. Someone was injured or damages resulted because of the operator's failure to use reasonable care.

Managers are held responsible for their own actions. In most cases, they also can be held responsible for the work-related acts of their employees. In some cases, managers can even be held responsible for the wrongful acts of their guests. The degree to which a manager could be held responsible for the actions of others typically depends on the foreseeability of the action. For example, if a dangerous situation was foreseeable, and no action was taken by management to warn others about it or to correct the situation, then the manager could be held liable.

If a manager acts in a way that shows a total disregard for the welfare of others, that manager could be found guilty of gross negligence. The difference between negligence and gross negligence is a critical one because the legal penalties for gross negligence are greater than those for ordinary

Manager's Memo

As noted, a seller of alcoholic beverages may face criminal charges if he or she breaks a state, county, or local law related to alcohol. In these circumstances, most states will hold managers criminally liable:

- If they serve alcohol to a minor.
- If they serve a guest who is or appears to be intoxicated.
- If they possess, sell, or allow the sale of drugs on the premises.

The consequences of these actions can be very serious. Depending on the state in which managers work, they could be placed on probation, fined, or even sentenced by the court to jail time. In Arizona, for example, serving alcohol to minors is considered a Class 1 misdemeanor, punishable by up to 6 months' imprisonment or up to a $2,500 fine, or both.

negligence. Sometimes it is hard to determine the difference between them. In a lawsuit, however, a jury's decision about whether a manager was negligent or grossly negligent can mean the difference of millions of dollars of compensation awarded to an injured party.

If an injured party suffers a loss due to the acts of others, the law requires that the person or company responsible for the loss be held accountable. The process for doing so is by awarding damages to the injured party. There are two types of damages of most interest to hospitality managers: actual damages and punitive damages.

Actual damages are real, identifiable losses that are the direct result of wrongful acts. If a guest is physically injured in a bar, actual damages could include such items as doctor and hospital bills, lost wages, and money to compensate the guest for pain and suffering. The amount of the "compensation" given for real losses can be subject to some dispute, but in most cases it can be calculated objectively.

The purpose of punitive damages is to punish those who have done wrong, and to serve as a warning to others not to commit the same act. Punitive damages are awarded when an individual or company was so grossly negligent it is required to pay damages in excess of the actual losses suffered by the injured party. By assessing punitive damages, society makes a statement that the behavior in question absolutely will not be tolerated. In the restaurant and foodservice industry, an operation could be required to pay punitive damages if, for example, it knowingly served alcohol to large numbers of underage drinkers without concern for the safety of the underage drinkers or the safety of others that could be harmed by them.

DRAM SHOP (THIRD-PARTY LIABILITY) LEGISLATION

Most people would agree that individuals should not consume so much alcohol that they pose a danger to themselves or to others. If a person drinks to excess, most would agree that the individual should be held responsible for his or her actions. To illustrate, assume a man drinks so much alcohol at his home that his driving is impaired. Despite that, the person drives his car. While doing so he causes a traffic accident. There is little doubt that the person in this example was irresponsible. He should be held liable, or legally responsible, for any damages caused by his actions.

Consider, however, the situation if this same person were involved in the accident after having consumed only one drink that was served to him at a local establishment. In nearly all cases, having only one drink with dinner (and no drinks prior to dinner) will not impair a driver's ability to drive. If, after dinner, the guest was involved in a car accident identical to the one identified in the earlier example, the guest would still be personally liable for the damages resulting from his actions. The establishment in which he was served only one drink likely would not be held responsible for the driver's actions.

In both of the examples cited, most people would agree that the driver, and the driver alone, should be held responsible for the damages he caused. Consider, however, a third scenario. In this scenario, the man is drinking in an establishment that is legally licensed to sell alcohol. The man drinks a very large number of drinks in a very short period of time. In fact, the man drinks so much that the person serving him knows, or should reasonably have known, that the drinker is intoxicated. If the man continues to request and is served drinks, what liability for the drinker's subsequent actions should be borne by the individual who served the drinks?

The societal response to this question is addressed by dram shop legislation. A dram shop is any type of drinking establishment where alcoholic beverages are sold for on-premise consumption. Traditionally, these facilities, which include restaurants, bars, taverns, and clubs, sold spirits by the *dram*, a small unit of liquid.

The dram shop laws are based on the principle that anyone who profits from the illegal sale of alcoholic beverages should be held liable for any damage that is the direct result of the sale. For a seller to be held liable, it is unnecessary to show that he or she is negligent. The seller will be held liable simply if it is proven that the seller sold alcohol to an intoxicated person, because that act is, by itself, illegal.

Under dram shop legislation, an individual who is injured by an intoxicated person can sue the seller of liquor. In most cases, the person who became intoxicated *cannot* sue the seller if he or she is injured. Dram shop legislation is intended to protect the general public from the hazards of serving alcohol to minors or those who are intoxicated. These laws have drawn criticism by some who claim they downplay the role of personal responsibility. However, beverage managers must understand the dram shop laws that apply to their own operations.

There is no question that alcohol can significantly change the behavior of those who are intoxicated. For that reason, it is illegal in all states to knowingly serve alcohol to an intoxicated person, just as it is illegal to sell alcohol to minors. In cases where intoxicated individuals cause damage or injury to themselves or others, society has deemed it appropriate to place a portion of responsibility on those who sold or served the alcohol.

The laws that address liability for serving alcohol illegally are complex. Managers must understand that there are at least three (not two) parties involved when an accident results from the illegal sale of alcohol:

- **First party:** the individual consuming the alcohol
- **Second party:** the operation serving the alcohol
- **Third party:** the injured person(s) not involved in this instance of selling or consuming the alcohol

To illustrate the third-party perspective of improper alcohol service, assume that Mark, a guest (the first party), is served an excessive amount of alcohol by Erick, the bartender, at an establishment (the second party). As a result, Mark drives a car and causes an accident that severely injures Don (the third party).

In such a situation, this establishment (and, in some states, even Erick the bartender) may be held liable for Don's injuries. This legal concept, known as third-party liability, forms the basis for dram shop legislation. This legislation has the intent to penalize those who serve alcohol improperly and to compensate innocent victims.

Prior to the 1990s, most state laws did not hold those who were licensed to serve liquor responsible for the damages caused to third parties. Today, 43 states and the District of Columbia have some variation of dram shop law in effect. Managers should know that there can be criminal as well as civil liability when alcohol is sold irresponsibly. Civil liability, under state dram shop laws, could require an alcohol establishment to pay the expenses of injured or deceased persons. These can include paying for such items as medical bills, property damage, lost wages, and cash awards to surviving family members. These damages are both real damages for pain and suffering and punitive damages. Criminal liability also can subject a hospitality operator to loss of liquor license, fines, and jail time.

Managers must recognize that society views the proper serving of alcohol to be of critical importance. As a result, many communities require those serving and selling alcohol to receive specialized training. Even if an operation is located in a community that does not require specialized alcohol server training or certification, it is always a good idea to make the responsible service of alcohol a priority. Because that is true, the entire next chapter of this book addresses the important topic of responsible alcohol service.

SUMMARY

1. **Explain why the ability to serve alcohol is a privilege, not a right.**

   Alcohol is classified as a depressant. Properly used, it is harmless and even promotes good health. Its excessive use, however, can lead to addiction, harm to the drinker and to others, coma, or even death. As a result, the consumption and sale of alcohol is closely regulated by society. Only those individuals and companies that have proven themselves responsible in the serving of alcohol are granted the right, and allowed to retain the right, to sell alcohol. Serving alcohol without the express consent of the state in which it is served is illegal and can lead to fines and imprisonment.

2. **Explain the concept of *duty of* care as it relates to the serving of alcohol.**

   A duty of care is a legal concept that requires managers to use reasonable care when performing any act that could potentially harm others. Some examples of common duties of care include duty to provide a safe facility, duty to warn of unsafe conditions, duty to train staff appropriately, and duty to serve alcohol safely.

3. **Explain the concept of *standard of care* as it relates to the serving of alcohol.**

   A standard of care is the industry-recognized amount of care appropriate to meet a manager's duties. These duties include the duty to provide a safe, secure facility and to warn guests of any conditions that are known to be unsafe. Additional duties include hiring qualified staff, training them appropriately, and terminating them if needed to protect guests or employees. Managers also have a duty to serve only wholesome products and to serve alcohol responsibly. By using reasonable care in the fulfillment of their duties, managers help protect their operations from charges of negligence: the failure to use reasonable care.

4. **Identify the three major governmental entities responsible for regulating the sale of alcoholic beverages and explain each entity's role.**

   The three major entities that are responsible for the regulation of alcoholic beverage sales in the United States are the federal, state, and local governments. The federal government primarily ensures the safe production of alcoholic beverages and their appropriate taxation. State governments are responsible for the issuing of liquor licenses and many of the rules and regulations related to alcohol sales including allowed time of sales, location of sales, and allowable promotions and advertising practices. Local governmental agencies inspect the health and safety of beverage operations and are primarily responsible for enforcing construction standards and establishing the allowable occupancy limits for buildings housing beverage operations. Local police departments help manage customer behavior and assist local operators in ensuring that guests who drink legally can do so in a safe, nonthreatening environment.

5. **Describe the concept of *legal liability* as it relates to the sale of alcoholic beverages.**

   In a lawsuit related to the sale of alcoholic beverages, the plaintiff is the party that claims to have suffered a loss as the result of something the defendant did or did not do. A manager or company that is a defendant and has not used reasonable care in a specific situation that required a duty of care and that resulted in damages to the plaintiff will, in most lawsuits, be declared legally negligent. As such it will be potentially liable, or legally responsible, for the consequences of what it did or failed to do. If it is determined the plaintiff is correct and the defendant is found to be liable for damages done to the plaintiff, the penalty assessed can include actual (real) damages or punitive damages (damages designed to punish and prevent future occurrences).

6. **Explain the concept of third-party liability as it relates to the sale of alcoholic beverages.**

To understand dram shop (third-party) liability legislation, managers must recognize that when an illegal sale of alcohol occurs and an accident or injury results, there are three (not two) parties involved in the incident. The first party is the individual who has consumed the alcohol. The second party is the operation or individual who served the alcohol. The third party is the injured person (or persons) who was not involved in either the selling or drinking of the alcohol. Society increasingly considers that the liability for any damages to the third party is borne by both the first and second parties. As a result, it is important that managers take all reasonable steps to ensure they serve alcohol responsibly and legally.

APPLICATION EXERCISE

Bart Stubbens entered Winthrop's Mayflower Tavern at 3:00 p.m. on a Monday afternoon. He seated himself at the bar, looked at the bartender, and said "draft." Witnesses would later agree that was all he said. Because the Mayflower offered only one beer on draft, the bartender nodded and served Bart a pint of lager and accepted the $10 bill offered in payment. Bart left the bar some 20 minutes later, never having said a word to anyone and leaving the change from his $10 bill on the bar counter.

Subsequently, Bart was involved in an accident in which a 14-year-old boy riding his bicycle was hit by Bart's car and was injured. Bart's BAC at the time of the accident was found to be 0.14% and he was arrested for DWI (driving while intoxicated).

The boy's parents sued the Mayflower and another operation, the J-Town Bar. The J-Town was sued because Bart had consumed seven 20-ounce beers in two hours at that establishment just prior to leaving it and driving to the Mayflower.

The manager and bartender at the Mayflower said they did not know, nor could they have known, Bart's condition when he arrived and that they were acting responsibly because they served him only one beer. Attorneys for the injured boy's parents stated the Mayflower served alcohol to an intoxicated person, an act that was illegal, and as a result under the state's dram shop laws was partially responsible for the injury suffered by the youngster.

1. Do you think the Mayflower served an intoxicated person?

2. Did the Mayflower's bartender act responsibly?

3. If you were the judge in this case, would you hold the Mayflower partially liable?

4. What would you advise the owner of the Mayflower to do in the future to avoid a similar incident?

REVIEW YOUR LEARNING

Select the best answer for each question.

1. What classification of drug includes alcoholic beverages?
   A. Narcotics
   B. Stimulants
   C. Depressants
   D. Hallucinogens

2. Which duty of care is addressed when managers buy beverage products only from those vendors properly licensed to sell them?
   A. Serve wholesome products
   B. Provide a secure facility
   C. Serve alcohol safely
   D. Train staff

3. Which duty of care is addressed when managers require all patrons to show a valid ID prior to serving them alcohol?
   A. Provide a secure facility
   B. Provide a safe facility
   C. Hire qualified staff
   D. Sell alcohol safely

4. Which governmental entity contains an alcohol beverage commission (ABC) that grants licenses and regulates the sale of alcohol?
   A. Federal government
   B. County government
   C. State government
   D. City government

5. Which law requires public accommodations to provide access to people with disabilities on a basis that is equal to that of the general public?
   A. EEOC
   B. Eighteenth Amendment
   C. Twenty-First Amendment
   D. ADA

6. Which governmental entity controls the Bureau of Alcohol, Tobacco, Firearms and Explosives (ATF)?
   A. Federal government
   B. County government
   C. State government
   D. City government

7. Who sets the limit on the number of guests who may be served at one time in an operation holding a liquor license?
   A. The operation's owner
   B. The operation's manager
   C. A local governmental entity
   D. A federal governmental entity

8. What are the series of laws that can hold sellers of alcohol responsible for those they serve?
   A. Dram shop legislation
   B. The requirements of ADA
   C. EEOC regulations
   D. ABC rules and regulations

9. What is the legal intent of punitive damages?
   A. To discourage lawsuits
   B. To reimburse for actual losses
   C. To punish and prevent specific behavior
   D. To require plaintiffs to reimburse defendants for their legal fees

10. Don owns an establishment. Lamar is a bartender at Don's establishment. One night Lamar serves Susan six drinks. When driving away from the establishment, Susan's car strikes Amy's vehicle. If a third-party liability lawsuit resulted in this scenario, who is the third party?
    A. Don
    B. Lamar
    C. Susan
    D. Amy

3

The Professional Service of Alcoholic Beverages

INSIDE THIS CHAPTER

- **The Importance of Serving Alcohol Responsibly**
- **The Importance of Training**
- **Management Steps** for the Safe Service of Alcohol
- **Professional Guest Intervention Procedures**

CHAPTER LEARNING OBJECTIVES

After completing this chapter, you should be able to:

- Explain the importance of understanding BAC to the responsible service of alcohol.

- State the two main purposes of a responsible alcohol service training program.

- List the four steps managers take to train employees in the responsible service of alcohol.

- Explain how managers ensure employees serve alcohol responsibly.

- Describe the role that bartenders and servers play in effective guest intervention procedures.

- Describe the role that managers play In effective guest intervention procedures.

KEY TERMS

action plan, p. 68

Alcoholic Beverage Control (ABC), p. 55

bond, p. 64

breached (duty of care), p. 54

certification (professional), p. 54

coaching, p. 65

competencies, p. 56

cost-effective (training), p. 56

incident report, p. 60

last call, p. 68

on-the-job training, p. 57

public intoxication, p. 52

CASE STUDY

"Look, I'm staying in Room 600," said the guest sitting at the bar in the Claremont Hotel lounge. "I had a few. But I'm taking the elevator home. I'm not driving! I just want one more to take back to my room."

Brad, the Claremont's bartender, considered what the man had said and took a look at the man's open drink tab. Based on the bar's computerized point-of-sale system, it looked like the man's first drink was served to him at about 3:00 p.m. and between then and now he had consumed eight drinks: Eight drinks over a three-hour period.

Brad knew it was illegal to serve an intoxicated guest. And in his opinion, based on the number of drinks served, this guest was intoxicated—or pretty close to it. That meant no more alcohol. "Eight drinks," thought Brad. "This would be the ninth, but he's not driving. He's staying in the hotel."

1. How important to the hotel would it be for Brad to follow the law regarding the overservice of alcohol to this guest?

2. Who do you think would be responsible for the acts of this guest if he is served "just one more" but then changes his mind and decides to drive to another bar to continue drinking?

THE IMPORTANCE OF SERVING ALCOHOL RESPONSIBLY

Recall from chapter 2 that blood alcohol content (BAC) is the amount of alcohol in a drinker's blood. Increasing levels of BAC directly affect drinkers' mental and physical capabilities. A variety of factors affect the BAC of each individual who drinks alcohol. As a result, managers must do two important things:

1. Understand BAC thoroughly
2. Train staff in the responsible service of alcohol

Blood Alcohol Content (BAC)

It is illegal to serve alcohol to an intoxicated guest. Intoxication is the physiological state that occurs when a person has a high level of alcohol in his or her blood. When a person is intoxicated, an elevated BAC level inhibits that person's normal capacity to act or reason. In the eyes of the law, the definition of intoxication differs depending on the situation to which it is applied.

DRINKING AND DRIVING

Every state has laws against driving under the influence (DUI) or driving while intoxicated (DWI). It is illegal to drive with a BAC level of 0.08 or higher. In some states there are enhanced DUI or DWI penalties as BAC levels increase. However, the BAC that triggers those harsher consequences varies by state. Many states also have zero tolerance laws for underage drinking and driving policies. However, zero does not always mean zero. In some states zero means 0.01 percent or greater, whereas in others it means 0.02 percent or greater. In still other states zero actually means zero (0.0 percent).

While some laws vary from state to state, there is one law that managers everywhere must remember: All states outlaw the service of alcohol to intoxicated guests.

PUBLIC INTOXICATION

The intoxication standard for a nondriving drinker is subjective. In Texas, for example, an individual is publicly intoxicated when that person is dangerous to himself or herself or others. The U.S. Constitution does not grant Congress the specific right to control public intoxication. As a result, public intoxication laws in the United States are entirely a product of state and local, not federal, laws. These laws vary widely from state to state, but many are similar to that used in the state of Texas.

Chapter 2 stated that dram shop liability legislation holds operators responsible for the acts of their intoxicated customers. This is the case whether those guests will be driving or whether they are publicly intoxicated. For that reason, it is critical that operators ensure their facilities serve alcohol responsibly and can prove that they do.

Implementing policies and procedures designed to ensure intoxicated guests are not served alcohol may seem easy. On the contrary, experienced managers know it can be challenging. The biggest challenge to not serving intoxicated guests is the fact that individuals process alcohol at different rates. Two drinkers could be served the same number and type of drinks, in the same time period. Despite near-identical circumstances, one drinker may become intoxicated while the other would not. The BAC of individual drinkers is not measured directly prior to serving alcohol. Therefore, managers must be able to show they have used reasonable care in prohibiting the service of alcohol to intoxicated guests.

It also is important to understand that, in some cases, even serving those who *do not* have elevated BAC levels is illegal and could result in the loss of an operator's liquor license. While specific laws related to illegal alcohol sales vary by state, most states have designated some very specific alcohol service–related acts as illegal:

- Serving alcohol to a minor
- Selling alcohol without a license
- Serving alcohol before permitted hours of service
- Serving alcohol after permitted hours of service

The test for deciding whether a bartender or server should have realized the extent of a patron's intoxication is also subjective. Courts look at the condition of the intoxicated person. They consider whether it should have reasonably been *foreseeable* to the employee serving him or her that the person was already "visibly intoxicated" or presented "a clear danger" to himself or herself and others and thus should not be served any more alcohol.

For managers, the most important point to remember is that it is not how many drinks the person has had. Rather, it is how the alcohol affects a guest's behavior and his or her BAC level that is critically important. Of course, establishing policies to avoid serving alcohol recklessly is something all professional managers seek to do. The practical difficulty in developing effective alcohol sales–related policies can be illustrated by actual cases settled in court.

CASE 1

The Complaint: A female guest was injured in an unprovoked assault by an intoxicated guest (also female) who had earlier been confrontational toward the attacked guest and her group of friends. It was agreed during the trial that the plaintiff (the attacked guest) had, on two occasions, complained and asked the bar staff to eject the offending drinker or at least to stop serving that guest alcohol. Despite the requests of the plaintiff and in spite of the intoxicated guest's hostile behavior, the operation's beverage staff continued to serve alcohol to the aggressive guest.

Manager's Memo

Recall that a variety of factors can influence the BAC of an individual drinker:

- Drinking rate (amount consumed)
- Drink strength
- Body size
- Body fat
- Gender
- Age
- Emotional state
- Medications taken
- Foods eaten
- Carbonation of drinks

Because all of these factors can directly affect the BAC of drinkers, managers and their beverage service staff have the important responsibility of always using reasonable care to ensure no intoxicated guest is served alcohol.

THINK ABOUT IT ...

Some observers believe that guests should not be allowed to drink alcohol before driving. They favor laws that prohibit all alcohol sales to those driving. Would you support such a law? Why or why not?

The Ruling: The bar was found to have breached, or violated, its duty of care to the plaintiff. The bar was found liable for the plaintiff's injuries.

Message to Managers: Be aware of situations where a guest's conduct indicates that he or she is likely to do harm to someone else. In such cases, it is the manager's duty to see that the disruptive guest is removed from the premises as soon as possible. If the manager fails to do that and the guest becomes violent, the operation may be held liable, or legally responsible, for any resulting injuries to others.

CASE 2

The Complaint: A regular guest with no history of violence or troublemaking assaulted another guest in an operation that served alcohol. Both guests had been at the bar for several hours before the incident occurred. Neither guest was served an amount of alcohol that was deemed excessive.

The Ruling: The court held that this act of violence was not reasonably foreseeable and that the defendant, the operator, was not liable.

Message to Managers: If a guest suddenly becomes violent and there were no warning signs that this was about to occur, the operator will likely not be held liable for resulting injuries—that is, as long as it can be shown that the operation served alcohol responsibly.

These two similar legal cases, the subjective nature of BAC levels, and the subjective definitions of public intoxication should lead thoughtful observers to one important conclusion:

> *Managers must be able to prove, in an objective manner, that they and their employees consistently exercise reasonable care in the service of alcohol.*

The best way to prove, in an objective manner, that an operation consistently exercises reasonable care in the service of alcohol is by training all employees in safe alcohol service and enforcing "serve-safe" alcohol policies.

The Responsible Alcohol Service Program

Managers whose operations serve alcohol must ensure that they or their staff members do not serve intoxicated persons and others not permitted to drink. To perform this task, managers must use professionalism and good judgment. The need for professional qualifications is not isolated to the restaurant and foodservice industry. Society recognizes that many jobs require the jobholders to be qualified and to prove it, if they are to perform their assigned duties well. One way to ensure professional jobholders are qualified is by requiring or encouraging their certification (*Exhibit 3.1*).

Certification refers to the confirmation that a person possesses certain skills, knowledge, or characteristics. In most cases, this confirmation is supplied by some form of external review, education, or assessment. One of the most common types of certification is professional certification. In most cases, the certified person has demonstrated an ability to competently complete a job or task. Typically he or she does so by passing an examination.

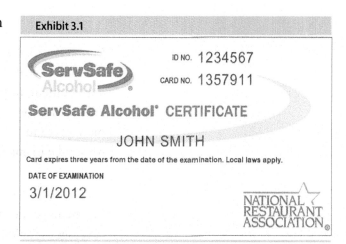

Exhibit 3.1

There are two general types of professional certification: Some are valid for a lifetime after the qualifying exam is passed, whereas others have to be recertified again after a certain period of time. In some professions, certification is a requirement prior to employment or practice. Doctors, teachers, certified public accountants (CPAs), and airline pilots are examples.

Increasingly, states require that establishment managers and, in most cases, bartenders and other beverage servers complete an alcohol service training course to become officially certified in the safe service of alcohol as a condition of keeping an operation's liquor license. In many cases, those companies that provide insurance to beverage-serving operations make the same requirement.

State requirements surrounding training and certification in the safe service of alcohol vary. In some states, the only accepted responsible alcohol service program is provided by the state Alcoholic Beverage Control (ABC), which is responsible for granting licenses and regulating the sale of alcohol. There are three states where this is true:

- Delaware
- Hawaii
- New Mexico

Several states require that supplemental information and, in some cases, a state-specific quiz be administered during a responsible alcohol service class. In most states, training and certification in the safe service of alcohol is provided by several organizations, including the National Restaurant Association. ServSafe Alcohol is the name of the responsible alcohol server program developed by the association. The print version of ServSafe Alcohol has been accepted as an Approved Program by the Alcoholic Beverage Control (ABC) Commission in 47 states.

Whether managers are required to be certified by their employer, by the state issuing their liquor license, by their insurance companies, or simply because they wish to improve their professional skills, training in the safe service of alcohol is important for them, for their entire beverage service staff, and for their customers. The purpose of an effective alcohol service program is twofold. The first purpose is to comply with the law. The second is to learn how to do what every manager and all beverage service employees should always want to do: serve alcohol safely.

THE IMPORTANCE OF TRAINING

Managers are responsible for ensuring their entire beverage staff is trained in the safe service of alcoholic beverages. They also are responsible for the development, implementation, and monitoring of alcoholic beverage service policies and procedures used in their facilities. To accomplish these two goals, managers must understand the training process and the specific steps they must take to ensure their operations continually serve alcohol safely.

Training Fundamentals

The manager of a bar, restaurant, or foodservice operation selling alcoholic beverages should be certified or otherwise able to demonstrate they are highly trained in the safe service of alcohol. Regular employees do not automatically know the many things they must be aware of to serve alcohol safely. Therefore, qualified managers must train their beverage service and other employees on their own operation's beverage service policies and procedures. Before managers can begin to train, however, they must understand how to train.

Training must be cost-effective: it must yield time and money savings that are greater than what it costs. The best training is performance-based, and it is planned and delivered in an organized way so employees will learn how to correctly perform all their beverage service–related tasks in the ways they are supposed to.

The need for training to be performance-based is important, but it creates challenges:

- Each important task and all required knowledge for each employee position must be identified.
- The specific knowledge and skills needed to do each task must be recorded.
- Training to provide all of the knowledge and skills to perform each task must be developed.
- Competencies (standards of knowledge, skills, and abilities required for successful job performance) must be known and considered when training programs are developed.
- An evaluation process is needed to learn if the training has been successful.

TRAINING BENEFITS

In addition to ensuring laws are followed, there are several additional benefits to effective alcohol service training:

- **Improved job performance:** Trainees learn how to perform required tasks more effectively and this improves their overall job performance.
- **Reduced legal risk:** Proper employee training helps an operation avoid the potential risk resulting from the illegal or irresponsible service of alcohol.

- **Reduced costs:** Improved job performance helps reduce errors in alcohol service. Fewer errors can lead to reduced lawsuits and lessens the risk of costly liability judgments against the business.

- **More satisfied customers:** Effective alcohol service programs make all guests feel safer. In addition, the proper training can help employees handle difficult situations in a more customer-friendly manner.

- **Reduced work stress:** Not knowing how to handle a new situation can be stressful for employees. Effective training and specific procedures provide employees the tools they need to address new or difficult situations. Having these tools reduces the stress associated with these situations.

- **Increased job advancement opportunities:** Competent employees are more likely to receive promotions than are less competent staff members.

- **Fewer operating problems:** Busy managers can focus on other priorities and not spend time on routine problems and issues caused by a lack of training.

- **Higher levels of work quality:** Effective training helps employees work at levels that meet management's standards of performance.

Exhibit 3.2

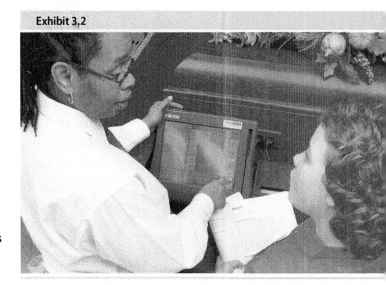

ON-THE-JOB TRAINING AND EVALUATION

On-the-job training is commonly used in the restaurant and foodservice industry, and it occurs when the manager or another trainer teaches job skills and knowledge to one trainee at a time, usually at the work site (*Exhibit 3.2*). For a variety of reasons, it is an excellent method to use for safe alcohol service training when it is well organized:

- It uses basic adult learning principles such as considering the trainee's attention span and providing immediate feedback about performance.

- It addresses what the trainee must know and be able to do.

- It can be used to train both new and experienced staff.

- It is well accepted by employees.

There are four steps to effective on-the-job training. These steps are presented in *Exhibit 3.3*.

Step 1: Training Preparation

Managers or other employees who will be training staff should do several things as they prepare for the training activity:

- Preview the training objectives and determine what the trainees will learn.

Exhibit 3.3

Phase 1:
Training Preparation

↓

Phase 2:
Training Presentation

↓

Phase 3:
Trainee Practice and Demonstration

↓

Phase 4:
Follow-Through

- Present the training content. It also may be helpful to duplicate copies of any relevant information for the trainees.
- Consider the training schedule. Know the length of the training activity and where in the overall training plan specific activities should occur.
- Select the training location. When possible, the training should occur in the work area where the task will be performed.
- Assemble training materials and equipment. Get everything needed for the training before it begins.
- Prepare the trainee. A new employee should know that the training will help him or her perform all job tasks correctly. An experienced staff member should understand that the training will provide the knowledge and skills needed to perform a task differently, to learn a new beverage service task, or to review current alcohol service procedures.

Step 2: Training Presentation

To review effective training presentation practices, think about how a manager might train an employee to understand the importance of BAC to the safe service of alcohol. First the employee would need to be taught the meaning of BAC. He or she would be told why it is important to understand the factors affecting a guest's BAC. The factors would be presented. The trainee would then be told what to do if he or she suspects a guest's BAC is approaching a critical level that might require server or manager intervention. Note: *Bartender, server, and manager intervention procedures are presented in the final portion of this chapter.*

As the presentation is made, the manager-trainer follows several training principles:

- He or she speaks in simple terms.
- Simple concepts are presented before more concepts are addressed.
- All important concepts are explained slowly and clearly, using examples.
- A questioning process is used, and the trainer asks open-ended questions such as "Why do you think it is important to monitor the BAC levels of guests?"

Step 3: Trainee Practice and Demonstration

Several principles are important as the trainee demonstrates understanding about what is being learned:

- The trainee should be asked to repeat or explain key points.
- The trainees should explain the importance of applying what they have learned.

- Each trainee should be able to explain what could happen if he or she does not apply what has been learned as it relates to these factors:
  - Guests
  - The business
  - Their own jobs
  - Trainees should be praised for their participation and learning with, at least, a compliment or "thank you."

Step 4: Follow-Through

The final step in on-the-job training is for the trainer to ensure that the training has been effective and to document the training. For example, at the end of the training session, the trainee should encourage trainees to ask questions about any areas the trainee does not understand fully. Close supervision immediately after training and occasional supervision after a concept has been mastered can help ensure that the trainee is able to consistently demonstrate understanding of what has been taught.

Training evaluation such as testing can be useful to determine the extent to which the training was successful. Evaluation also can help identify the strengths and weaknesses of training, and can be used to collect information to help improve future training programs.

Experienced managers know that there are several possible training evaluation methods:

- **Objective tests:** These tests can be written or oral. A separate test should be used for each training session.

- **Observation of after-training performance:** Managers and trainers can manage by "walking around" and noting whether the knowledge and skills that were taught are being applied.

- **Interviews with trainees and trainers:** The use of open-ended questions such as "What factors affecting BAC do you think are most important with the guests we serve in our operation?" may provide useful input to evaluate current training and improve future training.

- **Exit interviews:** Formal and even informal conversations with staff members leaving the operation can provide information helpful for training evaluation.

Finally, documentation concludes the training effort, and training information should be maintained in each trainee's personnel file and should include several pertinent details such as: the name of trainee, the training dates, and the training topics discussed. Notes about the successful completion of training and any other pertinent information should also be saved.

Should it ever be required, the written documentation of training is important to demonstrate that management has taken reasonable care in preparing its staff to serve alcohol responsibly.

Manager's Memo

Assume that an employee attends a training session and missed only 2 of 20 questions on an after-training test. Most managers would probably assume the training was successful because the trainee answered 90% of the questions correctly:

18 correct questions ÷ 20 questions = 90% correctly answered questions

However, the training could have been a waste of money and time if, before the training began, the trainee already knew the concepts covered by the 18 questions answered correctly.

Trainers who use pretests and posttests address this concern. They identify key training concepts and give a before-training pretest to learn a trainee's existing knowledge or skills. They then use the same test at the end of the training as a posttest, and improved scores measure training effectiveness.

MANAGEMENT STEPS FOR THE SAFE SERVICE OF ALCOHOL

In addition to training, managers must make sure they have the right policies and procedures in place to protect themselves, their guests, and their operations. Managers must take a number of important steps to help ensure the safe service of alcohol in their operations and to demonstrate to others, if the need arises, that they have done so:

1. Develop an incident report form.
2. Provide staff training.
3. Monitor licensing and certificates.
4. Monitor alcoholic beverage service.
5. Resolve beverage service problems and concerns.
6. Review resolutions of service-related problems and concerns.
7. Take corrective action if alcohol service–related problem patterns emerge.

Develop an Incident Report Form

Managers must be prepared if a critical incident related to alcoholic beverage service occurs. If it does, some operation may require managers to document the event. An incident report is the form used to document what happened and what was done in response. There are a variety of situations in which managers may decide to mandate the completion of an incident report:

- If alcohol service has been stopped to a guest
- If alternative transportation has been arranged for an intoxicated guest
- If an illegal activity has been observed
- If a fight or altercation occurs
- If a guest becomes ill and requires medical treatment

If a significant event such as those listed occurs, it can be stressful and emotions can run high. A manager must take control of the situation immediately for two reasons: (1) to ensure the safety of the guests and (2) to protect the operation legally.

Managers can accomplish these goals if employees are trained to respond properly in an emergency situation. Part of that training involves promptly completing and filing an incident report. Employees such as bartenders or servers who witness or who are involved in an incident should be taught to notify the appropriate person, communicate the problem, and take the steps needed to keep themselves and guests safe. When they do, managers or other responsible persons may record the event, depending on the operations policy. Doing so will allow owners or insurers to know about the event in the future. *Exhibit 3.4* shows an incident report form that can be

---

OPEN FOR BUSINESS

KEEPING IT SAFE

Assume you were on a jury, hearing two different lawsuits in which establishments were accused of not demonstrating reasonable care in the service of alcoholic beverages. In one case, the operation has well documented its beverage service training program, which includes certification for all managers and thorough and ongoing training for all staff. The other establishment can provide no evidence of any beverage service training for its manager or any of its employees. Would documented evidence of extensive training make you more or less inclined to believe the operation that provided it had used reasonable care? Why?

Exhibit 3.4

INCIDENT REPORT FORM

(Facility Name and Location)

Date Prepared _____

Completed By (*print*) _____ Title _____

Date of Incident _____ Reported By _____

Time of Incident _____ (AM) (PM) Location _____

Summary of Incident:

_____

_____

_____

Type of Incident: ☐ Guest Refused Service ☐ Injury/Fight ☐ Other

If Injury:

Was 911 called?	☐ Yes	☐ No
Was injured party capable of requesting medical attention?	☐ Yes	☐ No
Did injured party request medical attention?	☐ Yes	☐ No
Was medical attention provided? (*If yes, provide information below.*)	☐ Yes	☐ No

Nature of Medical Attention: _____

_____

If Fight/Disturbance:

Were police summoned?	☐ Yes	☐ No
Was a report taken?	☐ Yes	☐ No
Was an arrest made?	☐ Yes	☐ No

Attending Officer's Name (*Print*) _____ Badge Number _____

If Other:

Description of Action Taken: _____

_____

Witness to the Event _____

Name _____ Position _____

Contact Information _____

_____

Telephone _____

Report Submitted To _____ Title _____

Date of Submission _____

used to record critical information about beverage service–related issues. It is advisable to consult with an attorney before creating and implementing an incident report form.

If an incident related to beverage service should occur, managers must ensure the appropriate staff members are familiar with the incident report and know how to fill it out properly. Keeping a record of beverage service issues as they occur helps managers prevent future issues, modify training if needed, and be prepared for potential legal action against the operation. In addition, how managers respond to and document an incident may affect their operation's insurance coverage.

Provide Staff Training

In many states, the ABC mandates who on an operation's staff must be trained in responsible beverage service. Typically those positions identified as requiring mandatory training include key beverage service positions:

- Managers
- Bartenders
- Servers

In some cases, the requirement for training will include certification or the completion of a specific state-mandated training program. When certification is required, managers typically can choose from state-approved certification programs such as the National Restaurant Association's ServSafe Alcohol program. If certification is not required, managers must determine any externally offered courses or training requirements that are in place and document their operation's compliance with the requirements.

If no mandatory state training is required, managers must develop their own training programs. Because the needs of each operation differ, it is up to the manager to decide who will be trained and what they will be taught. There are a large number of possible training topics and knowledge areas related to responsible beverage service, and managers must choose the ones that make the most sense for their own operations. For beverage service training purposes, employees can be segmented into groups with similar responsibilities.

SPECIAL EVENTS SERVERS

Special events servers are those individuals involved in direct service of alcoholic beverages for temporary or special occasion events such as banquets or receptions where alcohol service is a minor part of the server's function.

For these individuals, only a few hours of alcohol service training may make the most sense. The topics that may be of concern in training these employees, however, are still significant and may include the following:

- Hours of legal operation
- Service to minors
- Possession by minors
- Drinker's age identification
- Service to obviously intoxicated persons
- Signs and stages of intoxication
- Intervention
- Incident reporting

PROFESSIONAL SERVERS

Professional servers are involved in direct service or sales of alcoholic beverages and can include bartenders, servers, cashiers, hosts, door attendants, bouncers, and valets. The employment status of these individuals may be part time, full time, temporary, or permanent. For these employees, more extensive training is typically required. The topics that may be of concern in training these employees include all of those identified for special events servers as well as additional topics:

- Alcohol-impaired driving
- Interaction of alcohol and drugs
- Physiology and factors affecting blood alcohol content (BAC)
- Alcohol tolerance
- Insurance
- Food promotion
- Guest safety assurance
- Drink size and limits
- Clues of intoxication

BEVERAGE SERVICE SUPERVISORS

Beverage service supervisors have the responsibility of managing sellers or servers of alcohol and thus require the most extensive training. The topics that may be of concern in training these employees include all of those which

OPEN FOR BUSINESS

RESTAURANT TECHNOLOGY

Training is one of the areas of restaurant and foodservice management that has been most impacted by advancements in technology. Today, training lessons on a variety of topics including responsible alcoholic beverage service can be delivered via the Internet or downloaded to personal computers, notebooks, and other mobile devices.

Using advanced technology as a training tool allows employees to complete training sessions at the times that are most convenient for them. It also allows managers to track the progress of their employees' training activities and can provide automatic documentation of training completion.

have been identified for special events and professional servers as well as additional topics:

- Laws, policies, rules, and regulations
- Administrative liability—ABC license sanctions
- Criminal and civil liability
- State ABC laws and regulations
- Age of alcohol sellers and servers
- State DUI or DWI penalties
- Suspension of service to intoxicated guests
- Assurance that intoxicated guests travel safely
- Handling of potentially violent situations
- Handling of illegal activities
- Handling of medical emergencies
- Summoning of local law enforcement
- Management of incident reports
- Legally permitted promotions of alcoholic beverages
- State and local operating laws
- Other operation-specific alcohol service policies and procedures
- Maintenance of required records of training

Managers carefully choose all of the training topics that are appropriate for their staff. They also use sound training procedures such as those indicated earlier in this chapter, including documentation of completion, as they prepare their team for the important task of serving alcohol responsibly.

Monitor Licensing and Certificates

Every state requires sellers of alcoholic beverages to be licensed. Applying for and maintaining a liquor license is a complex process. To maintain a liquor license, most states require managers to comply with, and document their compliance with, a variety of policies or laws. Managers must be very familiar with these licensing and certifying requirements. They must also ensure that they are in compliance at all times to maintain their licenses to sell alcohol.

To illustrate, consider just a few of the laws related to maintaining an establishment liquor license in the state of Utah. Operation managers in that state must be aware of a variety of requirements they must meet, and be able to document, information related to insurance, bonds (a guarantee of the ability to pay in case of a liability), and food sales if they are to keep their liquor licenses. Some examples are quoted here:

Insurance

Public liability and dram shop insurance coverage required in Section 32A-4-102(1)(h) and (i) must remain in force during the time the license is in effect. Failure of the licensee to maintain the required insurance coverage may result in a suspension or revocation of the license by the commission.

Bond

No part of any corporate or cash bond required by Section 32A-4-105, may be withdrawn during the time the license is in effect. If the licensee fails to maintain a valid corporate or cash bond, the license shall be immediately suspended until a valid bond is obtained. Failure to obtain a bond within 30 days of notification by the department of the delinquency shall result in the automatic revocation of the license.

Food Sales

The restaurant shall maintain at least 70% of its total business from the sale of food pursuant to Section 32A-4-106(23).

(a) The restaurant shall maintain records separately showing quarterly expenditures and sales for beer, heavy beer, liquor, wine, set-ups, and food. These shall be available for inspection and audit by representatives of the department, and maintained for a period of three years.

(b) If any inspection or audit discloses that the sales of food are less than 70% for any quarterly period, an order to show cause shall be issued by the department to determine why the license should not be immediately suspended by the commission. Any suspension shall remain in effect until the licensee is able to prove to the satisfaction of the commission that in the future, the sales of food will meet or exceed 70%.

Failure of the licensee to provide satisfactory proof of the required food percentage within three months of the date the license was suspended, shall result in the revocation of the license.

All state ABCs attach a large number of conditions to maintaining a liquor license. Therefore, monitoring the status of licensing and required certificates is a critical step in maintaining a liquor license in every state.

Monitor Alcoholic Beverage Service

Personally monitoring alcoholic beverage service is one of a manager's most important steps. Managers should observe servers and bartenders as they follow policies and procedures designed to ensure that they serve alcohol safely.

Beverage staff that has been properly trained must still be monitored and coached to ensure they do their jobs well. Coaching occurs when managers

Exhibit 3.5

Coaching is an important part of every beverage manager's job.

emphasize that employees are working correctly, called positive coaching, and when they discourage employees from working incorrectly, called negative coaching. Coaching is not usually a formal activity, and it often involves simple conversations with employees as they work (*Exhibit 3.5*).

Positive coaching occurs when a manager observes an employee doing something correctly: "Alex, you're doing a great job checking customers' IDs. Thanks a lot; I really appreciate it." Negative coaching involves correcting an employee: "Alex, I know you can get really busy, but we still need to check IDs carefully. Let's talk about how we can make sure we do that when we are busy."

Almost all employees want to know how their manager views their work. They like coaching input, and, since it costs no money and takes so little time, it should be a "must" tactic used by all managers.

Simple coaching can correct many beverage staff performance problems, and the use of several principles can help ensure coaching is effective:

- **Be tactful:** If corrective actions are required, focus on the employee's behavior, not on the staff member himself or herself.

- **Emphasize the positive:** Managers who interact with well-trained and motivated employees have many more opportunities to provide positive rather than negative coaching.

- **Demonstrate and review appropriate procedures:** Spend more time showing the correct way to do something than criticizing or complaining about improper performance.

- **Keep communications open:** A workplace that supports ongoing coaching conversations reduces concerns such as an employee thinking "What did I do wrong now?" every time the manager approaches.

- **Allow employees to contribute to their work:** Employees can be asked for their ideas when procedures are evaluated, revised, and implemented, and they can be asked about suggestions to address operating challenges.

- **Conduct most corrective coaching sessions in private:** Praise employees in public and conduct conversations to improve performance in private.

- **Evaluate the work of employees by comparing their performance against standards:** Avoid comparing one employee's work to that of another employee.

THINK ABOUT IT ...

Coaching gives workers feedback. Most employees like to know how their manager feels about their work. What approaches to coaching have worked best for you, either as the coach or the worker?

- **Establish and agree on time frames for improving performance:** If performance is not acceptable, the manager and employee should agree upon what must be done to improve performance. Then a schedule for acceptable performance or for a review of performance can be determined.

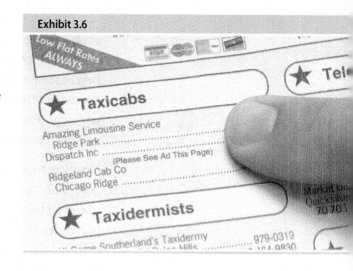

Resolve Beverage Service Problems and Concerns

Another of a manager's most important tasks is to help resolve beverage service problems and concerns as they develop. Despite excellent staff training, incidents such as the following ones will likely occur and will require management intervention:

- Refusing entrance to intoxicated guests

- Refusing service to underage drinkers

- Ensuring drink preparation procedures are carefully followed

- Stopping service to drinkers who appear intoxicated

- Assisting intoxicated guests to find safe transportation as they leave the operation (*Exhibit 3.6*)

In all of these examples and more, managers must be prepared to provide leadership to their beverage service teams. They also must follow their operation's stated policies and procedures when doing so.

Review Resolutions of Service-Related Problems and Concerns and Take Action If Problem Patterns Emerge

Sometimes managers will find that the same beverage service–related issues occur frequently and that simple employee coaching will not resolve the issues. When this happens, managers can use a formal problem-solving process to address and correct the recurring issue. For example, assume that a manager finds that when a certain bartender works, the operation serves guests past the legal time allowed for beverage service. This action places the operation's liquor license at risk, and coaching of the bartender has not corrected the problem. The manager can address this recurring problem by a series of actions:

DEFINING THE PROBLEM

The best way to define a problem is to think about who or what is affected, and a questioning process can be used for this purpose. Depending on the problem, different groups including employees, managers, owners, or even customers could be asked to help explain why the problem exists. In this example, the problem is that alcohol service is continuing beyond the legally allowed time period.

DETERMINING THE CAUSE OF THE PROBLEM

Problems affecting policies and procedures are often blamed directly on affected employees. However, problems often can have other causes. Most beverage operations are made up of a series of complex systems including those for admitting guests, taking orders, serving guests, and collecting payment. Problems can occur when one or more of these systems break down or were not carefully developed in the first place.

One way to identify the root cause of a problem is to examine all of the potential causes. Managers often use a questioning process to do this. In this example, the question of why guests are served too late could be related to the bartender, the operation's servers, or to other factors the bartender may not be able to control. In this example, assume that the manager discovers all servers announce last call (the statement used to notify guests alcohol service is about to end) five minutes before the hour alcohol service is to end. Last call causes a flood of final drink orders. The bartender is unable to fill all of these orders before the legal serving period ends.

ASSESSING ALTERNATIVE SOLUTIONS

An alternative is simply a possible solution to a recurring problem. A beverage service–related problem likely has a number of possible solutions. For example, terminating the offending bartender in the previous example would stop *that* bartender from serving guests after the allowable time period. It would not, however, solve the underlying problem.

After potential alternatives have been generated, they should be analyzed to determine which would best correct the problem. Key questions can be asked:

- What will happen if we use this alternative?
- Who will be affected and how will they be affected?
- Is the alternative better than any other alternative?
- Is it cost-effective? Will the solution cost more than the problem?
- Is it reasonable? Does the alternative have a good chance to succeed?

SELECTING THE BEST COURSE OF ACTION

Wise managers chose solutions carefully. An incorrect solution will likely create the need to repeat the problem-solving process, and the negative impact of the problem will also continue. After a manager chooses the best solution, he or she develops an action plan. An action plan is a series of steps that can be taken to resolve the problem. The action plan for the beverage service problem in this illustration may be to move forward the announced time for last call.

Communicating the action plan is essential. Managers also should communicate the action plan's expected outcomes to everyone involved so they know what must be done and how they will be impacted. In the earlier example, servers will need to be retrained and a procedure to inform guests about the change will need to be developed.

DOCUMENTING THE ACTION

The purpose of documentation is to record information for future use. Changes in job procedures and activities used to implement the solution should be recorded so training, coaching, and ongoing supervisory action can be modified as needed. In this example, a change in the timing of last call should be monitored to ensure that it does, in fact, correct this last call–related service problem. If it does not, the problem-solving procedure should be repeated. The continual review and modification, if necessary, of all alcohol service activities, policies, and procedures are an essential part of every beverage manager's job.

PROFESSIONAL GUEST INTERVENTION PROCEDURES

Managers of beverage operations know that they must please their guests. They also know that they and their employees must follow the law. In most cases, it is easy to do both. In some situations, however, it is not so easy. This can be the case, for example, when a guest who appears to be intoxicated wishes to purchase additional drinks. If the guest is refused service, he or she likely will not be happy. While that is unfortunate, experienced managers know that in such situations, guest safety is more important than short-term guest happiness.

Sometimes difficult situations require intervention on the part of the operation. When they do, it is essential that both employees and managers know how to perform their respective roles well. Doing so ensures that all guests will be provided a safe environment. It also ensures that the operation will fulfill its duty of using reasonable care in the service of alcohol.

Intervention by Bartenders and Servers

As has been noted, it is illegal in all states to serve alcohol to an intoxicated guest. As a result, all bartenders and servers should be trained to identify the signs that indicate a guest has had too much to drink. Effective intervention by bartenders and servers begins the moment a guest enters the operation. Keeping guests from becoming intoxicated is just as critical as is stopping service to them after they have become intoxicated.

Bartenders and servers should evaluate customers when they order their first drinks. This is done simply by greeting the guest, initiating a brief conversation with them, and noting key guest characteristics:

- Will the guest be ordering food?
- Does the guest appear tired, stressed, or depressed?
- Does the guest speak clearly (not slurring his or her words)?
- Is the guest already intoxicated?
- Does the guest make comments, either seriously or in jest, indicating his or her desire to "get drunk"?

The bartender or server should look for indications that the guest has already consumed some alcohol or is consuming alcohol at a rate likely to elevate the guest's BAC dramatically. When guests meet these criteria, bartenders and servers may encourage the guest to eat or to switch to nonalcoholic drinks (coffee or water), lower-alcohol drinks, or to "slow down" their consumption. Some servers also slow service to such guests, but this approach must be approved by management. In many operations, it is a policy that managers be alerted to the potential intervention issue so they are aware of the possibility of their future involvement.

In addition, bartenders and servers must be made aware of the times they must stop serving guests additional alcohol:

- If the guest shows physical or behavioral signs of intoxication
- If the bartender or server is concerned about the impact of the number of drinks the guest has consumed on the guest's BAC

Some operations allow bartenders and servers to stop service in such situations but require them to notify management. Other operations require managers to stop the service. In all cases, bartenders and servers should know, and follow, their own operation's guest intervention policies.

Intervention by Managers

In many operations, it will be the manager's job to intervene when a guest is refused service of alcohol. In such cases, it is essential that the operation's pre-established policies be followed and that the incident is documented in an incident report. In addition to stopping service to a guest, managers may face other intervention challenges, including guests who arrive intoxicated and intoxicated guests who seek to drive away from the operation.

KEEPING IT SAFE

In some cases, guests who are refused alcohol service may become threatening or even violent. In such cases employee safety, as well as the safety of other guests in the operation, should take first priority. Employees in an operation serving alcohol should avoid physical confrontations with guests at all costs. While it is uncommon, guests have been known to go to bars and nightclubs with unregistered weapons or concealed sharp objects. As a result, the best way for employees to survive a fight is to avoid it.

Employees should be carefully taught about the circumstances in which local law enforcement officials should be summoned to deal with unruly guests, but employees should never be instructed to place their own personal safety at risk.

GUESTS WHO ARRIVE INTOXICATED

Sometimes guests who are already intoxicated arrive at an operation that serves alcohol. In this situation, managers have a legal obligation *not* to serve such guests. Many managers feel they also have a professional obligation to help the guests depart safely. Managers can take specific steps if guests arrive intoxicated:

- Try to refuse entry.
- Ensure that guests are not served alcohol if they insist on entering.
- Call local law enforcement personnel to have the guest removed if he or she causes a disturbance.

INTOXICATED GUESTS WHO SEEK TO DRIVE AWAY FROM THE OPERATION

Sometimes guests who arrive intoxicated or who appear to become intoxicated while in the operation may decide to drive away when they are refused service. In such a case, managers should take specific actions:

- Determine if the guest is the only available driver or if a safe driver is available to drive him or her.
- If the guest is the only driver, ask for his or her keys (*Exhibit 3.7*).
- If the guest agrees not to drive, arrange for alternative transportation.
- If the guest refuses to surrender his or her keys and insists on driving, notify local law enforcement.

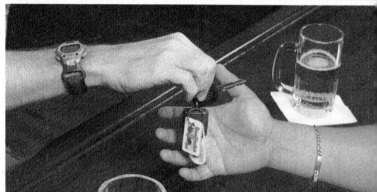

Exhibit 3.7

Managers are responsible for following the law related to the service of alcoholic beverages, but laws in this area do change. As a result, it is essential that managers stay abreast of legal changes regarding beverage alcohol service. Professional managers who seek to stay up-to-date with changes in the legal requirements of alcoholic beverage service take specific actions:

- They learn as much as possible about current laws.
- They develop a relationship with a state ABC staff member.
- They interact with a qualified attorney familiar with state law.
- They regularly read newspapers or visit an Internet news site.
- They are active in their state or local restaurant association(s).

All these activities help managers know about changes in the law and the resulting need to modify their operating policies to ensure they always serve alcoholic beverages legally and responsibly.

SUMMARY

1. **Explain the importance of understanding BAC to the responsible service of alcohol.**

   The key thing to know about blood alcohol content (BAC) is that its level in an individual is impacted by a variety of factors. Thus, it can be challenging to determine if an individual drinker's BAC has been elevated to the point where that drinker is intoxicated. It is illegal to serve an intoxicated person. BAC is one key factor indicating intoxication, but because it cannot be measured directly, managers must take steps to ensure they continually demonstrate reasonable care in the service of alcohol. To do so, managers must train staff and implement policies to minimize the chances of serving a guest who is intoxicated.

2. **State the two main purposes of a responsible alcohol service training program.**

   The purpose of an effective alcohol service program is twofold. The first purpose is to comply with the requirements of the state Alcoholic Beverage Control (ABC) or with the mandates of other entities that require proof of competency in the service of alcohol. These other entities may include employers and insurance companies. The second and equally important purpose of a responsible alcohol service training program is to learn how to do what every manager and all beverage service employees should always want to do: serve alcohol safely.

3. **List the four steps managers take to train employees in the responsible service of alcohol.**

   Managers responsible for the safe service of alcohol perform a number of critical tasks. These include providing comprehensive staff training at all employee levels. This training consists of four important steps. In training step 1, managers consider their training objectives and prepare their training plans. In step 2, managers actually present the training to employees. Step 3 in the training process is the one that provides employees with the opportunity to practice what they have learned and demonstrate their knowledge. Step 4 of the training process is management's follow-up and documentation. The purpose of this step is for the trainer to ensure that the training has been effective and to identify the need for additional training. The careful documentation of successfully completed training concludes this important step.

4. **Explain how managers ensure employees serve alcohol responsibly.**

   Effective managers take several steps to ensure their operation serves alcohol responsibly. Depending on the operation's policies, they may begin by developing an incident report form to document any problems that their operation experiences. All managers must ensure that staff is adequately trained. They also monitor all state licensing and certificate requirements as well as continually monitor alcoholic beverage service in their facilities.

Finally, managers resolve beverage service problems and concerns as they occur and take appropriate corrective action if alcohol service–related problem patterns emerge.

5. **Describe the role bartenders and servers play in effective guest intervention procedures.**

Because it is illegal in all states to serve alcohol to an intoxicated guest, bartenders and servers should be trained to identify the signs that indicate a guest has had too much to drink. Effective intervention by bartenders and servers begins when guests order their first drinks because it is usually easier to prevent guests from becoming intoxicated than to deal with them after they are intoxicated. Bartenders and servers should first greet and then initiate a brief conversation with each guest and then, as the guest is served, monitor any behavioral changes that indicate alcohol service should be stopped. This should be done in keeping with their employer's intervention policy.

6. **Describe the role that managers play in effective guest intervention procedures.**

Managers play a variety of roles in guest intervention as needed. They develop policies to address what is to be done if guests who are intoxicated arrive at the operation. They are also involved in all situations where guests are denied the service of additional alcoholic drinks. In addition, they establish policies for addressing those intoxicated patrons who are leaving the operation. Finally, managers are responsible for ensuring they are continually up-to-date with all current laws regarding the legal service of alcoholic beverages.

APPLICATION EXERCISE

Assume you are the manager at a popular nightclub. Despite your best efforts at monitoring the sale of alcohol, you recognize that some guests may drink too much and be incapable of driving themselves home. Draft a policy for your club that will be shared with your employees that addresses the topic of handling intoxicated guests who drove to the club and now are attempting to leave. Be sure to answer these questions as you draft your policy:

1. How should employees communicate to the guests that they should not be driving?

2. How should staff members request that guests voluntarily give up their keys?

3. What should employees do if the guests refuse to surrender their keys?

4. How should staff members arrange for alternative transportation?

5. When would you or your employees contact local law enforcement for assistance?

REVIEW YOUR LEARNING

Select the best answer for each question.

1. **Who in the United States is responsible for establishing laws regarding public intoxication?**
   A. The federal government
   B. The Department of Justice
   C. State and local government
   D. The Bureau of Alcohol, Tobacco and Firearms

2. **What has happened if managers have breached a duty of care?**
   A. They have met the duty
   B. They have violated the duty
   C. They have explained the duty to their staff
   D. They understand the requirements of the duty

3. **What is the name of the responsible alcohol service certification program offered by the National Restaurant Association (NRA)?**
   A. Safety First
   B. Alcohol 101
   C. ServSafe Alcohol
   D. Safe Alcohol Consumption

4. **In which phase of training do managers preview training objectives and determine what the trainees will learn?**
   A. Trainee practice and demonstration
   B. Training preparation
   C. Training presentation
   D. Follow-through

5. **The purpose of an incident report is to**
   A. discipline employees.
   B. prevent a disturbance.
   C. record events or actions.
   D. prevent illegal service of alcohol.

6. **What responsibility must managers assume if no mandatory state training is required of beverage service staff members?**
   A. Managers must hire only employees with previous training.
   B. Managers must not provide training for any of their employees.
   C. Managers must develop their own employee training programs.
   D. Managers must encourage employees to complete training on their own time.

7. **What do a pretest and posttest of employee skills help managers identify?**
   A. What employees think are the most important tasks addressed in training
   B. How much trainees learned as a direct result of a training session
   C. How trainees evaluate the training they received
   D. What employees learned most quickly

8. **Which is a principle of effective coaching?**
   A. Compare one worker's performance to another's
   B. Emphasize positive performance
   C. Discipline workers in public
   D. Give praise in private

9. **Which is the last step in correcting a recurring beverage service–related problem?**
   A. Determining the problem's cause
   B. Defining the problem
   C. Documenting action
   D. Assessing solutions

10. **An intoxicated guest becomes very agitated. In such a case, what should be management's top priority?**
    A. Ensuring the guest pays his or her bill
    B. Preventing damage to the facility
    C. Keeping the guest quiet and escorting him or her out
    D. Protecting the safety of employees and other guests

FIELD PROJECT

Training employees in the safe service of alcohol is one of a beverage manager's most important jobs. Prepare a short training program for use by servers indicating what they should do if they believe a guest is too intoxicated to be served additional alcohol. You may want to interview an operation or bar manager as part of your research for this project. Indicate these factors for this training program:

1. List the method you will use for teaching.

2. Give the basic steps employees should take to implement the intervention (i.e., the training session content).

3. Explain the method you will use to ensure trainees have mastered the information. (Note: *Consider objective testing as well as role-playing.*)

4. Create a timetable listing the frequency of refresher training on this topic that is appropriate for ongoing operation employees.

4

Beer

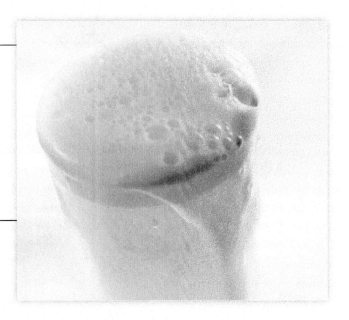

CHAPTER LEARNING OBJECTIVES

After completing this chapter, you should be able to:

- Describe the importance of malt in the making of grain-based alcoholic beverages.

- List and state the purpose of each of the four key ingredients found in beer.

- List the steps required to brew beer.

- Describe the three major forms of beer packaging.

- Explain how to serve quality draft beers.

KEY TERMS

CASE STUDY

"This beer tastes funny," said the customer to Angie, the bartender at the Stamford Carriage Restaurant and Lounge.

"What do you mean it tastes funny?" asked Angie. Angie had just served the man one of the specialty beers the Stamford Carriage offers on draft.

"It just tastes off," said the customer. "Could it be old? How long has it been since you changed the keg?"

"Maybe *you* just don't like it," said a second guest as he thoughtfully sipped his beer.

Angie wasn't sure what the problem was, but she knew it was her job to fix it. Angie took the glass of beer and checked the color and the odor to see if she could learn a possible reason for the customer's dissatisfaction.

1. Why is it important to the reputation of this operation to ensure the beer product being sold is of the highest quality possible?

2. Assume you own the Stamford Carriage Restaurant and Lounge. What would you want Angie to know about this product before she responded to the customer?

BEER

Beer is the world's most popular and likely the oldest form of alcoholic beverage. Hospitality managers know that beer drinkers enjoy beer by itself or with a wide variety of food ranging from burgers and pizza to fine-dining entrées. There are a variety of beer styles and types on the market today. The popularity of any one style or brand is heavily influenced by the location of the operation serving the beer and the food or activities that accompany its sale.

Today, the beer-brewing industry is a diverse and dynamic global business. The beer industry consists of a few extremely large multinational companies as well as thousands of small brewpubs and regional breweries. The alcohol content of beer typically ranges from 4 to 6 percent, although some beers are produced with higher or lower alcohol levels. Beers are popular and profitable menu items. Therefore, it is helpful for managers to understand how beers are made and how they can best be served to guests to maximize their enjoyment.

BEER PRODUCTION

Recall from chapter 1 that fermentation is what happens when living yeast cells convert the sugar contained in a liquid into ethyl alcohol and carbon dioxide. For example, in wine production, fructose and glucose are the two natural sugars found in grape juice. These sugars provide the needed nutrients for fermentation. But what if fruit and their natural sugars are not readily available for the making of alcoholic beverages? Can sugar be obtained from another source? The answer is yes, and the process for doing so explains the production of beer.

Beer is an alcoholic beverage product made by using grains rich in starch rather than fruit rich in sugars. Starch cannot be converted directly into alcohol. Rather, through the use of enzymes, the starches are converted to sugar. The newly formed sugar is then converted to alcohol through the normal fermentation process.

Ingredients

One reason beer has been made by so many people, and in so many countries, is that to brew it requires only four ingredients:

- Starch source
- Water
- Hops
- Yeast

In making beer, as in making any fine food, the quality of ingredients used to prepare the item and the skill in which they are combined have a tremendous impact on the quality of the finished product.

STARCH SOURCE

Grains used as a starch source in beer production are referred to as malt. Malted grains are cereal grains that are first germinated and then dried in a process known as malting. Because of its ideal chemical composition, barley is the most commonly used malted grain in beer production. However, brewers can also use wheat and rye, and for this reason, there are a variety of wheat and even some rye beers and blends on the market today.

In fact, until the early sixteenth century it was common in Germany to use rye malt for making beer. However, after a period of many bad harvests a law, known as the *Reinheitsgebot*, was passed in 1516. This law stipulated that rye would be used only for making bread and barley would be one of only three ingredients allowed in the beer making (the other two ingredients are water and hops). Yeast was not considered in this early law because it was not until the 1800s that Louis Pasteur discovered the role of yeast in the process of fermentation. In the 1500s no one yet knew about yeast and its important role in fermentation. The German brewing law *Reinheitsgebot* is also known as "The German Beer Purity Law." Many German and American brewers today still follow the guidelines set forth almost 500 years ago.

Malting is a three-step process that includes steeping, germination, and drying the grains. To begin the malting process, the barley or other grains are steeped, or soaked in water, until they begin to germinate (sprout). The germination process allows the grains to produce the enzymes required to convert the grains' starches to sugars. But before the grains can germinate completely, the process is stopped either by drying the grains or roasting them in a hot air kiln. The time, temperature, and ventilation in the kiln determine the color and flavor of the final malt. This entire process develops the characteristic grain flavors for beer.

From the perspective of the brewer, the quality of barley malt used to make beer is incredibly important. In fact, the process of preparing the highest-quality malt is so precise that brewers typically purchase their malts from companies that specialize in the process. Maltsters, as the makers of malt are known, have strictly defined processes to control the temperature at which the barley is roasted, how long it is roasted, and even the temperature at which it is cooled. Each of these variables plays an important part in the flavor and color the malt imparts to the beer.

WATER

Because beer contains 85 to 90 percent water, the quality of water used to produce it is of utmost importance. In earlier days, the location of breweries was driven by two factors: where starch sources were available and where there was a constant supply of fresh, clean river or spring water. The mineral

> ## THINK ABOUT IT . . .
>
> In addition to beer, malted grains are used to make whiskey, milk shakes (malts), candies, and drink flavorings. Aside from beer, what food or beverages have you had that contain malted grains?

content of the available water supply directly affects the beers produced. Hard waters, or waters with a high concentration of minerals, produce a different beer than do soft waters, or waters containing lesser amounts of dissolved minerals.

Water that makes a good beer of one type such as a pilsner may make a poor beer of another type, such as a porter. That is one reason why certain regions of the world are noted for beers of various styles and types. Today, brewers worldwide filter and condition their water to control hardness levels and salt content, thus ensuring a known and consistent quality of water for every batch of beer they brew.

HOPS

The hops used for beer making are the female flower clusters of *Humulus lupulus*, a plant species in the hops family. The flower looks like a small pinecone and has very soft petals. Carefully harvested at exactly the right time, hops are then dried to preserve the oils that contribute the aroma and bitterness to beer. The hops are stored under refrigeration until they are ready to be added in the brewing process.

Hops have not always been used to flavor beer. Until the fourteenth century, there were even laws in some areas forbidding the use of hops as a beer-flavoring ingredient. The first documented use of hops in beer as a bittering agent is from the eleventh century. Before this time, brewers used a wide variety of bitter herbs and flowers, including dandelion, marigold, ground ivy, and heather. Today, beverages brewed using bitter herbs and flowers rather than hops are called gruits.

Exhibit 4.1

Some beer brewers believe the finest hops are grown in the Czech Republic and Slovakia, formerly Czechoslovakia. Today many different types of hops are grown by farmers around the world, including the United States. The wide variety of hops allows brewers to experiment with different types to achieve different results.

Hops make several contributions to beer. They add flavor and chemical stability to it. Hops also contribute floral, citrus, and herbal aromas and flavors to beer. Finally, hops aid in head retention. Head is the term used to describe the frothy foam that forms on top of liquid beer when it is poured into a glass (*Exhibit 4.1*). Head is produced by bubbles of carbon dioxide rising to the glass's surface. Head retention is the amount of time the head will remain visible. Because head makes a beer more attractive to look at and enhances taste, the longer the head remains on the glass the better the guest's beer-drinking experience.

YEAST

Yeast is a one-celled microscopic plant that is responsible for the fermentation of the sugars used in brewing. Each strain of yeast yields a distinct beer. It is important to recognize that any type of yeast could be used to convert the sugars in unfermented beer into alcohol.

Before the role of yeast in fermentation was fully understood, fermentation involved wild or airborne yeasts. Today's brewers, however, carefully cultivate and preserve very specific strains of yeast to make their beers. The specific strain of yeast used directly influences the character and flavor of the beer it produces. Thus, brewers guard and preserve their yeast colonies very carefully!

OTHER BEER INGREDIENTS

The four ingredients used to make all types of beer are water, malt (typically barley malt), hops, and yeast. In the United States and in some other countries, other ingredients are often added to make beer. Some brewers add adjuncts, or additional cereal grains, to their beer to add flavor or reduce brewing costs. In the United States, popular adjuncts include the following:

- Wheat
- Corn
- Rice
- Oats
- Rye

Less widely used starch sources include millet and sorghum, as well as cassava root in Africa, potato in Brazil, and agave in Mexico. Basically any starch source, to some degree, can be used to brew an alcoholic beverage. Of course, the starch must be converted into fermentable sugar, and some adjuncts must be used in conjunction with malted grains because they lack the enzymes needed for starch to sugar conversion.

Brewers sometimes add ingredients other than grains to their beers. As with the use of adjuncts, these ingredients enhance the flavor or reduce the cost of the beers. Some brewers add sugars from corn, dairy products, or rice to their brews. Others add fruit such as cherries or raspberries, while still others age and flavor their brews by placing them in contact with wood or wood chips. Some brewers add one or more clarifying agents to beer, which are used to remove any solids in the beer, resulting in a bright, clear (not cloudy) finish.

Exhibit 4.2

STEPS IN MAKING BEER

Step 1:
Malting

Step 2:
Mashing

Step 3:
Brewing

Step 4:
Fermenting

Step 5:
Finishing

Brewing

The actual making of beer is a five-step process that is shown in *Exhibit 4.2.*

STEP 1: MALTING

As noted, it is usually a specialist known as a maltster who processes the raw grains used for brewing. The maltster begins the process by passing the barley over a filtering screen to eliminate any bits of debris and to select the best grains. Next, the maltster soaks the grains in water for several days to soften them. Workers transfer the grains to germination compartments for approximately three weeks. Here, the temperature and moisture content of the environment are controlled to maximize sprout germination.

When the sprouts are about an inch long, the grains are known as green malt. During the germination process, the enzyme amylase is produced. Amylase has the property of converting the remaining starch into the sugars maltose and dextrin, which will later be fermented by the addition of yeast into alcohol.

To stop the growth of the sprouts, the green malt is heated and dried (roasted). Light roasting of the grain will produce beers that are light in color, but the roasting can proceed until the grain is dark brown or black. These darker roasts are used to create dark beers.

STEP 2: MASHING

Mashing continues the process brewers use to convert starches into sugar. First the malted barley is ground into a coarse meal. Brewers combine the meal with hot water at a specific temperature. If the recipe calls for adjuncts such as corn or rice, brewers precook them and add them to the mixture at this time. The brewer holds the mixture at a low temperature, generally from 131°F to 162°F (55°C to 72°C), for one or more hours. The length and temperature of the mash help determine the characteristics of the finished beer. During this mashing process, the malt enzymes activate and begin the process of turning starch into sugar. Once the conversion is complete, the brewer drains and rinses the grains with more hot water to extract all of the sugars. The brewer transfers the resulting sweet liquid, called wort, to a brewing vat or kettle.

STEP 3: BREWING

At this stage, brewers begin adding hops to the wort in the brewing kettle at various intervals. The early additions of hops add bitterness and flavor, while late addition hops add aroma to the finished beer. The brewer boils the mixture, usually for one to several hours, depending on the style. Several things happen during this boil:

• The wort sterilizes.

• Some water evaporates.

• Some insoluble substances, those that cannot be readily dissolved, in the wort become soluble.

• The color of the mixture darkens due to carmelization.

At the end of the boil, the brewer filters the mixture again to remove all of the hops and other particulates that accumulate during the boil. Then the brewer cools the unfermented beer and transfers it to a fermenting vat. The temperature to which the wort is cooled and held depends on the type of beer the brewer is making.

STEP 4: FERMENTING

To begin the fermentation process, the brewer next adds yeast. The types of yeast depend on the style of beer the brewer is making. However, yeast can be divided into two main categories: bottom-fermenting yeasts used to make lagers or top-fermenting yeasts used to make ales (see *Exhibit 4.3*). The type of yeasts determine the temperature of fermentation: Lager yeasts need cooler temperatures, generally from 37°F to 49°F (3°C to 10°C), while ale yeasts ferment between 50°F to 70°F (10°C to 21.1°C).

Exhibit 4.3

COMPARING ALES AND LAGERS

	Ales	Lagers
Yeast	Top fermenting	Bottom fermenting
Fermentation Temperature	50°F to 70°F (10°C to 21°C)	37°F to 49°F (3°C to 10°C)
Fermentation Time	5 to 6 days	8 to 11 days
Postfermentation	Not needed	Lager is chilled
Aging Time	Typically served right away	Weeks to months
Flavor	More complex	Cleaner

There are many different types of lager and ale yeasts, with each strain imparting unique characteristics to the finished beer. Lager is typically fermented in 8 to 11 days, and then aged for weeks or months at cooler temperatures. The fermentation process for ales is completed in 5 to 6 days, after which time ales can generally be served. Lagers typically have a cleaner flavor, while ales tend to be more complex.

Fermentation produces alcohol, which remains in the beer. The process also produces carbon dioxide. Brewers may release the carbon dioxide or they may capture it to add it back to the beer. Ales are ready for finishing, although some styles call for cellaring in wooden barrels. Postfermentation, lagers typically undergo a chilling and resting process. During this resting period, chemical changes take place in the beer that will affect is taste and clarity. This storage period typically lasts for one to two months and the beer is held at a temperature near freezing. In fact, the word *lager* derives from a German term that means "storage."

STEP 5: FINISHING

When the storage is complete, it is time to carbonate the beer and ready it for packaging. Some brewers add a small bit of newly brewed wort to the nearly finished product. This process, called krausening, adds natural carbonation that results from renewed fermentation. If the beer is not naturally carbonated, the brewer will simply add carbonation back to the nearly finished beer using a process called forced carbonation.

Before the beer is packaged for distribution, the beer goes through the final finishing steps. Many beers undergo pasteurization, heating to 140°F to 150°F (60°C to 66°C) for a short time period to kill any bacteria and remaining live yeast cells. Some beers go through a filtration process. In this process, the beer is passed through very fine filters to remove yeast cells and any other impurities. Many craft breweries, breweries that focus on smaller batches of higher-quality beers generally using traditional brewing methods, sell nonpasteurized beer in bottles and cans. Nearly all beer distributed in kegs is also unpasteurized. All unpasteurized beer products must be kept cold to ensure their highest quality.

Although only four ingredients are used to make most beers, the variance in styles is great. When a beer is completely finished, its tastes and final coloring can differ significantly, as shown in *Exhibit 4.4*. These colors may be used in the products' names by the brewer to indicate the style or form of beverage produced.

Exhibit 4.4

BEER COLORS WHEN FINISHED

Beer colors range from light to dark. Words such as *pale*, *golden*, *amber*, *brown*, or *black* can be used to describe colors along this spectrum.

STYLES OF BEER

In general, beer is any fermented alcoholic beverage made from malted grain and flavored with hops. As noted, there are two basic styles of beer: lagers and ales. Each uses a different type of yeast and different methods of fermentation to give them different bodies and tastes.

Lagers

Recall that lagers use bottom-fermenting yeasts and lower fermentation temperatures. They are also traditionally aged longer than ales. It is believed that at some point during the medieval period German brewers began storing their beer in caves. These innovators of beer discovered that aging beer in caves after the initial fermentation produced a cleaner beer, as well as one that was less susceptible to contamination.

By the 1400s this process, which was called "lagering," led to the isolation of yeasts that thrived at lower temperatures more so than yeasts used for ale. This bottom-fermenting yeast created a drier beer with almost no flavor or aroma contributed by the yeast itself. When combined with lagering, the result created a simple, clean beer. Popular modern lager-style beers include pilsner, light lager, dark lager, bock, and malt liquor.

PILSNERS

Pilsner refers to the style of lager beer originally produced in Pilsen, Czech Republic, at the Pilsner Urquell brewery. A true pilsner-style beer is generally regarded as somewhat different from other lagers because of its more prominent hops character. True pilsners are generally all malt beers, meaning that adjuncts such as rice or corn are not part of the mash. While pilsners are best defined in terms of their characteristics and origin, the term is also used by some brewers in North America to indicate their "premium" beers, whether or not they have a particularly pronounced hop flavor.

LIGHT LAGERS

Light lagers make up the majority of beer sales in the United States. These beers are similar in origin to pilsners, yet tend to be lighter in body and flavor, largely due to use of corn and rice adjuncts (*Exhibit 4.5*). Light (often spelled *lite*) beers, or low-calorie beers, as well as their fuller-bodied counterparts, all fall under the light lager category.

Exhibit 4.5

These American-style lagers were originally made in a manner very similar to the original European lagers. That is because many first-generation immigrants to the United States brewed the beers. Adolph Coors, Frederick Miller, and Eberhard Anheuser (father-in-law of Adolphus Busch) for example, each formed the breweries that today still bear their names. These beers are among some of America's most popular.

In fact, the growth of the beer industry in Milwaukee, Wisconsin, was directly related to the city's large number of German immigrants. In the 1840s, Milwaukee began to take on a distinctly German character as waves of immigrants settled in the area seeking economic opportunity and, particularly, religious and political freedom. German consumers' demand for lager, a German brew, greatly expanded the city's beer industry and provided a large customer base for brewers. Many of these German immigrants were experienced brewers, saving brewery owners both time and money in training. The skills and experience of the German immigrants combined with Milwaukee's abundant natural resources including a good harbor, lumber for barrels, and ice for storage helped make Milwaukee a giant in the brewing industry.

Of course, America was certainly not Europe. The climate was different, summers were hotter, and the country had its own social attitudes. Thus, a beer somewhat lighter than the original European lagers matched perfectly with the American character and helps explain why beers of this type remain extremely popular today.

DARK LAGERS

This category actually encompasses several different styles, ranging from Oktoberfest beers and Vienna lagers to black lagers. In all cases, these lagers are darker in color and generally have a more pronounced malt character than pilsners and light lagers. The darker the color, the more likely the beer is to have pronounced caramel, toffee, or roasted flavors, with less emphasis on the flavor derived from the hops.

BOCK BEERS

Bock beer, called *bockbier* in German, is a special type of beer that is darker and sweeter than other lagers. Several substyles of bock beer exist including *maibock*, a paler, more hop-flavored brew traditionally made in the spring; *doppelbock*, a strong, heavily malted flavored beer; and *eisbock*, a strong version made by partially freezing the beer and removing some of the ice crystals that form. Modern bock beers can range in color from copper to dark brown and appeal to drinkers interested in a beer that is more flavorful than the typical lager-style pilsner.

MALT LIQUORS

The typical alcohol content for most beer is 4 to 6 percent. *Malt liquor* is a North American term referring to beer with greater than average alcohol content (typically 6 to 9 percent). It is often brewed like a stronger version of the light lager, with the use of corn and rice adjuncts.

The definition of malt liquor is not clear-cut because each state in the United States is permitted its own definition of the term. In some states, *malt liquor* refers to any alcoholic beverage made by fermenting grain and water; in these states, a non-alcoholic beer may also be called a non-intoxicating malt liquor. In other states, products labeled "beer" must fall below an established alcohol content, and beers that exceed the mark must be labeled as malt liquor.

Many critics see the malt liquor brewing process as targeting high alcohol content rather than quality. As such, malt liquors are seen as distinct from the traditions of brewing other types of high-alcohol, premium beers in the United States and Europe.

OPEN FOR BUSINESS

BY THE CUSTOMER/ FOR THE CUSTOMER

The growth of craft beer has coincided with the rise of social media. As a result, there are now several social media Web sites devoted to beer. These sites allow users to post reviews of beers, breweries, and bars. They also provide forums, where users can discuss trends in the industry, discuss their favorite beers, or relay favorable or unfavorable experiences at various establishments. Savvy beverage managers survey and participate in these sites to learn more about the public's opinion of beers and various establishments. These sites also allow managers to communicate directly with their current and potential consumers.

Ales

Recall that ales are fermented at higher temperatures than lagers and use top-fermenting yeasts. Ales generally have more complex aromas and flavor profiles than lagers, and are generally produced more quickly, with less aging. Popular ale styles include pale ales, wheat beers, brown ales, porters, stouts, and Belgian ales.

PALE ALES

Contrary to the name, most pale ales are more copper or amber than pale, or light in color. Their name derives from the use of pale malts, as opposed to darker malts used in brown ales, porters, and stouts. Pale ales tend to have a very high hop flavor and bitterness. This is especially true of India Pale Ales (IPAs), which were traditionally brewed with a higher alcohol content and more hops than regular pale ales because they were shipped from England to India during the time of British colonization. The increased alcohol and hops levels helped preserve the beers during the long voyage.

WHEAT BEERS

Ales brewed with wheat generally contain 50 percent or more wheat as the starch source. Wheat gives the beers better head retention and a slight bite in the finish. Wheat beers are often cloudy, due to the unfiltered yeast preserved from the brewing process. Wheat beers are most popular during summer months, and some customers prefer wheat beers served with a slice of lemon or orange.

BROWN ALES

Brown ales emphasize more malt character than hops, with an emphasis on caramel or toffee-like flavors. Some brown ales also have a nutlike flavor. The style originated in England, but American brewers have adopted and modified the style. Overall, brown ales tend to be lower in alcohol than pale ales, porters, or stouts.

PORTERS

Porters originated in England in the eighteenth century, but more or less disappeared in the mid-twentieth century. Porters saw resurgence in the late 1970s and early 1980s as American microbreweries resurrected the style. Porters tend to be heavy on malt flavors, with hints of chocolate and coffee. Some porters have a noticeable hop bite. The beers range from low to high alcohol content.

STOUTS

Stouts and porters are similar, although stouts tend to be a bit stronger, darker, and contain more roasted malt, given them more of a bite. Some traditional English stouts are sweet because they use lactose, or milk sugar, in their production. Irish and English versions of the style tend to be lower in alcohol than the Russian imperial stouts, which range in the 8 to 12 percent alcohol by volume range.

BELGIAN ALES

Belgian ales often defy single categorization. Belgian ales often use special yeasts, including those found in the wild, to cultivate distinct and unique flavors. Belgian ales range in color from light to dark, and in flavors from sweet to very sour. Some of the most prized Belgian and Belgian-style ales are those brewed by Trappist monks, some of whom sell only very small quantities of their beers.

Saké

Saké is a Japanese brew made from rice. Saké is sometimes referred to in English as "rice wine." However, wine is made by fermenting the sugar naturally present in fruit. Saké is more like beer than wine because in the making of both beer and saké the sugar needed to produce alcohol must first be converted from starch. Saké is produced using methods similar to beer production. Saké is unlike beer, however, in that the typical alcohol content of saké tends to be higher, ranging from 15 to 20 percent.

BEER PACKAGING

Beer is food. As with most food, beer is perishable. It deteriorates as a result of the action of bacteria, light, and air. However, unlike many other food products, packaged beer is not legally mandated to carry a "sell by" date. Some domestic beer sold in the United States does carry a freshness date. The Boston Beer Company was among the first to use freshness dating, as far back as 1985. Anheuser-Busch has followed suit with its much-publicized "born on" dates. There are still many breweries, large and small, that do not send all their beers to market with a freshness date, but the trend is certainly moving in that direction.

In general, beer goes bad when it exceeds its shelf life, the amount of time a product can be stored under normal conditions and retain its quality. Filtered beer tends to have a relatively short shelf life of rarely more than one year as components in the sterilized beverage break down into unpleasant-tasting ones. Live yeast inside the bottle, however, acts against these processes, giving the beverage a much longer shelf life. A good bottle of unfiltered beer can actually maintain its drinkability for many years, and some can be aged for decades.

There are essentially three factors that can impact a beer's shelf life:

- **Pasteurization:** Pasteurization kills microbes in the beverage but also can cause the product to deteriorate faster than a nonpasteurized product.

- **Sterile filtration:** In this method, beer passes through a mechanical system that removes any yeast or hops still present in the brew that could continue an undesired chemical reaction.
- **Alcohol content:** Beers with higher alcohol content or more hops in the formulation take longer to lose freshness than products with lower alcohol or hops. As a result, stouts, porters, barley wines, and strong ales have the longest shelf lives.

To ensure customers get the best-quality products, managers should look for freshness dating on every beer product they buy. Every brewery has its own way of indicating this date, naming it something such as "born on date" or "freshness date." The date may be on the bottle, case packaging, or cap, but it will be placed on the container. Its meaning should be shared by the beverage supplier.

In most cases, canned and bottled beer from major breweries has a shelf life of approximately six to nine months if stored properly. Draft beer, or kegged beer, is unpasteurized and thus should be kept refrigerated at all times. The ideal temperature for a keg of beer is 35°F to 45°F (2°C to 8°C). Beer that is kept too long in storage loses both flavor and aroma. Beer should never be frozen, because this causes the contents to permanently separate.

Bottles

Bottles are a traditional packaging method for beer. Brewers fill bottles with finished beer by drawing beer from a holding tank and filling bottles using a special filling machine. The bottles are capped, labeled, and packed into cases or cartons. Some smaller breweries send their bulk beer to large facilities for bottling, while some small boutique breweries bottle by hand.

The first step in bottling beer is to clean the empty bottles with water or air. Bottlers often inject bottles with carbon dioxide to reduce the level of oxygen within the bottle. Oxygen has a detrimental effect on the flavor of beers, causing cardboard-like off flavors. The bottling line fills the bottles with the appropriate amount of beer, plus sometimes a small amount of nitrogen on top to neutralize the effect of any oxygen remaining in the bottle. Finally, the bottle is capped and enters a labeling machine. The product is then packed into cases, ready for distribution.

Today beer is sold to operators in glass bottles of various sizes and shapes, although cases containing 24 twelve-ounce bottles are most common in the United States (*Exhibit 4.6*). Some managers wonder why most beer is sold in dark-colored bottles. The answer is simple: The full spectrum of daylight can have undesirable effects on a beer over a period of time. The ultraviolet portion of the spectrum is especially harmful, promoting chemical reactions that produce off flavors that diminish the aroma and taste of beer. Dark glass

Exhibit 4.6

KEEPING IT SAFE

Plastic is typically not the first choice of most brewers for the packaging of their beer. Plastic bottles, however, do make a great deal of safety-related sense in some restaurant and foodservice settings. Consider, for example, the hotel or resort that wishes to offer bar service to a pool or beach area that cannot be easily serviced by a draft beer system. In such a case, the dangers that are inherent in the case of broken glass beer bottles makes the use of plastic or cans an ideal choice. Other settings that have found plastic beer bottles appropriate include sports venues like stadiums and arenas, motor speedways, theme parks, and a variety of other outdoor and indoor entertainment facilities.

WHAT'S THE FOOTPRINT?

Keg beer not only tastes great, it is eco-friendly. The beer keg is returnable, refillable, and recyclable. It is not uncommon to find a metal beer keg 30 years old and still in service. Over a 30-year life, a single beer keg can dispense over 20,000 pints; that is the equivalent to more than 27,000 cans or bottles requiring production and disposal.

Keg beer costs the operator less per serving than an equal amount of bottle or canned beer. As a result, operators get lower costs, guests get great-tasting products, and the environment is protected—clearly a winning situation for all concerned!

inhibits this, whereas clear or light-colored glass leaves the beer vulnerable to being harmed by light. Although most brewers use dark glass, a few brands do bottle in clear or light-colored glass. Managers should take extra caution to ensure these beers are keep out of direct light.

Most recently, some brewers have begun experimenting with bottling beer in polyethylene terephthalate (PET) containers. PET is the material used to make plastic food containers. It is also used for soda and water bottles. Guest opinion on drinking beer from plastic bottles varies. Not surprisingly perhaps, acceptance is highest in the 21 to 25 age group and lowest in the 50+ age group. The generation that has grown up with soft drinks packed in PET is less concerned about being served beer in a plastic bottle. It may not be long before beer packed in PET bottles will become commonplace in restaurants, bars, and clubs.

Cans

Canning is a popular way to package beer. Early attempts at canning beer left a metallic aftertaste. This made canning an unpopular choice for all but the largest brewers. However, in recent years, advances in can lining technology have led to a resurgence in the packaging technique.

Canned beer has many advantages, some of which also appeal to restaurant and foodservice operators. Beer bottles are fragile, are about twice as heavy as an equal-sized can, and do not stack easily. Glass bottles also take longer to chill than cans do. Perhaps most important, if accidently dropped in handling or drinking, beer cans do not shatter!

Kegs

A keg is a small barrel used to store beer. Traditionally, a wooden keg was used to store and ship a variety of items such as nails, gunpowder, crackers, and a variety of liquids, including beer. Today, beer kegs are most often constructed of stainless steel or aluminum.

A beer keg has a single opening on one end covered by a self-closing valve. A coupler, a mechanism that allows beer to flow out of the keg, fits into this valve. The coupler has two openings. One allows gas, usually carbon dioxide, into the keg while the other opening allows the beer to flow out. The gas forces the beer out of the keg, through the opening, and into the lines that transport the beer to the tap, or faucet. A regulator gauge attaches between the tank of gas and the coupler. The regulator allows the right amount of gas to be released when the beer faucet is opened.

Historically, a beer barrel was a standard size of 50 gallons, as opposed to a wine barrel at 32 gallons, or an oil barrel at 42 gallons. Since keg sizes are not standardized, the keg cannot be used as a standard unit of measure across the restaurant and foodservice industry. In fact, the most popular keg sizes vary from country to country and brewery to brewery. Most countries use the metric system when packaging kegs, although most U.S. brewers do not.

In the United States, the most popular beer keg size is the half-barrel. A half-barrel contains 15.5 gallons of beer. A quarter-barrel has a volume of 7.75 U.S. gallons. In the United States, the terms *half-barrel* and *quarter-barrel* are derived from the fact that a U.S. beer "barrel" is legally defined as being equal to 31 U.S. gallons. Because keg sizes do vary, managers should carefully note the actual amount of beer product they are buying when they purchase a "keg" of beer from any of their beverage suppliers.

DISPENSING KEG BEER

Unpasteurized beer is a highly perishable food. It is susceptible to odors, bacteria, and yeast growth. Properly stored and served, it has a lovely, frothy head, tingles the tongue, and looks freshly effervescent. However, managers must pay close attention to proper temperature, dispensing, and cleanliness to ensure the quality of the product meets expectations.

Experts debate about the proper temperature for serving the best draft beer. The disagreement has to do with the chemistry of carbon dioxide in beer. Some opinions revolve around taste preferences. However, many experts suggest that managers maintain the keg at a temperature between 35°F to 45°F (2°C to 8°C).

Carbonation in beer is just as important as its serving temperature. Certain beers taste best at different carbonation levels. A fresh, untapped keg starts with the correct amount of dissolved carbon dioxide in it. To keep the right amount after tapping, a balance between the temperature of the beer and the pressure of the carbon dioxide must be maintained. If the pressure is maintained properly, the carbonation level of the beer remains stable. If the pressure is too high, the beer will overcarbonate. If the pressure is too low, the beer loses carbonation. It is the function of the regulator to control the carbonation in a keg of beer.

To properly pour a draft beer, a bartender starts with a beer-clean glass, one that is cleaned and prepared especially for draft beer. He or she holds the glass a half-inch to an inch below the tip of the faucet. The bartender tilts the glass at a 45-degree angle and the faucet is opened all the way, pouring down the side of the glass. When the glass is half full, the bartender stands it straight up. The remaining beer pours directly into the center of the glass. The faucet is then quickly closed, leaving a three-quarter-inch head at the top of the glass. This thick, creamy head should leave lacing on the glass as the beer is consumed.

Some managers are wary of selling draft beer because of problems related to its proper pouring and service. Beverage suppliers can be very helpful in this area. However, troubleshooting the problems that can occur is an important

Manager's Memo

Clean glasses are essential to the enjoyment of all beers. To ensure glasses are beer-clean, follow these steps:

- In a clean sink, wash the glasses with a low-foam glass cleaner.
- Rinse thoroughly with fresh water.
- Sanitize with the correct amount of sanitizer.
- Dry the glasses in a way that allows airflow inside the glasses, on a drying rack.
- Rinse the glasses with cold water before filling them with beer.

If a glass is beer-clean, bubbles will not form on the sides of the glass and head retention will be optimized. Wet the inside of a glass and place it upside down on the bar. If drops cling to the glass, it is not beer-clean!

part of a manager's job. Managers test their draft systems by placing a rinsed, beer-clean glass at a 45-degree angle under the faucet and by opening the tap all the way to draw a proper pour. *Exhibit 4.7* lists some of the things managers should consider if the pour does not result in a perfect beer.

LINE CLEANING

Beer-clean glasses are essential for the sanitation and the service of quality draft beer. Clean beer lines are just as important. Beer lines must be cleaned because over time, beer leaves mineral and protein deposits in the draft lines. Bacteria and molds can work their way into the lines, and yeast can form and multiply in them as well.

Exhibit 4.7

TROUBLESHOOTING DRAFT BEER ISSUES

Problem	Likely Causes
Faucet is open but no beer comes out.	Keg is empty. If it is, gas will rush from the faucet as gas escapes from the keg through the line. Coupler is set improperly. Carbon dioxide tank is not connected. Carbon dioxide tank valves do not open. Carbon dioxide tank is empty. Line is frozen.
Flat, headless beer comes out.	Regulator gauge is improperly set. Glass is not beer-clean. Carbon dioxide tank is not connected. Improper pouring technique is used.
Foamy, overcarbonated beer comes out.	Keg is near empty. Regulator gauge is improperly set. Proper keg storage temperature is not maintained. New keg has just been tapped.
The beer does not taste right.	Beer is past expiration date. Beer lines are not cleaned. Monthly cleaning is recommended. Glasses are not clean.
Beer is darker than usual, or cloudy.	Keg has been tapped for more than three weeks. Beer is past expiration date. Keg storage temperature is too high. Beer lines are not cleaned. Glasses are not beer-clean.
Black flecks or slimy chunks appear in beer.	Beer lines are not clean.
Quality of the pour changes throughout the day (i.e., starts well but worsens as the day goes on).	Beer cooler (keg storage area) is changing temperature, perhaps due to increased traffic in the storage area. As a result, pressure and temperature are not staying the same. Gas regulator is set to give a good pour at one temperature but that temperature is not being maintained. Limit access to storage.

The frequency of line cleaning depends in part on the volume of beer sold. However, most experts agree that beer lines should be properly cleaned at least every three to four weeks. The lines themselves should be replaced completely every four to five years. Some managers purchase the supplies and equipment required to clean their beer lines themselves. Others hire companies that specialize in the service.

One way for managers to determine if they are cleaning their lines often enough is to taste the same draft beer before and after a line cleaning. If the lines needed cleaning, there will be a significant difference in product taste. If the lines are being cleaned frequently enough, there should be very little difference in the before and after cleaning taste.

Beer faucets should be cleaned regularly. It is also a good idea to keep a spray bottle filled with an appropriate sanitizer mixed according to manufacturer's instructions. As part of the bar's closing each night, spray inside and out of all the beer faucets to help prevent unwanted bacteria, mold, and yeast growth.

NON-ALCOHOLIC BEERS

Not every person wants to, or can, drink alcoholic beverages. In some cases, health concerns, the presence of certain medications, or religious beliefs may cause people to prefer not to consume alcohol. Historically, if such individuals found themselves in a setting where alcoholic beverages were being served, they simply ordered a Shirley Temple. Named after a famous child film actor of the 1930s, a classic Shirley Temple consists of ginger ale and cherry juice served over ice and garnished with a maraschino cherry. It contains no alcohol.

Beginning in the 1970s, bartenders in the United States and other countries began to notice those individuals who elected not to drink increasingly ordered flavored soda waters. The increased demand for these products, increased penalties for drinking and driving, and consumer acceptance of "light" beers and other "light" products showed that there was a potential market for "de-alcoholized" beverages.

To meet this demand, non-alcoholic (NA) beers and, to a lesser degree, non-alcoholic wines were introduced. NA beers are fermented in the traditional way, but they undergo a process that removes the majority of their alcoholic content. The resulting products are not classified as alcoholic beverages because they contain less than 0.5 percent alcohol. The 0.5 percent alcohol level in NA beverages is so low that it is necessary to drink 24 glasses of non-alcoholic wine to match the alcohol contained in one 4-ounce glass of traditional wine. Drinking eight cans of NA beer would equal the amount of alcohol now found in one 12-ounce can of traditional beer.

Manager's Memo

Many states have implemented keg registration laws. Keg registration policies stipulate that beer kegs be marked with unique identification numbers, using metal or plastic tags, stickers, invisible ink, or engraving. When a keg is sold, the keg identification number is recorded along with the purchaser's name and contact information. These records must be kept for a specified length of time, usually six months to a year. The purpose of keg registration is to discourage those who are old enough to buy alcohol from providing beer to underage drinkers—an illegal act that should be opposed by all responsible beverage managers.

MANAGER'S MATH

Recall that beer kegs in the United States come in many different sizes, with two common sizes being a 15.5-gallon half-barrel and a 7.75-gallon quarter-barrel. Assume you purchased a standard half-barrel keg of beer.

1. Approximately how many 12-ounce glasses of beer can be drawn from the keg?

2. Approximately how many 16-ounce (1-pint) glasses of beer can be drawn from the keg?

3. Approximately how many 20-ounce glasses of beer can be drawn from the keg?

Hint: *There are 128 ounces in a gallon.*

(Answers: 1. 165 glasses; 2. 124 glasses; 3. 99 glasses)

Calorie counts for NA beers and wine are also lower. A standard glass of wine or beer contains about 150 calories while an NA glass of wine is about 40 calories. A standard beer has about 150 to 180 calories per serving, while a glass of NA beer contains only approximately 60 calories. Today, most major breweries offer one or more NA beers to their customers. Managers are recommended to stock at least one brand in bars serving beer.

SUMMARY

1. **Describe the importance of malt in the making of grain-based alcoholic beverages.**

   Malt is essential for the making of grain-based alcoholic beverages because yeast cannot directly cause fermentation in grain starch. Grain starch must first be converted to sugar before yeast can then convert those sugars to ethyl alcohol and carbon dioxide. During the malt preparation process, the enzyme amylase is produced. Amylase has the property of converting the remaining starch in a grain into the sugars maltose and dextrin, which will later be fermented by the addition of yeast into alcohol. While several grains can be used to perform the malting process, beer makers primarily use barley when making their products.

2. **List and state the purpose of each of the four key ingredients found in beer.**

   The four ingredients found in beer are starch sources, water, hops, and yeast. The type of water used to make beer gives the final product much of its character. The presence of minerals and salts in the water affect a beer's final flavor. Barley and other grains are used to create malt, the essential starch source. Hops are a variety of flower and are used to flavor beer and give it its characteristic bitterness. Yeast converts the sugar in wort to alcohol and carbon dioxide, and each strain of brewers' yeast lends its own unique flavor to beer.

3. **List the steps required to brew beer.**

   There are five steps involved in the brewing process:

   Malting: The malting process involves preparing grain (typically barley) for mashing. This process includes seed soaking, germination, and kilning.

   Mashing: Mashing is the process of holding ground malted grain at specific temperatures to allow the amylase enzymes to convert the starches to sugar. The converted grains are drained and rinsed, and the result is called wort.

   Brewing: Wort is flavored with hops in the brewing process. The wort is boiled, strained, and then filtered.

   Fermenting: Fermenting begins when yeast is added to the cooled wort. The yeast used to make lager beers works from the bottom, while the yeast used to make ale rises to the surface and works from the top. Lager yeasts prefer cooler temperatures, while ale yeasts prefer relatively warmer ones.

   Finishing: In the final step the beer may be filtered, pasteurized, and packaged for shipping.

4. **Describe the three major forms of beer packaging.**

The three major forms of beer containers are bottles, cans, and kegs. Bottles can be used to package pasteurized or unpasteurized beer products. Dark glass is best because exposure to light can harm beer. Cans are a popular packaging form for beer because of their light weight, their ability to be stacked easily, and the fact that they will not shatter if dropped accidently. Historically, beer has been stored and served in kegs of a variety of sizes. Today, beer kegs are made of stainless steel or aluminum and contain unpasteurized products. Because their contents are unpasteurized, keg beer must be kept properly refrigerated at all times.

5. **Explain how to serve quality draft beers.**

Quality draft beer can be served when managers control for temperature, pressure, and cleanliness. Proper keg storage temperature of 35°F to 45°F (2°C to 8°C) should be maintained. A properly working regulator should ensure the optimum amount of carbon dioxide is used to push the beer through the beer lines to the beer faucet. Finally, the beer lines and faucets should be cleaned regularly to ensure there is no growth of flavor-robbing bacteria or yeast in the lines. To properly pour (draw) a draft beer, a beer-clean glass is held a half-inch to an inch below the faucet. The glass is tilted at a 45-degree angle and the faucet is opened. When the glass is half full, it is stood straight up and the beer is poured directly into the center of the glass, leaving a three-quarter-inch head at the top.

APPLICATION EXERCISE

Beer is so popular that nearly every state or geographic region has a variety of breweries and microbreweries producing it. Use your favorite search engine to search for breweries in your state or region. Then answer the following questions.

1. How many breweries are operating in the state?

2. Is there a brewers' guild or association in the state? If so, where is it located?

3. Is there an annual meeting of beer enthusiasts in the state? If so, where and when is it held?

4. How would membership in such an association be helpful for a manager whose operation featured a wide variety of beer products on the menu?

5. Write a two-page paper summarizing your feelings about the importance of local microbreweries to the success of restaurant and foodservice operations in your area.

REVIEW YOUR LEARNING

Select the best answer for each question.

1. **What is the average alcohol content percentage of most beers?**
   A. 1 to 2%
   B. 4 to 6%
   C. 12 to 14%
   D. 18 to 20%

2. **What is first step in the beer-brewing process?**
   A. Malt is dried and roasted.
   B. Yeast is added to the wort.
   C. Starch is converted by enzymes to complex sugars.
   D. Barley is soaked in water until it begins to germinate.

3. **What creates the "head" on a glass of beer?**
   A. Carbon dioxide
   B. Ethyl alcohol
   C. Starch
   D. Sugar

4. **What is the purpose of krausening beer?**
   A. It slows down starch to sugar conversion.
   B. It eliminates excessive hops taste.
   C. It adds natural carbonation.
   D. It clarifies the beer.

5. **Which type of beer is top fermented?**
   A. Stout
   B. Pilsner
   C. Malt liquor
   D. Light lager

6. **Why is beer pasteurized?**
   A. To improve its flavor
   B. To kill microbes in the beer
   C. To increase its alcohol content
   D. To decrease its alcohol content

7. **Approximately how many 20-oz glasses of beer can be drawn from a keg containing 15.5 gal of beer?**
   A. 50
   B. 100
   C. 150
   D. 200

8. **At what temperature range is keg beer best stored and served?**
   A. 25°F to 30°F (−4°C to −1°C)
   B. 35°F to 45°F (2°C to 8°C)
   C. 55°F to 65°F (13°C to 18°C)
   D. 65°F to 75°F (18°C to 24°C)

9. **What is the average alcohol content percentage of non-alcoholic (NA) beer?**
   A. 0%
   B. 0.5%
   C. 2%
   D. 4%

10. **At what point in the pouring of a draft beer should the bartender stand the glass straight up to optimize the head on the beer?**
    A. At the beginning of the pour
    B. When the pour is 1/4 complete
    C. When the pour is 1/2 complete
    D. When the pour is 3/4 complete

FIELD PROJECT

About half of the states in the United States currently have keg registration laws. Go to your favorite Internet search engine and type in "Keg Registration" along with your state's name. Review the information you find to answer the following questions.

1. Does your state require keg registration?

2. What is the legal definition (in volume) for a "keg"?

3. What is the maximum alcohol content your state allows a beer to contain?

4. What identification must be shown to buy a keg?

5. What is the penalty for violating this law?

5

Wine

CHAPTER LEARNING OBJECTIVES

After completing this chapter, you should be able to:

- Classify wines by their characteristics.
- Identify the four major types of wine.
- Describe the basic differences between red and white wines.
- List the world's five major wine-growing regions.
- Identify how wine is packaged.
- State the different ways managers can prepare wine lists.
- Explain the procedures used to properly open and pour wine for guests.

KEY TERMS

aromatized wine, p. 104

bin number, p. 117

blush wine, p. 107

bouquet, p. 101

carafe, p. 115

cellar temperature, p. 107

dry wine, p. 102

fortified wine, p. 103

house wine, p. 114

oenology, p. 100

rosé wine, p. 102

semi-dry wine, p. 102

sommelier, p. 118

sparkling wine, p. 101

still wine, p. 102

sweet wine, p. 102

vintage, p. 118

CASE STUDY

"Normally I agree with you, Carol, but this time I don't!" said Sophia, the manager at the Bear and Bull restaurant. She was meeting with Carol, the operation's dining-room manager.

"Well," said Carol, "we should recommend a wine for each menu entrée, with the name of the wine under the entrée description. I can train my staff on each wine and how to sell them."

"But we have over 100 wines in stock," said Sophia. "We only have 20 entrées. How will we sell the other wines?"

"One hundred is too many," said Carol. "My servers don't know about 100 different wines. Same for our customers. With my idea, it's simple: one entrée, one best wine!"

"There are lots of good wines to go with each entrée," replied Sophia. "How do we recommend just one? Let's just list our wines and indicate the types of food that most people enjoy with them, like dry reds with steaks. Customers like lots of choices when they dine out. I know I do."

1. What is your opinion about the two approaches to selling wines at the Bear and Bull?

2. Assume you were the operation manager and it was your job to make a decision about which approach to use. Which would you choose? Why?

WINE CHARACTERISTICS

The history of winemaking is as old as human history. No one really knows when the first wines were made. In fact, it is most likely that the first wine was produced when a cliff dweller gathered grapes, left them in a container for a period of time, and then came back to find that the grape juice had, by itself, changed in a way that made it very pleasurable to drink. The sugar in the grape juice had been fermented by natural yeast, and the first wine was born.

Wine is an alcoholic beverage made directly from the juice of fruit, most often grapes. Oenology is the science and study of all aspects of wine and winemaking. It is a science studied all over the world because wines are made all over the world. Many restaurant and foodservice managers spend a great deal of time learning about the wines their customers will like best and the specific foods that go best with specific wines. The information about wine, winemaking, and wine drinking would fill not just many books, but many libraries. The most important thing to know about wines, however, is that they are produced to be enjoyed by wine drinkers. As a result, the best wine for any customer is the one that he or she enjoys drinking most.

Although wine (along with beer) has been made for centuries, it was not until the 1860s that Louis Pasteur proved that in the process of fermentation, yeast cells convert sugar to alcohol and carbon dioxide. With that knowledge, winemakers and brewers were able to control what was happening to their products and when it would happen.

It is important to recognize that wine, like human beings, goes through a predictable life cycle. That is, it is born, begins to grow, fully matures and, if not consumed it finally dies. As a result, the taste of the same wine, consumed at different periods in its life, can vary greatly.

Exhibit 5.1

Wine and the Senses

Wine drinking is a sensory experience. The color of the wine, the aroma, the taste, and even the feel of the wine in the mouth are all factors that affect the drinker's appreciation of wine.

COLOR

Most wines are made from the juice of grapes, an often colorless liquid extracted from grapes. Wines range in color from those that have very little color, like those that are the color of pale straw, to those that are a deep burgundy (*Exhibit 5.1*). The color of wine comes from the skins and not from the juice itself and gives an indication of the wine's character. Given two wines made from the same grapes and in the same style, the deeper the color, the fuller the flavor of the wine will be. It is in the evaluation of a wine's color that some wine drinkers conclude that white wines are milder than red wines. The important thing to remember about wines of all colors is that they should be brilliant and clear. Dark-colored wines are not "better" than lighter-colored wines, but they are different.

AROMA

The aroma of a wine is called its bouquet. A wine's quality can best be judged by its bouquet and its taste. The bouquet is more than the "smell" of a wine; it is the total aromatic experience of the wine. The bouquet of wine is best revealed by gently swirling the wine in a wineglass to expose it to more oxygen and release its aromatic essence. Sparkling wine, or wine that has bubbles caused by the presence of carbon dioxide, is not swirled as this would cause it to lose some of its carbonation and thus negatively affect its taste.

To understand why bouquet is important, know that scientists have found that well over half of the experience people normally called "taste" is actually their ability to "smell." The aroma of a wine gives good clues as to what will be experienced in the tasting. Wine drinkers often talk about aromas in sensory details. For instance, a wine drinker might swirl a wine, inhale the bouquet, and declare, "I can detect traces of blackberry!" Other wine drinkers might use adjectives such as *flowery, spicy, earthy*, or *oaky* to paint a picture of the wine's aroma.

TASTE

Color and aroma are important to the sensory evaluation of wine, but taste is critical. As with the aroma, wine drinkers often describe the taste in colorful terms. A drinker may describe a red wine as having fruity, spicy, or woody flavors. A white wine might be said to have hints of apple, pear, butter, herbs, or earthiness. Wine drinkers also talk about the overall experience—was the wine too sweet or too dry? Too crisp or too light? Tastes can be subjective, so not all drinkers will experience the same flavors in a wine.

Remember that when comparing the characteristics of two wines, it is best to compare wines of the same type and price point. In the comparison, questions like "Which wine has the better color?", "Which wine has the more pleasing bouquet?", and "Which wine tastes best?" are important. Comparing different wines at vastly differing prices makes little sense.

Wine Basics

For restaurant and foodservice guests, purchasing wine to be consumed by itself or with food should always be a pleasurable, nonthreatening experience. Some managers can be intimidated by the great variety and amount of information associated with wine. They need not be. While some beverage management positions require tremendous wine knowledge, most managers need not be experts in all aspects of wine and winemaking to facilitate a pleasant guest experience. They must, however, know wine basics, train their staff well, and oversee the responsible sale and consumption of quality wines.

To begin, know that wines can be grouped in a variety of ways. The country and region in which the wine was made, the wine's age, and the grapes used to make it are examples of ways wines can be classified. For instance, in France, wines are known by the region they come from. For example, Champagne, Beaujolais, and Rhone are all areas of France. In California and Germany, wines are primarily known by the grape, for example, Chardonnay, Cabernet Sauvignon, Gewürztraminer, and Riesling are all grape varieties. Wines can also be grouped on the basis of their sugar content. Thus, wines are often classified as dry, semi-dry, and sweet. These terms describe the sweetness of a wine and refer to the residual sugar content, or the amount of grape sugar remaining in the wine after fermentation has occurred.

Dry wines are the least sweet and have sugar contents below 0.8 percent. Semi-dry wines have 0.8 to 2.2 percent sugar content, and sweet wines have more than 2.2 percent sugar content. Although sugar content is an important wine characteristic, there are a variety of other ways to group wines.

Color is also a common method of classification. Interestingly, wine color does *not* depend on the type of grapes used to make it. A wine's color depends on how long the grape skins stay in the beverage during fermentation. Since all grape juice is clear in color, any juice can be used to make white (clear) wine. If red or purple grape skins are allowed to stay in contact with the juice during production, the juice will take on the color of the grape skins. If the colored skins stay in contact for a long time, red wine will result. If they are allowed to stay in contact for only a short time a light red, or rosé wine, will result.

Restaurant and foodservice managers also classify wines by other characteristics. One common way to group them is to use the following four types:

- Still
- Sparkling
- Fortified
- Aromatized

STILL WINES

When people think about wine, in most cases they are thinking about still wine. Still wine gets its name from the way it is produced. During fermentation, yeast consumes the sugar in grape juice and turns it into ethyl alcohol and carbon dioxide. If that carbon dioxide is allowed to escape, then the wine is referred to as a still wine.

A tremendous number of still wines are produced across the globe because the vast majority of wine consumed is still wine. The alcohol content of still wine ranges from 9–15 percent by volume.

SPARKLING WINES

Sparkling wine is wine that contains carbon dioxide. Remember that when the yeast interacts with the naturally occurring sugars in the grape juice, alcohol and carbon dioxide are produced. In a still wine this carbon dioxide is allowed to escape. In *méthode champenoise,* this carbon dioxide is captured and produces the bubbles so strongly identified with Champagne. In other areas where sparkling wines are produced, carbon dioxide from another source may be introduced to the wine in order to cause the bubbles.

Some wine drinkers mistakenly refer to all sparkling wine as Champagne. In reality, Champagne is a specific region in Northeastern France that produces a famous sparkling wine. It is not legal to call wine "Champagne" unless it specifically comes from this region. Some other wine-producing areas use their own terms to identify sparkling wines: Spain uses the term "*cava,*" Italy designates it "*spumante or Prosecco,*" and in South Africa the term used is "*cap classique.*"

Sparkling wines are available in many flavors, and can range from dry to sweet. Their alcohol content ranges from 10–14 percent by volume.

FORTIFIED WINES

Some wines that are not considered to be still or sparkling are a very important part of a beverage inventory. Among the most important are fortified wines. A fortified wine is one that has had a spirit added to it to increase its alcohol content. Fortified wines are popular for drinking and for use in cooking.

Recall from chapter 1 that spirits are made by distillation, the process of removing water from a liquid that contains alcohol. In most cases the spirit added to fortified wine is brandy. Brandy—from the Dutch word *brandewijn,* meaning "burnt wine"—typically contains 35 to 60 percent alcohol. When brandy, or another type of spirit, is added to wine, the wine's alcohol content increases. Fortified wine is different from spirits made from wine in that spirits are produced by distillation, while fortified wine is simply wine that has had a spirit added to it. Fortified wines are widely available and their alcohol content ranges from 14 to no more than 24 percent by volume.

Here is a list of many of the popular fortified wines.

PORT Port wine, also known as "*Porto*" or "port" for short, is a Portuguese fortified wine produced exclusively in the northern portion of Portugal. It is often produced as a sweet red wine, but also is made in dry, semi-dry, and white varieties. Fortified wines in the "style" of port are produced in many areas of the world, but only the product from Portugal may be labeled as *Porto.* The term *port,* however, is one that is used by makers in a variety of countries.

SHERRY Sherry is a fortified wine made from white grapes grown near the town of Jerez, Spain. In Spanish, sherry is called *vino de Jerez* and "sherry" is the English version of the name. Like the terms *Champagne* and *Porto*, the laws regarding which products can legally be called *Sherry* are extensive. Sherry-style fortified wines, however, make a popular before and after dinner drink as well as being flavorful ingredients in a variety of menu items.

Sherry is fortified with brandy after fermentation takes place. Therefore, because most of the sugar in the grape juice has been converted to alcohol, sherries are initially dry, with any sweetness added back later. Cream sherry is a version of sherry popular as a cooking ingredient and is used in items such as lobster bisque. The name can be deceptive. It is merely a sweet-style sherry; it contains no dairy products whatsoever.

MADEIRA Madeira is a fortified wine made in the Madeira Islands, located off the coast of Portugal in the North Atlantic Ocean. The Madeira Islands are noted for their unique winemaking process that involves heating the wine and deliberately exposing the wine to oxygen, which changes its character. Madeira is produced in a variety of styles ranging from dry wines, which can be consumed on their own, to sweet Madeiras that are served with desserts.

MARSALA Marsala is a fortified wine produced in the area surrounding Marsala, in Sicily. Originally, Marsala wine was fortified with alcohol to ensure that it would not spoil on long ocean voyages, but now it is fortified because of its popularity in foreign markets.

Marsala is an ingredient in a variety of Italian dishes, the most well known of which are scaloppine (e.g., scaloppine al marsala) and zabaglione, the very popular Italian dessert.

AROMATIZED WINES

Aromatized wines are those that have been flavored with something other than the grapes used for their production. Wines have been flavored with a variety of ingredients since their inception. The Romans flavored their wines with pepper, cypress, myrrh, poppy, aloe, chalk, and even boiled seawater. Today, wines are aromatized with a variety of herbs, roots, flowers, and barks, including quinine, the bark of the cinchona tree.

Vermouth is the most widely popular form of aromatized wine. Vermouth can be either sweet (Italian) made from white grapes or dry (French) made from red grapes. Like fortified wines, the alcohol levels of aromatized wines are most often increased after fermentation is complete. In the case of vermouth, the alcohol level is increased to around 18 percent (36 proof).

A *wine cooler* is the generic term used for wine mixed with fruit juice, a carbonated beverage, and sugar. Unlike fortified or aromatized wines, these products are popular for their *lowered* alcohol content (typically between 4 and 6 percent). Initially homemade, wine coolers have been bottled and sold by commercial distributors since the early 1980s, especially in areas where their lower alcohol content causes them to come under less-restrictive laws than wine itself.

In 1991, changes in alcohol-related tax laws made it much less profitable for U.S. wine cooler makers to produce these products. Fruit-flavored "coolers" are still produced today, but the alcoholic beverage used for the base is now a malt beverage (see chapter 4) rather than wine. Popular flavors of malt beverages include mango, watermelon, coconut, lime, lemon, black cherry, and strawberry. The products may be called malt beverages, malt coolers, or simply coolers, but many guests still refer to them as wine coolers.

Sangria, the Spanish mix of wine and fruit, is a popular form of homemade wine cooler. However, sangria is also mass-produced and can be a good addition to an establishment's wine list. Sangria can be purchased in bottles or made on-site.

As previously stated in chapter 5, there are also non-alcoholic (NA) wines on the market today; however, their acceptance among wine drinkers has been slow. Despite that, managers may consider having one or more NA wines on their wine lists as an option for guests. There are some occasions when customers including traditional wine drinkers will simply prefer an NA beverage:

- When they are out for a party or dinner but must drive a vehicle
- If a medical condition prevents them from drinking alcohol
- If they are pregnant and do not wish to drink alcohol
- If they enjoy the taste of wine but not the effects of alcohol

Still, sparkling, fortified, aromatized, or mixed with other beverages, wines of all types and flavors are made to be drunk and enjoyed at restaurant and foodservice operations throughout the world.

WINE PRODUCTION

Due to soil conditions, weather, and other geographic characteristics, some areas of the world produce spectacular grapes and wines while other areas produce either no wine or very poor wines. Many countries, however, produce a wine that is popular within its borders. Wine is a particularly fascinating area of interest to many because no two wines are ever exactly identical. There are significant differences in wines, even those made from the same grapes. Location, climate, soil, grapes used, the winemaker's skill, and the age of a wine are but a few of the characteristics that influence a wine's taste.

It is not surprising that some who study wines do so based on the grapes used to make them, whereas others focus on geographic location of the vineyards or wineries producing the wines. Each of these approaches (and many more!) can make good sense when beginning a study of wines. For restaurant and foodservice managers, one easy way to begin to learn more about wine is simply to consider wines of two basic types: red wines and white wines.

Red Wines

Red wines actually vary greatly in color. Wine can be dark red, light red, ruby red, deep violet, maroon, and a host of other hues. As noted earlier, grape skins, not grape juice, provide the color in red wines. When grape skins stay in contact with grape juice during the fermentation process, tannins in the grape skins color the juice. An individual wine's particular red hue depends on the grape type used in the process and the length of time the skin's pigmentation is in contact with juice. Worldwide over 100 different grape types are used to make red wine, and red wine is made in thousands of locations.

Wine drinkers often further classify red wines by their "body type." A light-bodied wine is one with lower levels of tannins from the grapes used to make it. Tannins are responsible for the mouth-puckering aspect of wines. Medium- and full-bodied red wines have more "pucker power" and, as a result, the types of food that go best with these full-flavored wines differ from the types of food guests might prefer with lighter-bodied red wines.

Exhibit 5.2

Despite the range of flavors available, red wines have traditionally been associated with hearty, full-bodied flavor. The classic red wines are made from the Cabernet Sauvignon (cab-er-NAY so-veen-YOHN) grape. This is the red wine made famous by the Bordeaux region of France. These wines are complex, outstanding products that make excellent food accompaniments and are fine for drinking by themselves. They are typical of the red wines sold to accompany menu items such as beef, wild game, and other dark meat entrées that require a bold, hearty flavor (*Exhibit 5.2*).

A second outstanding grape used for making red wines is the Pinot Noir (pee-NO NWAR). It is from this grape that the famous French burgundies are made. This is also the grape used to make Champagne. Other important grapes used for making red wine include the Merlot (mer-LOW); the Gamay, or Napa Gamay, grown in France and California; the Shiraz (or Syrah), popular with winemakers in Australia and South Africa; and the Zinfandel (ZIN-fand-el) grape grown in California and popular for making a very light red wine referred to as blush wine.

Blush wines are red wines that range from just barely pink to nearly red. They are called White Zinfandels (if they are made from that type of grape), blush, or rosé wines, and are especially popular in the summertime. In addition, they are frequently paired with light food such as fish and poultry. Generally, they resemble white wines in taste.

Some red wines are made from a blend of grape types. The blends are often noted on the labels. In some cases, red wine blends are simply labeled "Red" or "Table Red."

The most important thing for managers to remember is that red wines will very likely form an integral part of every operation's beverage menu or wine list. It is critical that the red wines selected for sale match the tastes and price range of targeted customers. It is also important to know that most red wines are best served at cellar temperature, generally considered to be between 65°F and 70°F (18°C and 21°C). Red wines are stronger in flavor and heavier in body than are white wines. They can range in taste from very sweet to very dry. The alcoholic content of red wines typically ranges from 10 to 14 percent.

White Wines

While red wines have traditionally been associated with robust food, white wines, with their more delicate taste, are the most popular wine for drinking by the glass in bars, at receptions, and with lighter food. White wines complement more delicate food such as fish, poultry, and pork.

White wines are not actually "white" at all, but rather range in color from very light (pale) straw color to deep gold. White wines are made from the grape juice *and* grape skin of green, gold, or yellowish colored grapes or from just the juice, not the skin, of select red grapes.

White wines are typically served chilled at refrigerator temperatures, or the bottles are immersed in ice prior to service. They range in flavor from those that are dry and tart to others that are sweet and mellow. White wines generally have a more delicate flavor than red wines. Like red wines, they can range from the very sweet to the very dry. They range in alcohol content from a low of 10 percent to as much as 14 percent. Most of the white wines served in the United States are produced in Italy, Germany, France, South America, South Africa, or California.

Grapes used to produce fine white wines vary according to the country that makes the wine. In the Rhine and Moselle valleys of Europe, the Riesling grape is most often used to produce the sweet, flavorful wines associated with German whites. Pinot Bianco, Pinot Grigio (its name in Italy, but Pinot Gris elsewhere), and Traminer are other popular grapes used for making white wine.

By far the most popular white wine in the United States is Chardonnay. This complex wine is aged in oak. Whereas many white wines are fermented in stainless-steel tanks, fermenting and aging in oak and other woods gives wines unique and quite complex flavor, color, and aroma characteristics. Like many red wines, Chardonnay wine will improve with age prior to its bottling. Chardonnay is made from the same grape used in the Burgundy and Champagne regions of France.

White wines are an essential component of nearly every operation's wine list because of the popularity of seafood, poultry, and pork entrées. In addition, white wines are an important part of every bar menu because drinking white wine by itself, without food, is one extremely popular way of enjoying it.

WINE-GROWING REGIONS OF THE WORLD

Wine grapes grow almost exclusively between 30 and 50 degrees north or south of the equator. The world's southernmost vineyards are in New Zealand, and the northernmost are in Sweden (*Exhibit 5.3*).

Wines of good quality are made all over the world. However, for restaurant and foodservice managers, the most important wines are those that can be purchased in a large enough quantity to be included on their operations' wine lists. Some very exclusive establishments may purchase wines in which availability is limited to only a few bottles or cases per year. For most establishments, however, wine suppliers will offer a large variety of wines from which to choose. These wines will be available in sufficient quantities to merit placement on an operation's wine list. In most cases, the wines readily available to managers will come from one of the five major wine-producing areas of the world:

- Europe
- North America
- South America
- Australia
- Africa and the Middle East

Exhibit 5.3

WORLD WINE GROWING MAP

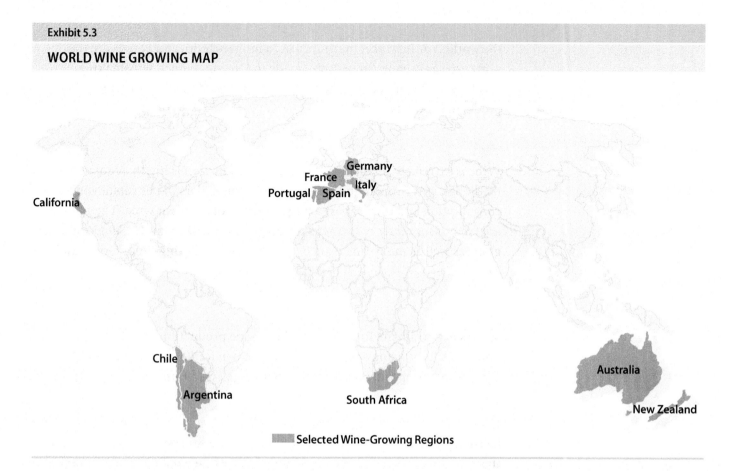

Selected Wine-Growing Regions

Europe

Not all grapes can be used to produce high-quality wines. Europe is by far the world's largest producer of the type of grapes (called *Vitis vinifera*) used to make fine wine and wine for exporting. It leads all areas in the world in per capita wine consumption and wine export. Wine is made in all European countries. However, four countries dominate the wine market:

- France
- Italy
- Spain
- Germany

FRANCE

France is well known for the quality of its cooking and its wines. French wines are carefully labeled to indicate where they are made and by whom. There are several world-class red and white wines produced in France, including Bordeaux, Burgundy, Chablis, and Champagne.

France is the source of many grape varieties that are now planted throughout the world. For instance, the grapes used in French Burgundy reds are the same type as used in Pinor Noirs made in Oregon. French winemaking practices and styles of wine have also been adopted in all other wine-producing countries.

ITALY

Wine is extremely popular in Italy and its production is highly regulated by the Italian government. Italians are among the leaders in per capita wine consumption and they export a large quantity of excellent wine. The Italians are famous for many red wines such as Chianti made from the Sangiovese grape as well as many fine blanco (white) wines including Pinot Grigio and Trabbiano.

SPAIN

Spain's harsh climate limits some of the grape production of its vast vineyards. That being said, Spain is well known for its sherry wine and for Cava, a sparkling wine made in the champagne tradition.

GERMANY

Germany is noted for the quality of its white wines. Especially noteworthy are the wines made from the Riesling grape. These fine wines range from very sweet to very dry. Located among the northernmost wine-growing regions of the world, German vintners have mastered the art of producing excellent wines in a variety of geographic areas:

- The Reingau
- The Rheinhessen
- The Nahe
- The Rheinpfalz
- The Moselle
- Baden

German wines are bottled and labeled to indicate four recognized quality levels:

1. *Deutscher Tafelwein* (**German table wine**): Made from normally ripe and slightly underripe grapes, this wine is primarily consumed in Germany with very little exported to the United States.
2. *Landwein* (**country wine**): This wine is a superior Deutscher Tafelwein with a minimum of 0.5 percent more alcohol.

3. *Qualitätswein bestimmter Anbaugebiet* (**quality wine from a specified area**): This middle-quality category consists of good-quality wines that come from one specific wine-growing region. The wines are made of approved grape varieties and have reached sufficient ripeness for a quality wine.

4. *Qualitätswein mit Prädikat* or *Prädikatswein* (**quality wine of distinction**): This is the category for the best of German wines.

Of course, quality wines are produced in other European countries, and managers should explore with their wine suppliers those countries producing wines their guests may enjoy.

North America

The United States dominates wine production in North America. Interestingly, it can be said that there are two wine industries in the United States. The first and oldest wineries produced products from native grapes hardy enough to survive the New England winters endured by the country's earliest settlers. This native grape, *Vitus labrusca*, produced quality wines, but these wines tasted different from their European counterparts. Efforts to grow the traditional European wine grape, *Vitis vinifera*, were not initially successful due to the harsh weather. Today, many wineries in the United States still make wines using native American grapes.

In time, winemakers discovered that European-style wine grapes grow well in California. Today, that state accounts for the majority of all wine produced in the United States. California produces all types of wines, many of the same outstanding quality as those produced in Europe. Most restaurant and foodservice guests are now familiar with the quality of California wines as well as good-quality wines produced in nearly all other states. As a result, guests often look for California wines as well as locally produced wines on the menu.

South America

Chile and Argentina have become significant suppliers of good-quality wine from the world's southern grape-growing regions. Catholic missionaries introduced winemaking to South America in the sixteenth century. Today, Chile's sunny climate allows that country to produce excellent wine. Due to the high altitude and low humidity of the country's main wine-producing regions, Argentine vineyards rarely face the insects, fungi, molds, and other problems that can affect grape production. This allows cultivating with little or no pesticides, thus allowing even organic wines to be easily produced in that country.

Manager's Memo

Following the creation by the United States Department of Agriculture (USDA) of the National Organic Program (NOP), an organic wine is defined as "a wine made from organically grown grapes without any added sulfites."

By this restriction, the vast majority of what customers would assume to be called organic wines can only be referred to as "wines made from organic grapes" or organically grown grapes, since wines are allowed to contain up to 100 parts per million (ppm) of added sulfites.

Despite some labeling confusion, managers should be aware that consumer interest in organic products of all types, including wine, continues to grow.

Australia

The history of wine production in Australia is not a long one. Captain Arthur Phillip brought the first grapevine cuttings to the country when he arrived in New South Wales in 1788. While good wine is produced in all parts of Australia, the main wine-growing regions are in the southern, cooler parts of the country:

- South Australia
- New South Wales
- Victoria
- Western Australia

The products most exported include those made from Shiraz, Cabernet Sauvignon, Chardonnay, Merlot, Semillon, Pinot Noir, Riesling, and Sauvignon Blanc grapes.

Africa and the Middle East

The southern geography of South Africa makes that country ideal for growing wine grapes. South Africa is located at the southern tip of the African continent and most of its wine regions are located near the ocean coasts. These regions have a Mediterranean climate that is characterized by abundant sunshine and dry heat. Today, the focus in the South African wine industry has been on increasing the quality of wine for export, thus more of it is available for manager's consideration for inclusion on wine lists.

While the first wines were likely made in the Middle East, the Islamic religion forbids the use of alcoholic beverages. Because the Middle East is primarily a Muslim region, little wine is produced there today. However, Cyprus and Turkey produce limited amounts of wine for export, as does Israel.

WINE PACKAGING

Wine comes in several package types. Most wines come in bottles, although some wines are sold "boxed" and others come in single-serve containers of several types.

Wine Bottles

For many guests, ordering wine means ordering a bottle of wine sealed with a cork. Glass bottles have been used to package wines for hundreds of years, and many of the best wines made today tend to be packaged in glass bottles with cork stoppers.

The wine bottle sizes that can be legally sold in the United States are listed in *Exhibit 5.4*. Note that the common names for these bottles date to before the U.S. beverage industry's conversion to metric measurements in the 1980s.

Exhibit 5.4

WINE BOTTLE SIZES AND CAPACITIES

Bottle Size (Capacity)	Common Name	Description
0.100 L	Miniature (mini)	A single-serving bottle
0.187 L	Split	¼ of a standard bottle
0.375 L	Half-bottle	½ of a standard bottle
0.750 L	Bottle	A standard wine bottle
1.5 L	Magnum	Two bottles in one
3.0 L	Double magnum	Four bottles in one

Note: L = liter. 1 U.S. quart (qt) = 0.946 L; 1 U.S. gallon (gal) = 3.785 L.

Wine bottles must contain standard amounts of wine but can vary widely in shape and color. For example, the Bordeaux tradition calls for dark green bottles to be used for red wines, light green for dry whites, and clear bottles for sweet whites. German wines tend to be bottled in dark to medium green–colored glass bottles, although some producers have traditionally used amber. Champagne is usually packaged in dark to medium green bottles. Clear bottles have recently become popular with white wine producers in some countries, but most red wines worldwide are still bottled in green glass.

Regardless of their size, shape, and color, for more than 400 years most wine producers have preferred to seal their bottles using cork stoppers:

- **Impermeability:** Cork is very resistant to moisture penetration. It is used in life jackets!

- **Lightness:** Cork weighs little and is low in density.

- **Compressibility:** Cork can be compressed to half its dimension with no loss of its flexibility. It can be compressed in diameter without expanding its length.

- **Flexibility:** When removed from compression, cork will recover about 85 percent of its initial volume immediately and more than 98 percent after 24 hours.

- **Adherence:** Cutting the surface cells in forming a cork stopper produces a cupping effect. Millions of cork cells are opened and function as suction cups. This provides an exceptional power of adhesion to wet, smooth surfaces such as wine bottles. In addition, the cork easily compensates for small imperfections in glass.

- **Temperature and age stability:** Cork retains its properties at both high and low extremes of temperature and usually lasts approximately 20 years without any deterioration.

- **Environmental impact:** Cork is biodegradable and comes from a renewable resource.

THINK ABOUT IT . . .

Do you think most wine drinkers perceive boxed wines to be of a lower quality than bottled wines? What can managers do to help change the perception of those who do?

OPEN FOR BUSINESS

WHAT'S THE FOOTPRINT?

Wine in aluminum bottles? Why not? Some winemakers are experimenting with canning their wines in aluminum "bottles." The reasons include changing market structures as well as new trends in consumer behavior. Small-sized cans with a volume of 200 to 250 milliliters are particularly attractive to consumers who enjoy wine only occasionally or in single-serve quantities.

The metal packaging also offers a way of reaching young consumers who are not traditional wine drinkers. Further, cans are unbreakable, lightweight, and compact, making them ideal for outdoor consumption. Aluminum bottles can be recycled almost infinitely and the bottles require less fuel to transport than their heavier glass counterparts. Wine in metal bottles also has a particular appeal to market segments where ease of transport, weight, storage, and safety are important. This is the case for airlines, passenger ships, and trains.

Cork is harvested from Cork Oak trees that are cultivated in Portugal, which accounts for approximately half the world's annual production, as well as in Spain, Algeria, France, and Italy. Cork trees can live to be hundreds of years old. Their cork is harvested approximately every 10 years. The harvesting of cork does not harm the tree; in fact, no trees are cut down during the cork harvesting process. Only the bark is extracted, and a new layer of cork regrows, making it a renewable source for the life of the tree.

Research has shown that most wine consumers assume that a wine packaged in a bottle with a cork stopper is superior to those wines packaged in other ways. Whether consumers will continue to maintain this belief over time remains to be seen. However, it is true that there are alternative forms of wine packaging available to restaurant and foodservice operators and their guests. These include bottled wines sold with screw-off caps, or with synthetic (artificial) corks. Both of these options are gaining popularity and are used by winemakers primarily because each alternative is less expensive than a traditional cork stopper.

Boxed Wine

Some wine is sold in cardboard boxes containing a bag that holds the wine. These boxes of wine contain the interior bag and a faucet that dispenses the wine. The primary benefit that this packaging offers to consumers is that it prevents oxidation of the wine during dispensing. After opening, wine in a bottle is affected by the air that displaces the poured wine. The oxygen in that air can transform the flavor of a wine. Wine in a bag is not touched by air and thus is not subject to oxidation until it is dispensed. The result is a wine that can be stored for several days with little loss of quality. This can make some boxed wines a good choice for use as a house wine, a wine designed to be sold at a low cost and often in single servings.

Boxed wine also has environmental benefits. Boxed wines are sold commercially in 2- to 20-liter sizes. As a result, far less packaging mass is required. Boxed wines chill quickly, are recyclable, and do not break if dropped. As is true with non-corked wines, however, there is some evidence that wine drinkers currently perceive boxed wines to be inferior to bottled wines. As a result, managers should carefully watch consumer trends related to wines as they decide the best choices to offer their own guests.

Single Service

A recent development in wine packaging is the single-serve disposable unit. It is different from the 100-milliliter mini-bottle because the wine comes prepacked in a hygienically sealed, convenient, and stylish polyethylene terephthalate (PET) plastic *wineglass*. PET is the same material bottlers use for bottled water and most carbonated soft drinks. The PET wineglass holds

175 to 200 milliliters of wine. To maintain wine quality and freshness, the wineglass is injected with inert gas prior to sealing, giving the wine a shelf life of one year. It can be consumed in places where glass is considered to be unsafe, illegal, or environmentally unsound.

CREATING WINE LISTS

Managers purchase wines in a variety of container sizes. Wines are then sold to guests in a number of ways, including by the glass, in carafes (a glass container used to serve wine or water) of various sizes, and by the bottle. Managers list the wines they have available for sale on a wine menu, or list. Sometimes the wine list is a separate menu; at other times, it is incorporated into the regular food menu. The wine list, like the food menu, should reflect the personality of the establishment and, when properly created, should include wines that complement and harmonize with the operation's food menu offerings.

Wise managers know that when wine is served with a meal, it can increase the dining experience to one of a special occasion that, in turn, will result in increased guest satisfaction and greater profits (*Exhibit 5.5*). There is a long tradition of suggested wine and food pairings. The concept of pairing is that some wines go better with specific types of food than do others, and that a wine should be selected *after* the food item to be served with it has been chosen.

Since wine should complement the food with which it is served, many diners seek to match, or pair, specific wines to specific menu items. Although there are traditional wine and food pairings that managers should be aware of (see *Exhibit 5.6*), equally important are the preferences of individual guests. Experienced managers know that, regardless of any tradition, the best wine to accompany a menu item is always the one the guest likes and wants to buy.

Exhibit 5.5

Wines can be enjoyed before, during, or after full meals.

Exhibit 5.6

COMMON WINE AND FOOD PAIRINGS

Type of Food	Traditional Service Recommendation
Hors d'oeuvers	Champagne
Soups	Sherry
Fish and poultry	White wines
Pork and veal	White or rosé wines
Beef	Red wines
Cheeses	Port or White Zinfandel
Desserts	Champagne
All food	The guest's preferred wines

Some operators seek to recommend a single wine with each of their menu offerings. However, managers must think carefully about doing so. Consider, for example, a couple dining out, one of whom has ordered a beef dish and the other a pork item. If the menu suggests only one wine for each dish, it will likely be a red wine for the beef and a white or rosé wine for the pork. If the suggested wines are available for purchase only by the bottle, it is possible that neither person will order the suggested wine because it is not available by the glass. Despite that possibility, it is usually a good idea for managers and servers to have a basic understanding of the characteristics of all the wines included on the establishment's wine list as well as which specific menu items these wines best complement.

Order of Presentation

Managers creating wine lists can choose from several alternative presentation formats. Managers may list wines:

- **In the order they would be consumed:** appetizer wines, entrée wines, and dessert wines

- **By their origin country or state:** Italian, French, German, or Californian

- **By color:** white wines followed by rosé wines followed by red wines

- **By serving size:** glass, carafe, or bottle

- **By selling price:** from least expensive to most expensive or most expensive to least expensive

- **Using a combination of two or more formats:** listing wines by their origin and by their price, for example

The wine pricing is heavily influenced by the type of establishment selling them and the quality of wines sold. In all cases, managers should price wines in a way that encourages sales and generates a profit (see chapter 10). Managers should keep wine prices in line with the overall pricing structure of the operation. Typically, less-expensive establishments will not sell only higher-priced wines, and higher-priced operations would lose revenues if they offered only inexpensive wines.

As a general rule, each wine list should include some inexpensive wines so cost-conscious guests can enjoy a special occasion with the opportunity to include wine with their meal. Similarly, a wine list should include some higher-quality and higher-priced wines for those customers who enjoy drinking finer wines with their meals.

Characteristics of an Effective Wine List

An operation's wine list can be extensive or simple, but it should always include basic characteristics that help ensure the list is appropriate for the establishment. Careful attention must be paid to a number of factors.

The wines selected should complement the food on the menu and the character of the establishment. The most important feature of a good wine list is that it consists of wines that go well with the food items served, and that it is in keeping with the overall objectives of the establishment. For example, if the wine list is created to complement a mid-priced Italian-style establishment, the wines selected should reflect the style and atmosphere of the cuisine being served. Guests visiting this type of operation will have some expectations that can be met, in part by the wine list. These expectations may include inexpensive house wines, some wines produced in Italy, and in other European countries as well, and good-quality domestic wines with which these guests are likely to be very familiar. Each wine should have a role on the wine list. That is, each should be selected for its ability to complement the food items served or to further the establishment's character.

The wines selected should complement the pricing structure of the establishment. Some guests, but certainly not all, may desire a high-quality and relatively expensive wine to complement their meal. Others will prefer a more modestly priced wine. The best wine lists offer something for both types of guests. In all cases the price of the wines offered should be in keeping with the menu's entrée prices. If they are not, less wine will be sold. Extremely rare and expensive wines will not sell on a wine list that accompanies a menu designed for a mid-priced establishment.

The selection of a wine from the menu should be made easy for the diner. Most but not all guests are less familiar with wines than are the wine list planners. Also, many of the best wines made and sold today are of foreign origin and have names that may be difficult to pronounce. A result is that it can sometimes be difficult or potentially embarrassing for diners to buy wines.

When appropriate because of potential ordering difficulty for guests, the establishment should offer pronunciation assistance or use the common technique of assigning a bin number to each wine to ease the guests' task of selecting a wine. A bin number tells the location in a wine cellar where a specific wine is being held for service. Bin numbers are often provided to allow guests to order wines by number, rather than by names that can sometimes be hard to pronounce properly.

The wine list should include "by the glass" offerings. While wine has traditionally been perceived as the alcoholic beverage of moderation, diners are more cautious than ever about excessive alcohol consumption. More diners are limiting alcohol consumption during meals to one or two drinks. Sales of wine by the glass appeal to these diners because they can enjoy their preferred beverage with their meal and still moderate their total consumption of alcohol.

Descriptions of the wines should be included whenever possible. When space allows, provide as much information about the wines as is practical. Interesting information such as origin, flavor, and special characteristics make the wine list more appealing to the diners and will typically result in increased wine sales.

The wine list should avoid repetition. A smaller offering of quality wines is better than a larger offering of wines that are very similar. Wines that do not sell rapidly result in excessive inventory costs.

Wine information listed on the menu should be accurate and spelled correctly. This is a common error. Always obtain the spelling of the wine directly from the bottle's label. Accuracy in identifying vintage (the year in which grapes used to make the wine were grown) and region or vineyard is also important. Bottle sizes should also be properly identified where appropriate.

The wines listed on the wine menu should be readily available. Avoid listing wines that cannot be kept in inventory in good supply. Just as menu planners do not want to list items on the menu that cannot be served at all times, wines that will not be stocked consistently should not be listed.

The wine list must be clean and attractive. Whether the wine list is part of the main menu or is provided separately, it should be eye-catching, stain-free, and in good condition. Just as food menus must be kept immaculately clean, so too should the wine list.

The wine list should be made available to every diner who is of age to drink. While this is an operational issue rather than one directly associated with the wine list itself, a wine list that is not readily seen by the guests cannot help sell wine. If the wine list is not part of the regular food menu, it should always be presented to diners at the same time as the food menu.

Wine lists that incorporate each of these characteristics help the restaurant or foodservice operation sell more wine and, therefore, better satisfy its wine-drinking guests.

WINE SERVICE

Establishments with high-volume wine sales may employ a sommelier, a service employee with extensive knowledge about wine including its storage and wine and food pairings. Sommeliers advise customers about wine selection, take wine orders, and present and serve the wines that are selected. Most operations do not have this specialized assistance available, and the food or beverage server is responsible for assisting customers with wine selection.

An important first step in selling wine is to have some product knowledge about the wines available. Servers should also know how to properly pronounce the name of each wine. In some establishments tables are set with wineglasses, often a glass for white wine and a separate glass for red wine. In this instance, if a wine is not ordered, both glasses should be removed from the table. If one type of wine is requested, the glass that is not needed is removed. In other establishments, wineglasses are not set on the table before the customers arrive and, instead, they are brought to the table if wine is ordered.

Exhibit 5.7 outlines the 10 steps that form the basis for professional wine service.

Step 1: Present Wine List

Wine lists, like food menus, represent the operation's brand. They should be clean and neat because they are significant selling tools. They should be brought to the table for presentation to the customer with a comment such as, "I am proud to present our wine list." This can be followed with the suggestion, "If you have any questions about our wines, I will be happy to answer them. Otherwise, please take a few moments to look over the list." In some establishments, wine lists are placed on the table when it is set for service. In this case the server should point out the wine list on the table.

Step 2: Assist Customers with Wine Selection

Some customers are likely to be very knowledgeable about wine and will not desire or appreciate assistance. Others may have questions about the type of wine to select relative to the food being ordered or the quantity to order. Note: *There are approximately five servings (5 ounces each) per bottle; a full bottle holds 25.6 ounces. Therefore, a full bottle will likely be sufficient for two to three people depending on portion size.*

Step 3: Take Wine Order

The wine order should be taken and repeated to ensure there is no communication problem.

Step 4: Collect Wineglasses and Obtain Necessary Wine

Some establishments use the same wineglass regardless of the wine type selected; others use specific glasses for specific types. Establishments use various systems for servers to obtain the wine ordered. White wines are typically served chilled; red wines are typically served at approximately room temperature. These factors influence where the wine will be stored until it is issued to service staff (see chapter 8).

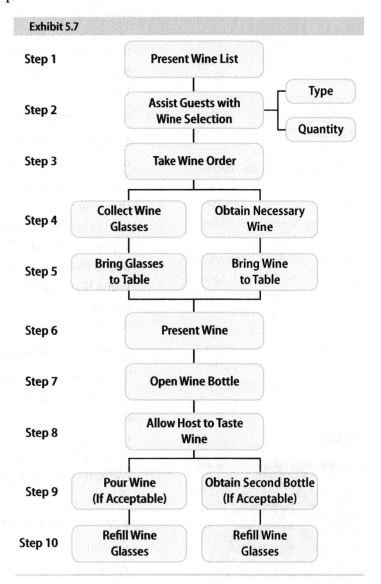

Exhibit 5.7

Step 1 — Present Wine List
Step 2 — Assist Guests with Wine Selection → Type / Quantity
Step 3 — Take Wine Order
Step 4 — Collect Wine Glasses / Obtain Necessary Wine
Step 5 — Bring Glasses to Table / Bring Wine to Table
Step 6 — Present Wine
Step 7 — Open Wine Bottle
Step 8 — Allow Host to Taste Wine
Step 9 — Pour Wine (If Acceptable) / Obtain Second Bottle (If Acceptable)
Step 10 — Refill Wine Glasses / Refill Wine Glasses

One reason for the popularity of social media sites is that they allow users to easily share information of common interest. Wine is one area of great common interest among diners. Managers who understand this can develop lively conversations about the wines offered on their menus. In such a case it is not the role of the manager to "push" or promote any one wine on the wine list, but rather to provide an easy forum for customers to share their perceptions and experiences with the wines they have ordered during their meals. Some guest comments will no doubt be glowingly positive and others less so. As long as the wine service delivered was professional and prompts feedback that stimulates discussion about an establishment's wines and wine list, it is a win–win for managers and their guests.

Exhibit 5.8

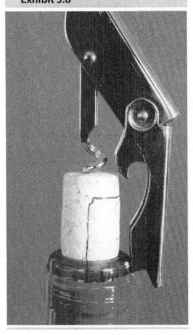

Step 5: Bring Glasses and Wine to Table

If wineglasses are not pre-set, they should be brought to the table on a small serving tray and handled by their stems, not by their bowls or rims. They should be placed to the customer's right. Red wines can be brought to the table on a tray or in a wine basket. Chilled white and sparkling wines should be brought to the table on a small serving tray or in a wine cooler (bucket). In some establishments, wine coolers are placed on the table; in others, a cooler stand is placed on the floor to the host's (the person who ordered the wine) right to provide more table room.

Step 6: Present Wine to Guests

In most cases, the host should be presented with the wine; however, the decision of who at the table will taste the wine is the host's, not the server's.

The host should be allowed to read the label while the server pronounces the name. For example, "This is a bottle of the Robert Mondavi Fumé Blanc that you ordered." The server may also mention any information about the wine that he or she feels could be of interest to the guests and add to the enjoyment of the wine. For example, "This is the original Fumé Blanc. Robert Mondavi created the term in 1966 to distinguish his dry Sauvignon Blanc from the sweeter-styled Sauvignon Blanc wines made at the time."

Step 7: Open Wine After Guest Approval

The server should use the knife blade attachment on a corkscrew to remove the foil, which is placed in the server's pocket or apron. The corkscrew is inserted into the center of the cork and is screwed in as far as it will go. The lever is placed on the bottle's lip, and the cork is levered up until it can be removed (*Exhibit 5.8*). Once removed from the corkscrew, the cork can be presented to the host, who may want to examine it.

Step 8: Allow Guests to Taste

A small sample of the wine is poured into the host's glass for sampling. When the wine is poured, the bottle's label should be facing the customer, and when pouring is complete, the bottle should be twisted at the same time it is tipped up to reduce drips. Glasses are not removed from the table as wine is poured unless, for example, the customer is seated against a wall or in a booth, or there is another reason pouring in place is impractical. If the host does not approve the wine, the server should retrieve a second bottle. Improper processing, transporting, or storing conditions sometimes yield an unsatisfactory bottle of wine. Sometimes, however, the customer may just be unsatisfied with the wine's taste. Care should be taken that this is not caused by an improper description on the wine list or by the server. Alternatively, the server may suggest a different wine or request that the manager or other staff member with more extensive wine knowledge assist the customer. When a new bottle of wine is brought to the table, steps 6 through 8 should be repeated.

Step 9: Pour Wine After Guest Approval

Begin with the woman nearest the host's right; serve all other women, then male guests, and finally the host. The manager should establish the portion size to be poured in wineglasses, and this decision will be based in part on the shape and size of wineglass.

Step 10: Refill Wineglasses

Servers should know when to refill glasses. When a guest's wineglass is almost empty, the server can inquire, "Would you care for more wine?"

There is a great deal of tradition and showmanship in professional wine service. Proper use of these procedures is appreciated by many customers and is an important part of their enjoyment of the wine and of the meal itself.

OPEN FOR BUSINESS — MANAGER'S MATH

A manager is trying to decide how much he should charge for a new wine by the glass that he is thinking about adding to his operation's wine list. The wine he is considering comes in both 750-milliliter and 1.5-liter bottles. The advantage of the smaller bottle is that it is less likely to go bad if the entire bottle is not served at one time. Also, he feels it simply "looks" better because it is smaller. The advantage of the large bottle is its lower cost per serving.

He is also considering whether to offer a 4- or 5-ounce portion of the wine. Before he considers his selling price, he would like to know his product costs. Consider the costs of the two wine bottle size options available in this example. Then fill in the empty cells with the costs per glass.

Which bottle size would you recommend he choose? Why?

Bottle Size	Cost per Bottle	Number of Ounces per Bottle	Cost per 4-Oz Glass	Cost per 5-Oz Glass
A: 750-ml bottle	$ 6.50	25.4	$	$
B: 1.5-L bottle	$ 10.75	50.8	$	$

(Answers: Bottle A's cost per 4-oz glass is $1.02, and the cost per 5-oz glass is $1.28; Bottle B's cost per 4-oz glass is $0.85, and the cost per 5-oz glass is $1.06.)

SUMMARY

1. **Classify wines by their characteristics.**

   There are a variety of ways to classify wines. For restaurant and foodservice managers, two of the most important ways relate to the color of the wine (white, rosé, and red), and the wine's sugar content (dry, semi-sweet, and sweet). Other common methods used to classify wine include the grape from which the wine was made; the country, region, or state in which the wine was produced; and its vintage (the year in which the grapes used to make the wine were grown).

2. **Identify the four major types of wine.**

   The four major wine classifications are still, sparkling, fortified, and aromatized. Still wines are made by fermentation of fruit juices, mainly grapes, where the carbon dioxide resulting from fermentation is allowed to escape from the wine. Sparkling wines are made by fermentation of juice where the carbon dioxide resulting from fermentation is captured or added back to the wine. Fortified wines are those in which the spirit is added to the wine to increase its alcohol content. Aromatized wines are those in which a flavoring ingredient is added to the wine. Ingredients commonly used to flavor aromatized wines include a variety of herbs, roots, flowers, and barks, including quinine.

3. **Describe the basic differences between red and white wines.**

   The same type of grape can be used to make red or white wine. Red wines gain their color from extended exposure to the tannins found in grape skins. As a result, most red wines have a fuller body than white wines. In general, red wines are best consumed at cellar temperature, generally considered to be between 65°F and 70°F (18°C and 21°C). White wines are best served chilled at refrigerator temperatures. Red wines tend to improve when bottle aged, while white wines are typically best consumed shortly after they are bottled.

4. **List the world's five major wine-growing regions.**

   Quality wines are made all over the world; however, many wine experts would agree that there are five major wine-growing regions in world. These are Europe, North America, South America, Australia, and Africa and the Middle East. In Europe, wine production is dominated by the big four producers: France, Italy, Germany, and Spain. In North America, California dominates the wine market but wines are also made from many native American grapes in the northeastern part of the country. Chile and Argentina dominate wine production in South America. Australia has recently become known as a producer of fine wines, as has South Africa and some areas in the Middle East where winemaking is an ancient art.

5. **Identify how wine is packaged.**

Wine is sold commercially in several package types. Restaurant and foodservice managers typically purchase wines for sale to customers in bottles or in boxes. The standard bottle size is 750 milliliters (approximately 25.4 ounces per bottle), but other bottle sizes are commonly available for sale in their bottled form or for sale in carafes or glasses.

Boxed wines are also sold to restaurant and foodservice operations for use in serving wines by the carafe or single glass. Boxed wines are those sold in cardboard boxes containing a bag that holds the wine. Most recently, single-serving wines are also available packaged in plastic, aluminum, or small-sized boxes.

6. **State the different ways managers can prepare wine lists.**

Managers can choose from a variety of options as they present their physical wine lists to guests. A first option is to present wines in the order in which a guest's meal would be consumed. A second choice is to list wines by their origin. Wines may also be listed by their color or by their serving size. Some operators prefer to list their wines by price, while still others use combinations of two or more of these approaches to create their own unique wine list presentation formats.

7. **Explain the procedures used to properly open and pour wine for guests.**

To open and pour wine, the server first presents the wine to the host (the guest who ordered the wine). The host should be allowed to read the label. After the host has given approval, the server uses the knife blade attachment on the corkscrew to remove the foil, inserts the corkscrew, and uses its lever to remove the cork from the bottle and present it to the host. A small sample is then poured for the host, who is allowed to taste it first. Upon approval, the glasses of all guests drinking wine are then served in an order that is in keeping with the operation's policy, with the host's glass being filled last. When a guest's wineglass is almost emptied, the server can inquire whether the guest would care for some additional wine.

APPLICATION EXERCISE

Wines are made in nearly every U.S. state. Conduct an Internet search of the wineries in your state or in another geographic area in which you are interested. Choose three wineries to research and answer the questions that follow:

Winery 1:

What is the name of the winery?

_____

How long has it been producing wines?

_____

What grape types are used to produce its wines?

_____

What types of wines are produced?

_____

Winery 2:

What is the name of the winery?

_____

How long has it been producing wines?

_____

What grape types are used to produce its wines?

_____

What types of wines are produced?

_____

Winery 3:

What is the name of the winery?

_____

How long has it been producing wines?

_____

What grape types are used to produce its wines?

_____

What types of wines are produced?

_____

REVIEW YOUR LEARNING

Select the best answer for each question.

1. **What is the approximate alcohol content of a nonfortified still wine?**
   A. 1 to 5%
   B. 9 to 15%
   C. 29 to 45%
   D. 49 to 65%

2. **What is the classification for wines that have been flavored with something other than the grapes used for their production?**
   A. Still
   B. Fortified
   C. Sparkling
   D. Aromatized

3. **What is the wine classification for Champagne and wines made in the Champagne method or style?**
   A. Still
   B. Fortified
   C. Sparkling
   D. Aromatized

4. **What ingredient gives Chardonnay its unique flavor?**
   A. Grape skins
   B. Tannin
   C. Wood
   D. Cork

5. **Who is served first after a host (the guest who ordered the wine) has tasted and approved a wine that he or she has ordered?**
   A. The host
   B. The female sitting to the left of the host
   C. The female sitting to the right of the host
   D. The individual (male or female) sitting to the right of the host

6. **In which major wine-growing region are Bordeaux wines produced?**
   A. Europe
   B. Australia
   C. South Africa
   D. North America

7. In which major wine-growing area is the Napa Valley located?

A. South America

B. North America

C. Australia

D. Europe

8. Which is the best serving temperature for most red wines?

A. Room temperature

B. Slightly warmer than room temperature

C. Slightly cooler than room temperature

D. Refrigerator temperature

9. Which is the best serving temperature for most white wines?

A. Slightly warmer than room temperature

B. Slightly cooler than room temperature

C. Refrigerator temperature

D. Room temperature

10. Approximately how many 5-oz glasses of wine are contained in a 750-ml wine bottle?

A. 3

B. 5

C. 7

D. 9

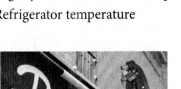

FIELD PROJECT

Managers can choose from a variety of approaches as they design their wine lists. These options include listing wines in the following ways:

1. In the order they would be consumed

2. By their origin

3. By their color

4. By their serving size (e.g., bottle, carafe, or glass)

5. By their selling prices

6. By a combination of two or more of these formats

Consider a type of establishment you would like to manage that sells wine. Then choose three different approaches you could use at the establishment to build your wine list. Identify advantages and disadvantages for each of your selections.

Your First Choice: _____

Advantage _____

Advantage _____

Advantage _____

Disadvantage _____

Your Second Choice: _____

Advantage _____

Advantage _____

Advantage _____

Disadvantage _____

Your Third Choice: _____

Advantage _____

Advantage _____

Advantage _____

Disadvantage _____

6

Spirits

INSIDE THIS CHAPTER

- Spirit Production
- Spirit Products
- Mixology

CHAPTER LEARNING OBJECTIVES

After completing this chapter, you should be able to:

- Explain the relationship between spirit distillation and proof.

- Identify the seven major spirit types.

- Explain the importance of standardized recipes to profitable drink production.

- Describe how standardized drink recipes are developed.

- Explain the importance of standardized drink recipes to serving alcohol responsibly.

- Identify and state the purpose of each of the major ingredients in a mixed drink.

KEY TERMS

blender drink, p. 148

call brand (spirit), p. 144

cocktail, p. 129

cordials, p. 135

distilling, p. 128

drink recipe evaluation, p. 141

free pour, p. 137

highball, p. 148

house brand (spirit), p. 144

infusion, p. 130

mixology, p. 136

neat, p. 129

on the rocks, p. 129

overpour, p. 137

shaken cocktail, p. 149

specialty drink, p. 138

standard drink (spirit), p. 129

still , p. 128

stirred cocktail, p. 149

straight up, p. 129

underpour, p. 137

well brand (spirit), p. 144

CASE STUDY

"Well, it's still confusing to me," said Lynn, one of the bartenders at the Goldstar Bar and Grill.

"What's so confusing?" asked Barry, the Grill's manager as he approached Lynn and Oscar, the two bartenders currently on duty at the Grill.

"Last week, we took a class on serving alcohol safely," explained Lynn. "We understood in the class when the instructor talked about the importance of keeping track of how many drinks we serve each guest. But today, Oscar made a guest a Funky Cold Medina—you know, the drink with a one-ounce shot of vodka, a one-ounce shot of peach-flavored bourbon, and a one-ounce shot of blue curacao, with a splash of cranberry juice."

"OK," said Barry, "I'm familiar with the drink. So what's confusing?"

"What's confusing," said Lynn, "is that it has three different spirits in it. So, should we count that as one drink, two drinks, or three? Oscar says it's only one."

1. Why is it important to monitor the alcohol consumption of guests?

2. What could happen if Lynn and Oscar use different drink-counting systems for monitoring their individual guests' alcohol consumption?

SPIRIT PRODUCTION

The Chinese are generally credited with being the first to create a spirit by distilling an alcoholic beverage (rice beer) to increase its alcohol content. It is the Arabs, however, who are responsible for the term *alcohol,* a discovery they made when using the *alembic* (still). A still is the device used to "distill" an alcoholic beverage. Distilling is the process of purifying a liquid by boiling it and condensing the vapors.

While beer is the result of the fermentation of a grain-based beverage and wine is the result of the fermentation of grape juice, spirits are the distillation of these and other fermented sugar products. For example, vodka is a spirit made from grain, rum is distilled from sugar cane, and brandy is the result of distilling grape juice. Other spirits include whiskey, gin, and tequila.

Today, spirits are legally defined as any unsweetened, distilled alcoholic beverage containing at least 20 percent alcohol. Technically *liqueurs* are not spirits, but rather they are spirits to which a sweetener has been added. In common industry usage, however, the distinction between spirits and liqueurs is widely unknown or ignored. Consequently, all alcoholic beverages that are not beer or wine are generally referred to as spirits.

Their flavors and body differentiate spirits. Flavor and body are determined by the food product used to make the beverage, the amount of alcohol in the beverage, and special product treatments during processing such as aging, flavoring, blending, and bottling. As a result, taste differences occur among different types of spirits (for example, gin versus vodka), within product categories (Irish whiskey versus Scotch whisky), and among different brands of the same product (one brand of vodka versus another).

Distillation

Spirits are the most potent alcoholic beverages, created by separating the alcohol from water after the fermentation process. Water and alcohol boil at different temperatures, allowing distillation, or the concentration of alcohol in a beverage, to occur. The boiling point of water is 212°F (100°C). Alcohol boils at 173°F (78.3°C). Thus, if a distiller can boil a liquid mixture containing alcohol at a temperature above 172°F (77.8°C) but below 212°F (100°C), the alcohol will vaporize but the water in the mixture will not (see *Exhibit 6.1*). The distiller captures the alcohol and converts it back to a liquid before the vapor escapes into the air, creating the basis for a distilled beverage. The distilled alcohol is generally blended with pure water and flavoring elements to create the finished spirit. The amount of blending with water and other ingredients determines the alcohol content, or proof, of the beverage.

Exhibit 6.1

°F   °C

220
Boiling Point of Water — 210 — 100
200
190 — 90
180
Boiling Point of Alcohol — 170 — 80
160 — 70
150
140 — 60
130
120 — 50
110
100 — 40
90 — 30
80
70 — 20
60
50 — 10
40
30 — 0
20
10 — −10
0 — −20

Proof

After the distillation process is complete, the job of the distiller is to combine the right amount of alcohol with the right amount of flavoring. In chapter 1, *proof* was defined as the percentage of alcohol content in a beverage. A unit of proof equals one-half of 1 percent of alcohol. For example, if a spirit product is 100 proof, it contains 50 percent alcohol. To calculate the amount of alcohol in a beverage, divide the proof number by two.

Unlike most beers and wines, which have very similar alcohol contents, the proof of different spirits varies tremendously. Some spirits are created and sold at 20 proof; others are produced and sold at well over 100 proof.

SPIRIT PRODUCTS

A **standard drink** made from spirits contains 1.5 fluid ounces (44 milliliters) of a 40 percent (80-proof) spirit (*Exhibit 6.2*). Restaurant and foodservice guests can choose from a wide variety of spirit product–based drinks and can order them in a variety of ways:

- **Neat:** When guests order a spirit *neat* they mean the beverage should be served by itself and at room temperature. Other terms guests may use to indicate drinks served in this manner are *straight* or *straight up* (see chapter 1).

- **Straight up:** The spirit is shaken or stirred with ice, then strained from the ice and served by itself.

- **On the rocks:** The spirit is served over ice.

- **With water:** The spirit is mixed with water.

- **With a simple mixer:** The spirit is mixed with, for example, club soda, tonic water, cola, or fruit juice.

- **As an ingredient in a mixed drink:** The spirit is combined with other drink ingredients or flavorings to create a mixed drink, called a **cocktail**.

Regardless of how they serve them, managers whose operations serve spirits typically offer their guests choices in those spirit categories most familiar to guests:

- Vodka
- Gin
- Rum
- Brandy
- Tequila
- Whiskies
- Liqueurs

Manager's Memo

Because spirits are produced at a wide variety of proof levels, it is difficult to determine how much alcohol is actually contained in one drink that has been made with a spirit.

In the United States, the standard drink contains 0.6 fluid ounces (18 milliliters) of alcohol. This is approximately the amount of alcohol in a 12.0-fluid-ounce (350-milliliter) glass of beer, a 5.0-fluid-ounce (150-milliliter) glass of wine, or a 1.5-fluid-ounce (44-milliliter) glass of 40 percent (80-proof) spirit.

By understanding the number of standard drinks contained in a single mixed drink containing spirits, managers and their staffs can effectively monitor the drink consumption of their guests and count the number of standard drinks served to guests regardless of what specific mixed drink those guests are ordering.

Exhibit 6.3

VODKA

Vodka was relatively unknown in the United States prior to the 1950s. Today it is the largest-selling spirit in the U.S. market. Unlike most other spirits, vodka is noted for the fact that it is distilled and filtered in a way that makes it odorless and tasteless. This makes it a popular product for mixing with carbonated beverages and fruit juices. It is also noted for its refreshing bite, which makes it a good accompaniment to oily and smoked food such as caviar and salmon. Vodka is famous for the warming sensation it provides the body as it is consumed, perhaps one reason for its popularity in colder climates.

Vodka was invented in Poland, probably in the tenth century, but was adopted by the Russians as their official drink. In fact, the word *vodka* is a variation of *Voda*, the Russian word for "water." In the United States, it was introduced in the late 1940s as the principal ingredient in the Moscow Mule, a mixed drink combination of vodka and ginger beer.

Contrary to popular opinion, the best vodka is made not from potatoes but rather is distilled from fermented grain mash at high proof. Vodka is bottled for sale in proofs ranging from 80 to 100. However, the most popular vodka products are those of the lower proofs. In the United States, vodka must contain a minimum alcohol content of 40 percent (80 proof).

Unlike whiskey or gin, which are lightly flavored by the distiller, vodka is produced with the objective of creating a tasteless, colorless, odorless product. To achieve this result, the vodka is filtered through charcoal, often multiple times. It requires no aging, and mixes easily with other beverages because of its neutral qualities. It is this neutral quality that is responsible for vodka's great popularity.

In eastern Europe, vodka is typically consumed neat. That is not common in the United States. Rather, it is substituted for gin in such popular drinks as the gin and tonic and martini, creating the vodka and tonic and the vodka martini. It has also become the spirit of preference for making the Bloody Mary, which contains vodka and spiced tomato juice (*Exhibit 6.3*). Vodka also mixes well with fruit juice, which makes it popular in the vodka and orange juice screwdriver and the sea breeze, an increasingly called-for cocktail consisting of vodka and cranberry and grapefruit juice.

Most recently, flavored vodkas have appeared on the market. Most of these products are the result of **infusion**, the process by which a flavoring ingredient is left in contact with vodka in a sealed container until the ingredient imparts (infuses) its flavor into the vodka. The infusion period can range from hours to months. After the spirit maker is satisfied with the vodka's flavor, the flavoring ingredient is filtered out, leaving a clear, flavor-infused spirit. Vodka is infused with a variety of flavors including berries, citrus fruit, oak, honey, pepper, and vanilla.

In the United States, popular vodkas are sold from U.S., Russian, and Swedish producers, as well as those from other countries. Many beverage managers instruct their bartenders to keep vodka in the freezer, for it is believed to improve its drinkability. It certainly makes for a good show for the consumer, and is one of the techniques that can help make vodka drinks special. And often, special translates into more profitable.

Exhibit 6.4

GIN

In the 1950s, gin outsold vodka in popularity in the United States by nearly a three-to-one margin. It is a favorite among those nostalgic for the gin martini made from gin and dry vermouth, and is an important part of every bar's basic stock (*Exhibit 6.4*).

The flavor of gin comes from juniper berries. The beverage was invented in Holland in the 1600s. Today, gin is available in two basic types: Dutch and English. Dutch gin is meant to be consumed straight and cold, and is rarely mixed. English (dry) gin is made in both England and the United States, and is used most often in mixed drinks. The most famous of the gin cocktails is the martini. The gimlet (gin and lime juice), the Gibson (gin and vermouth garnished with a pickled onion), and the orange blossom (gin, vermouth, and orange juice) are also popular.

The martini was originally a drink made with equal parts of gin and dry (French) vermouth. Over the years, the amount of vermouth was reduced until eight-to-one became the accepted standard. Today, many people order a "martini," but ask that the vermouth bottle just be "waved" over the gin. The lesser the amount of vermouth in a martini, the "drier" the martini is said to be.

Aquavit, a Scandinavian spirit, is very similar to gin. The main difference is that caraway seeds rather than juniper berries are used for its flavoring. The product called sloe gin is actually a liqueur and is discussed later in this chapter.

RUM

Rum is perhaps the oldest distilled beverage. It is a spirit with a significant history in the development of the New World. It is said that Columbus brought sugarcane cuttings to the Caribbean Islands on his second voyage, in 1493. Molasses, which is produced when sugar crystallizes, became to Caribbean countries what malted barley was to the Scots and grape juice was to the French and Italians—the essence of a unique and flavorful distilled spirit.

Rums of many flavors and colors are produced throughout the Caribbean, as well as Central and South America. They can be either light- or full-bodied. The great majority of rum sold in the United States is of the light Puerto

Rican variety. Darker rums tend to be fuller flavored than the lighter varieties. Jamaican-style rums tend to be more full-bodied and are also popular.

Customers often request spiced and fruit-flavored rums. These flavored rums can be spiced with a variety of ingredients. Popular spiced rums include those flavored with apricot, fig, vanilla, coconut, and other ingredients. Rum mixes well with fruit and fruit juices. It sells strongly year-round, but particularly well in the summer and year-round in warm climates and near the winter holidays, when it is used to make eggnog.

Exhibit 6.5

BRANDY

Brandy is a distilled spirit made from a fermented mash of fruit. The fruit used is generally grapes, but brandies can also be made from apples, cherries, apricots, and plums. If brandy is made from grape juice, the term *brandy* stands alone on the label. If it is made from other fruit, the name of the fruit appears with the term *brandy*, such as *apricot brandy*. Brandy is traditionally drunk at room temperature from a special glass called a snifter (*Exhibit 6.5*). Brandies must be bottled at 80 proof or more.

There are a variety of different types of brandy:

- **Cognac:** Considered the finest of brandies, Cognac is produced in the Cognac region of France. Cognac is the distillation of the juice of grapes only.

- **Apple brandy:** This was an American favorite in early New England days.

- **Calvados:** The French produce Calvados from apples, and it is the equivalent to apple brandy.

- **Kirsch** or **Kirschwasser:** This German brandy is made from cherries.

- **Ouzo:** This Greek brandy is colorless and has a licorice-like taste.

- **Per William:** This brandy is made from Swiss or French pears.

- **Elderberry:** This brandy is made from the elderberry.

- **Fraise:** Fraise brandy is made from strawberries.

- **Framboise:** This brandy is made from raspberries.

- **Slivovitz:** Slivovitz brandy is a plum brandy from central Europe.

Brandy is also an important kitchen ingredient as it is used to make many classic meat sauces, soups, and desserts.

TEQUILA

Tequila (tuh-KEE-luh) is a spirit made from the blue agave plant in the area surrounding the Mexican city of Tequila. The city is located northwest of Guadalajara in the western Mexican state of Jalisco. Mexican law requires that tequila can be produced only in the state of Jalisco and in very limited other areas. As a result, tequila is produced only in Mexico. Tequila is most often made to achieve a 38 to 40 percent alcohol content (76 to 80 proof), but can be made at proofs up to 110. Tequila is also aged in oak and, to earn its name, must contain at least 51 percent fermented agave juice.

Tequila was extremely popular in the United States in the 1970s and 1980s. It was consumed straight as a "shooter" (shot) with salt and lime. It is the principal spirit ingredient in the popular margarita, a fruit juice and tequila cocktail that can be served frozen or over ice. In the late 1990s, American consumers' interest in tequila waned until some of the traditional tequila distillers launched premium tequila products. These upscale products contain as much as 100 percent agave juice and can be sipped or used to make premium margaritas. Premium tequila products are now very popular. Tequila is most often bottled in one of five categories:

- *Blanco* ("white") or *plata* ("silver"): This tequila is aged less than two months in stainless-steel or oak barrels.

- *Reposado:* *Reposado* tequila is aged a minimum of two months, but less than a year, in oak.

- *Joven* ("young") or *oro* ("gold"): This tequila is a mixture of *blanco* and *reposado* tequila.

- *Añejo* ("aged" or "vintage"): *Añejo* tequila is aged a minimum of one year, but less than three years, in oak.

- Extra *Añejo* ("extra aged"): Extra *Añejo* tequila is aged a minimum of three years in oak.

WHISKEY

Whiskey is a brown, or colored, spirit (rather than a white, or clear, spirit). In the recent past, the sale of brown spirits has been declining in the United States whereas the sale of white spirits (vodka, rum, and tequila) has increased. For every professional bar and beverage manager, however, a basic understanding of whiskey is absolutely essential for success.

The four steps in producing whiskey are malting, fermenting, distilling, and aging. Aging is what gives whiskey its color. Whiskey is aged in wood. The type of wooden barrel used in the process adds flavor and aroma. After whiskey is bottled, the aging process stops.

The terms *straight* and *blended* are used differently depending on whether they are applied to Scotch whisky or American whiskey. Straight Scotch whiskies are unmixed or are mixed with whisky from the same distiller or distillation period. Blended Scotch whiskies are a mixture of similar straight whiskies from different distillers or distillation periods. When referring to American whiskey, blended whiskey is a product comprised of a minimum of

20 percent straight whiskey mixed with grain-neutral spirit. By government standards, an American whiskey can be labeled as straight if the mash used to make it contains at least 51 percent of a specific grain.

WHISKY OR *WHISKEY*? Labels read both ways. Scottish, Japanese, and Canadian distillers typically spell *whisky* without an *e* while Irish and American distillers include the *e*. Fittingly, whiskies are most commonly categorized according to their country of origin:

- **Scotch whisky:** This is the whisky of Scotland and is light-bodied and smoky-flavored. The base grain is barley, although sometimes corn is substituted. Most Scotch whisky is blended rather than straight, and is bottled at 80 to 86 proof. The base grain is dried over open peat fires that give the product its smoky taste. The grain is then combined with water (mash), fermented, distilled, and aged at least four years in uncharred oak barrels. Age is not necessarily a guarantee that a Scotch whisky is of high quality. While there are many high-quality Scotches that are at least 12 years old, there are also 12-year-old inferior products that should be distinguished from higher-quality products.

- **Canadian whisky:** This is a blended product and is light in body. It may contain corn, rye, wheat, and barley as base grains. It is aged three years or more and bottled at 80 to 90 proof.

- **Irish whiskey:** This spirit uses the same ingredients and is made in a way that is similar to Scotch whisky. The main difference is that the malted barley is not exposed to peat smoke when it is dried, so there is no smoky taste. The product also goes through a triple distillation process and uses several grains in addition to malted barley. The result is a very smooth, high-quality whiskey that must be aged for at least three years but is usually offered for sale after aging a minimum of seven years.

- **U.S. whiskey:** These whiskies include several subcategories: bourbon, rye, corn, bottled in bond, and blended.

  - Bourbon is the most popular U.S. whiskey. It is a straight whiskey distilled from a fermented mash containing a minimum of 51 percent corn. It is aged in charred oak barrels from 2 to 12 years, and reaches peak mellowness in about 6 years. Bourbon has a strong flavor and a full body. It is generally bottled at 80 to 90 proof, but some brands are bottled at 100 proof or slightly more.

  - Rye is produced in much the same way as bourbon except it is distilled from a fermented mash containing at least 51 percent rye. True rye is an unblended whiskey.

  - Corn whiskey is produced from a fermented mash containing no less than 80 percent corn grain. It is aged in uncharred oak containers for at least two years.

- Bottled in bond whiskey refers to American-made spirits that comply with the production requirements set out in the Bottled-in-Bond Act of 1897 (see the Manager's Memo).

- Blended whiskey is a combination of at least 20 percent straight whiskey combined with grain-neutral spirits. Close to one-half of the U.S. whiskies consumed are blends. They are designated by the words *American Whiskey* on their labels. If a blended whiskey contains 50 percent or more of one type of straight whiskey, it must use the name of that specific whiskey. One example is blended rye whiskey.

LIQUEURS

Liqueurs, which are also called cordials, are spirits that have had flavorings steeped in them like tea, or redistilled. That is, the leaves, peels, seeds, or other flavorings used to make the liqueur are placed in a still, covered with an alcoholic spirit, and distilled. The final product carries the flavor of the various ingredients and when finished is a high-proof spirit. This high-proof spirit is reduced in proof by the addition of syrup (sugar and water) at bottling.

When the sugar content is high, liqueur has a creamy quality and is designated "crème de" (as in *crème de cacao*). There are many popular liqueurs:

- *Anisette* has a red or clear color with an anise or licorice flavor.
- *Amaretto* is an almond-flavored liqueur made from apricot stones.
- *Coffee liqueur* is made from coffee beans.
- *Crème de bananes* is a yellow-colored, banana-flavored liqueur.
- *Crème de cacao* has a brown or clear color with a chocolate–vanilla flavor.
- *Crème de menthe* has a green or clear color with a mint flavor.
- *Crème de cassis* has a deep red color with a red currant flavor.
- *Curacao* is orange, blue, or clear color with an orange peel flavor.
- *Triple Sec* is a white curacao (orange flavored).
- *Kummel* has a clear color with a caraway seed flavor.
- *Maraschino* liqueur has a clear color with a nutty, cherry flavor.
- *Rock and rye* is whiskey and rock candy syrup.
- *Sambuca* is a licorice-flavored liqueur usually clear in color.
- *Sloe gin* has a red color with a plum flavor, made from the sloe berry.

Schnapps are sometimes confused with liqueurs. In Germany, schnapps is a spirit distilled from fermented fruit but bottled with no added sugar. Schnapps produced in the United States have sugar added to the distilled

Manager's Memo

To be "bottled in bond," products must meet specific criteria:

- Be made by only one distiller at one distillery
- Be aged for four years under government supervision
- Be bottled at 100 percent
- Be labeled in a way to identify the product's producer

While any spirit can be bottled in bond, the majority of them are American-made whiskeys. Because of the quality control involved, many customers have come to view the term *bottled in bond* as a sign of high product quality.

spirits, so these products are technically liqueurs. In the United States, schnapps has traditionally been associated with peppermint-flavored liqueurs, but modern schnapps producers make products in a wide variety of other flavors, including banana, amaretto, pear, orange, peach, strawberry, apple, raspberry, root beer, licorice, and cola.

MIXOLOGY

There are hundreds of popular spirits and literally thousands of recipes for mixed drinks or cocktails. Appendix A lists 25 of the most popular ones in the United States. Because of the large number of potential combinations, the art of mixology, or the making of mixed drinks, is one that must be well understood by managers. The key to mastering mixology is the understanding of its two key components, standardized drink recipes and professional drink production.

Standardized Drink Recipes

A bartender is similar to a chef because both, regardless of experience, must follow standardized recipes. While experienced bartenders do not have to review a written standardized recipe card before they prepare a common drink such as gin and tonic, bartenders do need to consistently prepare that drink with the same ingredients, quantities, portion sizes, and garnishes pre-established by management. The same bartender, however, may need to carefully study a written recipe before preparing a less common drink such as a horse's neck. All operations should use standardized drink recipes. Using standardized drink recipes to control alcoholic beverage preparation is important for several reasons:

- Drinks prepared incorrectly will not meet quality standards and will disappoint customers.
- Product costs must be controlled.
- The quantity of alcohol served to each customer must be known if the establishment is to serve alcoholic beverages responsibly.

Professional managers must standardize drink production, and this requires careful monitoring of drink recipes. The consistency offered by a standardized drink recipe benefits the customers and the establishment. Each time the drink is ordered it will look and taste the same. The size of the serving will be the same, and the same ingredients in the same amounts will be used. The customers will receive consistent value because they will pay the same amount every time they order an item, and the product will be of the same quality and quantity each time it is served.

A standardized drink recipe also helps ensure consistency for the establishment. A beverage menu item's selling price is often based, at least

THINK ABOUT IT . . .

Some bartenders resist standardized drink recipes because they are not accustomed to using them. Others may feel that standardized recipes make the bartenders replaceable. What would you say to bartenders who express these concerns?

in part, on ingredient costs. A standardized drink recipe ensures that the same ingredients and amounts of each ingredient are used every time the product is prepared. Then beverage costs and selling prices can be determined.

Finally, standardized drink recipes allow managers and bartenders to monitor the amount of alcohol consumption by guests. When using standardized drink recipes, extra attention must be given to portion size, especially to the amount of alcohol in each drink. For example, a standardized recipe for a gin and tonic may state two parts tonic water to one part gin (for example, 1.5 fluid ounces of gin and 3.0 fluid ounces of tonic water). Managers calculate the beverage cost using this ratio. When a drink is poured to recipe, the customer will find the drink acceptable, the alcohol consumption rate is known, and beverage costs will be in line with expectations as long as the drink actually contains these amounts of ingredients.

Exhibit 6.6 shows the number of drinks that are contained in a one-liter bottle of spirits when the amount of alcohol used in a drink varies. Managers who allow bartenders to free pour alcohol without using a portioning tool must ensure that bartenders neither underpour (use less alcohol than required by the recipe) nor overpour (use more alcohol than allowed by the recipe). Use of a measuring tool is one way to ensure consistency (*Exhibit 6.7*).

When managers make the decision to standardize drink recipes, communication is important. Bartenders and servers should be told exactly why the recipes are important and why the procedures to follow them are needed. Employees may also be asked to assist in recipe development activities. When employees are part of the process, there will likely be less resistance to recipe use because they are invested in the process.

STANDARDIZED DRINK RECIPE DEVELOPMENT PROCESS

The actual development of standardized drink recipes in an operation is a six-step process:

1. Choose the recipes.

2. Standardize the drink sizes.

3. Calculate the recipe costs.

4. Assess food safety issues, if applicable.

5. Finalize preparation and presentation.

6. Record and communicate final recipes.

Exhibit 6.6

NUMBER OF STANDARD DRINKS IN A 1-LITER (33.8-FLUID-OZ) BOTTLE AT VARIOUS DRINK SIZES

Drink Size	Number of Drinks
1.0 oz	33.8
1.25 oz	27.0
1.5 oz*	22.5
1.75 oz	19.3
2.0 oz	16.9

*Standard drink size.

Exhibit 6.7

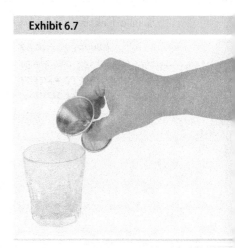

OPEN FOR BUSINESS
MANAGER'S MATH

Many spirits are sold in 750-milliliter bottles that contain 25.4 fluid ounces. Calculate the number of drinks that can be obtained from one 750-milliliter bottle with the following standard drink sizes.

Drink Size	Number of Drinks
1.0 oz	
1.25 oz	
1.5 oz*	
1.75 oz	
2.0 oz	

*Standard drink size.

(Answers: 1.0 oz = 25.4 drinks; 1.25 oz = 20.3 drinks; 1.5 oz = 16.9 drinks; 1.75 oz = 14.5 drinks; 2.0 oz = 12.7 drinks)

STEP 1: CHOOSE THE RECIPES. In many cases, guests determine the drinks that should be served in an operation. For example, the guest who orders Scotch and water has clearly stated the drink he or she prefers. The operation should, of course, be prepared to make and deliver that drink. It can do that in a consistent and profitable manner only if the production of a Scotch and water is standardized by the use of a standardized recipe. **Specialty drinks** are those unique drinks developed by an operation to respond to consumer trends or to assist in promoting the image of the operation. Both traditional and specialty drinks should be made according to their standardized recipes.

Exhibit 6.8 shows a sample standardized drink recipe for a sea breeze, a popular vodka-based cocktail.

Exhibit 6.8		
STANDARDIZED DRINK RECIPE		
Spirit Category: Vodka		
Name	**Quantity and Ingredients**	**Preparation**
Sea breeze	1 ¾ oz vodka 3 oz cranberry juice 1 oz grapefruit juice ½ grapefruit slice	1. Pour the vodka and cranberry juice into a 7-oz highball glass half filled with ice cubes. 2. Stir well. 3. Top off with the grapefruit juice. 4. Garnish with the grapefruit slice.

Note: *This recipe equals 1.2 standard drinks based on a 1.5-oz standard drink size made with an 80-proof spirit.*

Note that the recipe identifies key components of the drink:

- Spirit type used
- Drink name
- Specific ingredients required
- Quantity of required ingredients
- Preparation method
- Glassware to be used
- Garnish to be used
- Drink strength measured in standard drinks

A standardized drink recipe should be developed for each drink that will commonly be served in the operation.

STEP 2: STANDARDIZE THE DRINK SIZES. Note that the recipe in *Exhibit 6.8* calls for 1 ¾ ounces of vodka. It is important to understand that there is no legal requirement that a sea breeze be made with 1 ¾ ounces of vodka. It could, for example, be made with 1 or 2 ounces. Management will establish the amount of alcohol contained in *this* operation's sea breeze after its evaluation of a variety of factors:

- Recipe taste
- Proposed selling price
- Drink presentation
- Available glassware
- Operational concept and image
- Target customer

Recall that a standard spirit drink contains 1.5 fluid ounces of an 80-proof spirit. Variations from this amount may be appropriate; however, when such variations are made, they should be noted on the standardized drink recipe as shown in *Exhibit 6.8*. Managers can do this easily by using the following standard drink formula.

$$\frac{\text{Actual Alcohol}}{\text{Amount per Recipe}} \div \frac{\text{Alcohol Amount}}{\text{in Standard Drink}} = \frac{\text{Number of}}{\text{Standard Drinks}}$$

For example, if a standardized drink recipe calls for 2.0 fluid ounces of an 80-proof spirit, the calculation would be:

$$\text{2.0 oz} \div \text{1.5 oz} = \text{1.3 standard drinks}$$

It is important to understand that the alcohol content in a drink does not change when a nonalcoholic beverage (mixer) is added to the drink. For example, 1.5 fluid ounces of 80-proof vodka contains the same amount of alcohol (40 percent) if it is served neat or mixed with several ounces of mixer. For servers or bartenders to assist in monitoring guests' potential BAC (blood alcohol content) levels (see chapter 2), servers and bartenders must know the number of standard drinks in each beverage served.

When standardizing drink size, remember that adjustments in alcohol level may require other recipe modifications. For instance, the amount of mixer or the glassware used may be modified. The best mixed drinks are balanced and flavorful. It is that combination managers seek to achieve when they determine the amount of alcohol to include in standardized drink recipes.

Manager's Memo

Many beverage managers simply choose the spirit products that they will offer and allow guests to choose how they want their drinks served, while other managers create a number of specialty drinks that consist of unique combinations of spirits and mixers. These house specialties are often created to reflect trends or even fads in drink popularity. Specialty drinks can be very popular with guests and allow for the creation of printed beverage menus designed to help promote and sell the specialty drinks.

When choosing and creating such special drink recipes managers follow the same steps as those listed for standardizing drink recipes, but must add an additional step for taste testing the new recipes. These tests should address both the taste and the appearance of the specialty drink because in many cases a specialty drink's presentation will be of critical importance to how the drink is marketed and, as a result, the number of times it will be ordered by guests.

STEP 3: CALCULATE THE RECIPE COSTS. In many cases, the selling price of mixed drinks does not vary based on the cost of the individual drink. For example, the selling price of a Scotch and water is often the same as the selling price of a Scotch and soda, despite the fact that an ounce of soda may cost the operation more than an ounce of water. Product pricing in a beverage operation is often driven by marketing concerns as well as by product cost concerns (see chapter 10). However, it is still essential that managers calculate the costs of their standardized recipes. Accurate drink recipe costing is important for a variety of reasons:

- Managers can use recipe costs to determine the quantity and quality of spirits that will optimize customer satisfaction and value perception.

- Managers can use recipe costs to compare actual financial results with forecasted results to help determine the source and cause of any significant variations.

Exhibit 6.9 shows an example of a format managers can use to cost drink recipes. Note that the exhibit contains the name of the drink and seven key pieces of information:

1. **Ingredient:** This is the item ingredient used to make the drink.

2. **Amount:** This is the quantity for each item called for in the drink recipe, listed in either volume as for spirit or mixer, or number as for olives, lime slices, or cherries.

Exhibit 6.9

DRINK RECIPE COSTING WORKSHEET
Drink Category: Vodka
Drink Recipe: Sea Breeze

(1) Ingredient	(2) Amount	(3) Purchase Unit	(4) Cost per Purchase Unit	(5) Cost per Fluid Ounce or Piece	(6) Ingredient Cost
Vodka	1 ¾ oz	1 L (33.8 oz)	$11.00	$0.33	$0.58
Cranberry juice	3 oz	1 gal*	4.95	0.04	0.12
Grapefruit juice	1 oz	1 gal	2.75	0.02	0.02
Grapefruit	1 slice	1 piece (20 per)	1.09	0.05	0.05
				(7) Total Cost	$0.77

*Gal = gallon.

3. **Purchase unit:** In most cases the purchase unit will be the amount contained in the bottle purchased or, in the cases of mixers, the price paid per pint, quart, or gallon. Garnishes are typically priced by the piece.

4. **Cost per purchase unit:** This is the price paid by the operation to purchase the needed ingredient in its purchase unit.

5. **Cost per fluid ounce or piece:** This is the total purchase amount divided by the number of fluid ounces or pieces in a purchase unit.

6. **Ingredient cost:** This total per ingredient cost is calculated by multiplying the amount in column 2 times the cost in column 5.

7. **Total cost:** This is the total cost of the recipe and is calculated by summing all of the amounts in column 6.

In this example, the product cost required to make a sea breeze cocktail is $0.77. This cost assumes that the standardized recipe is carefully followed each time the drink is made. It also assumes that the recipe has been costed with current ingredient costs. Variations from either assumption can cause a fluctuation in actual costs.

STEP 4: ASSESS FOOD SAFETY ISSUES, IF APPLICABLE. Some drink recipes require little in the way of food safety considerations. For example, a Scotch and water requires merely a clean work area, proper staff hygiene, and clean glassware to deliver a quality product. Other drink items, however, are more complex and do require consideration of food safety issues.

For example, consider the operation that sells milk-based blender drinks. In their preparation, dairy products such as milk and cream are mixed with spirits, ice, and other flavorings to make individual drinks. In this case, the proper storage of the dairy products and the proper cleaning of the blender to eliminate or reduce bacteria to safe levels between uses are both food safety concerns. As a result, standardized recipes should address issues of this type. This can be done by including caution or warning statements in the recipe and by noting important recipe-specific information useful for training employees.

STEP 5: FINALIZE PREPARATION AND PRESENTATION. After recipes have been pre-costed and found to be acceptable, effective managers complete a final check for quality and for presentation. Drink recipe evaluation is a formal process in which a taste test panel may be used to assess whether a standardized drink recipe yields an acceptable product.

Who should serve on the taste test panel? Of-age bartenders and servers, managers, and owners are all potential panel members. In some cases, even the operation's "regular" guests would make good choices for taste test panels.

Some managers ask representatives from the establishment's target market to serve on a taste test panel, perhaps in exchange for complementary meals or a free drink at another time.

The use of customers on a taste test panel has the additional benefits of providing an opportunity to show the operation's concern for them and enabling the customers to learn more about how the establishment operates. It also validates customer opinions. Panels composed of any nonestablishment employees should be scheduled at times when employees are not participating, because doing so allows employees to be more candid in their own observation and comments.

Some managers formalize the specialty drink recipe evaluation process by asking taste panel participants to complete a survey similar to the one presented in *Exhibit 6.10*. Management carefully reviews the

---

Exhibit 6.10

STANDARDIZED DRINK RECIPE EVALUATION FORM

Standardized recipe name: _____   Recipe category: _____

Evaluation date(s): _____   Recipe no.: _____

Instructions: Check the box that best represents your analysis of each factor.

Evaluation Factor	Your Analysis						Comments
	Poor				Excellent		
Serving size	❏	❏	❏	❏	❏	❏	
Color	❏	❏	❏	❏	❏	❏	
Aroma	❏	❏	❏	❏	❏	❏	
Taste and strength	❏	❏	❏	❏	❏	❏	
Glassware type and size	❏	❏	❏	❏	❏	❏	
General appearance and garnish	❏	❏	❏	❏	❏	❏	
Ice or temperature	❏	❏	❏	❏	❏	❏	
Other: _____	❏	❏	❏	❏	❏	❏	
Other: _____	❏	❏	❏	❏	❏	❏	
Should we use this drink recipe as is?	❏ Yes			❏ No			

Comments: _____

_____

Name of evaluator: _____

completed surveys for indications that the recipe should be changed prior to including the recipe on the specialty drink menu. When several specialty drink options are being evaluated and not all can be included on the menu, the ranking column shown in *Exhibit 6.10* can be used to help decide which drinks are most liked by the rater. Those drinks with the highest scores should be added to the menu, rather than those drinks with lower scores.

STEP 6: RECORD AND COMMUNICATE FINAL RECIPES. The last step in the recipe standardization process is to record and communicate results to all concerned. It does little good to develop standardized drink recipes and not train staff in their use. After training, the recipes should be made readily available to those who will use them. This availability could take the form of a printed "book" of recipes stored at the bar, or behind-the-bar access to computerized recipe files. In some cases, managers help their bartenders by including pictures of the finished drinks as well as their recipes in the recipe file. In all cases, however, the recipes should be readily available for use, and their use should be mandated!

A final word about the development and use of standardized drink recipes relates to responsible alcohol service. Consider two different restaurant or foodservice operations that serve mixed drinks. In each operation, a guest left the facility and was later involved in an auto accident that caused serious harm to a third party.

In one of the operations, no standardized drink recipes were in place. In fact, it was common knowledge that each bartender in that operation served drinks containing the amount of alcohol he or she felt "the customer wanted." In some cases, servers in this operation tried to monitor the number of drinks consumed by those they served, but the waitstaff could not be sure about the quantity of alcohol in each drink they served. As a result, they did not always count as carefully as they could have. Management did not feel the standardization of drink production was an essential issue to be addressed on a regular basis.

In the other operation, however, standardized drink recipes were carefully followed every time a drink was made and served. Drink portions were determined in advance, standardized recipes were consistently used and, if drinks contained more than one standard-sized portion, it was clearly noted on the guest's open tab or check. Management consistently spot-checked accuracy of drink production. Servers were trained to notify management if any guest appeared to be intoxicated or was moving too quickly toward intoxication.

Manager's Memo

Managers must train their employees to know how to effectively handle all of the potential concerns related to the responsible service of alcoholic beverages. External programs such as the National Restaurant Association's ServSafe Alcohol program are excellent examples of a system that can be presented with modification as needed to fit the needs of the specific operation.

Restaurant and foodservice operations that are part of a larger, multiunit group may offer specialized training programs developed by their organization for properties within the chain.

For either type of program, information including attendance, training date, and certificates of completion issued should be filed in each employee's personnel records.

Exhibit 6.11

Recall from chapter 2 that in some cases, the establishment serving the alcohol can be held liable for accidents related to intoxicated guests. In which of these operations would a manager rather defend himself or herself against a legal charge of irresponsibly serving alcohol?

Professional Drink Production

After management develops and communicates the standardized recipes, the operation's beverage staff must prepare and serve drinks professionally (*Exhibit 6.11*). Doing so requires a complete understanding of the essential ingredients contained in a mixed drink and the methods used to produce them profitably and to the specified quality level. A quality mixed drink contains three to four key ingredients:

- Alcohol
- Mixer
- Garnish
- Ice (optional)

ALCOHOL

With very few exceptions such as a wine cooler or Champagne cocktail, bartenders use a spirit to provide the alcohol in a guest's mixed drink order. As a result, one of a manager's first spirits-related purchasing decisions involves choosing which liquors will be the establishment's well brands and which will be its call brands.

A **well brand** is the brand of liquor that is served by the operation when the guest does *not* indicate a preference for a specific brand. A well brand is also sometimes called the **house brand**. For example, a guest ordering a Scotch and soda would be served the establishment's well brand of Scotch and soda water. A **call brand** is a specific brand of liquor requested by a guest. Typically, these brands are more expensive and of higher quality than well brands. For example, a guest ordering a Walker Black and soda would be served only Johnny Walker Black Label Scotch and soda because he or she "called" for that specific spirit product.

Well brands are typically selected because they cost the operation less than better-known, more expensive, or more popular call brands. As stated, bartenders use well brands when guests do not specify the brand of liquor to be used in a beverage. These guests generally do not care what brands are used as long as the quality of the beverage is acceptable. If, however, guests view the well brands as too "cheap" or inferior, the operation's reputation may suffer. In practice, a middle-ground product, neither the most nor least expensive, is generally most desirable for well liquor. Liquor distributors can be very helpful in assisting managers in the selection of well brands that are in keeping with the quality image desired by a specific operation.

Managers should select their well and call brands based on what they know about market conditions and their guests' preferences. There are several important factors in selecting spirits:

- Quality relative to price
- Value relative to price
- Supplier prices
- Supplier payment terms
- Supplier services
- Product reputation
- Product availability
- Philosophy and needs of the operation
- Liquor proof
- Brands used by competitors
- Suggestions from knowledgeable sources

After deciding what to buy, managers must choose how to buy. In the United States, spirits of all types are sold to establishments in the bottle sizes listed in *Exhibit 6.12* if the specific bottle size is approved for sale within an individual state.

The common (but inaccurate) names for these bottles predate the U.S. beverage industry's 1980s conversion to a complete metric measurement.

Exhibit 6.12

SPIRIT BOTTLE SIZES AND CAPACITIES

Common Bottle Name	Metric Capacity	Fluid-Ounce Capacity
Miniature	50 ml	1.7 oz
Half-pint	200 ml	6.8 oz
Pint	500 ml	16.9 oz
Fifth	750 ml	25.4 oz
Quart	1.0 L*	33.8 oz
Half-gallon	1.75 L	59.2 oz

*1 liter (L) equals 1,000 milliliters (ml).

KEEPING IT SAFE

Behind-bar work areas can be especially dangerous for bartenders because of water, ice, and other liquids that can be spilled on the floor, especially during times of high production. While safety is always a priority concern, it is challenging to stop beverage production when, for example, spills occur behind the bar during peak business times. Slip-resistant flooring behind the bar makes good sense, as does a requirement that bartenders wear slip-resistant shoes. The best flooring behind bars can have another advantage: reduced glass breakage, with the safety hazards that result from the breakage.

MIXERS

Mixers are the second ingredient in most cocktails. Quality mixers should be used for all drinks produced. Mixers such as carbonated beverages, flavorings, fruit and vegetable juices, and dairy products directly affect the flavor of the final drink. Larger bars usually have soda "guns" (also called "arms" or "snakes") to supply carbonated mixers. In smaller establishments, bartenders usually keep a supply of bottled carbonated beverages on the front bar. A variety of quality mixers are commonly available at all bars:

- Carbonated mixers, including colas, tonic water, ginger ale, soda water, and lemon-lime soda
- Juice mixers including orange, cranberry, lime, and pineapple juice
- Sweet and sour or fruit blend mixers such as Bloody Mary, daiquiri, and sour mix
- Dairy mixers including milk, cream, half and half, and ice cream
- Syrups, such as simple syrup, and grenadine, a blood-red, strong syrup made from pomegranates and used to color and sweeten a variety of drinks
- Bitters, which are blends of herbs, spices, and other flavoring ingredients in a liquor base
- Other mixers such as coffee

GARNISHES

Many mixed drinks are served with traditional garnishes. For instance, a gin and tonic is served with a slice of lime, a Bloody Mary with a stalk of celery, and a martini with olives. In other cases, the operation will identify on the drink's standardized recipe the proper garnish to use with each drink it prepares. There are a variety of standard garnishes used in most bars:

- **Lemons:** Twists are the most popular, and customers who prefer a stronger lemon taste will usually request lemon slices or wedges.
- **Oranges:** Slices are most often used as garnishes.
- **Limes:** Wedges are used as garnishes, and also to flavor the rims of glasses used for certain drinks.
- **Cherries:** Maraschino cherries are a traditional garnish. Usually, customers prefer them with stems attached so the cherries can easily be removed from the drink.
- **Olives:** These are used for martinis, and are best when they are pitted, and *not* stuffed with pimento; however, some operations stuff them with unique flavoring ingredients such as bleu cheese, jalapeno pepper, or spiced pimento.
- **Cocktail onions:** These are used for Gibsons and some other drinks and are best if they are small in size.

- **Celery and other plants:** Celery is the traditional garnish for Bloody Marys. Pickles and cucumbers are other vegetables commonly used to enhance a drink's appearance or taste.

- **Coarse salt:** This is used on the rims of glasses for some drinks such as margaritas.

- **Coarse sugar:** This is used on the rims of glasses for some drinks such as the pink lady.

- **Nutmeg:** This spice is used for brandy alexanders, and also for eggnog drinks that are especially popular during the traditional holiday seasons.

ICE

Liquor, mixers, and garnishes are the three essential ingredients in most cocktails and simple mixed drinks. Ice, however, is an incredibly important but often overlooked ingredient in nearly all mixed drinks. Ice is the one ingredient universal to almost every cocktail. Ice chills a drink. As the ice melts or is shaken or stirred, the water that formed the ice becomes part of the drink itself. Basic science indicates that ice is simply water in a solid form. As a result, the cleaner the water, the cleaner the ice. And the cleaner the ice, the better the drinks it chills.

Managers should ensure their operations produce ice with quality water that would be good for drinking—for example, distilled, purified, natural spring, or bottled. All ice should be made from good-quality water, but there are several forms of ice important to drink making.

ICE CUBES Ice cubes may be shaped in a variety of ways and may be large or small. Large ice cubes leave space between them when they are scooped into a glass. This permits a larger amount of mixers to be added that can dilute the drink more than intended. Smaller cubes or shaved ice pack a glass and a smaller volume of mixer can be added. This may give the impression of a "stronger" drink. Proper-sized ice cubes are good for almost all mixing: for shaking, stirring, making drinks on the rocks, or for mixing with juices and sodas. The larger, thicker surface area makes a cube melt slowly and causes less dilution.

CRUSHED ICE Smaller than cubes, crushed ice melts faster and adds more water to drinks. Usually this is used when making frozen drinks such as margaritas or daiquiris because cubes can become clogged in blender blades and result in inconsistent sizes and undesirable "lumps" in the drink. Two-thirds to one cup of cracked ice is typically the recommended amount used for single-serving frozen margaritas or daiquiris.

BLOCK ICE Ice blocks are very large pieces of ice. Block ice is primarily used for chilling punch bowls and can take any shape desired. Ice rings are popular and there are many novelty shaped molds available. In some cases, fruit or other garnishes can be frozen within the ice block to add interest to the beverage item being served.

OPEN FOR BUSINESS

KEEPING IT SAFE

Bartenders should be trained to always use a plastic or metal ice scoop when filling drink glasses. They should never use the glass itself or any other device made of glass for this purpose. When a glass is broken in ice, the entire ice bin must be carefully cleaned to remove all glass fragments including small slivers. This cannot be done during a busy shift, so bartenders and customers will be inconvenienced while another source for ice and a means to store it is quickly implemented.

Even experienced bartenders can be stumped when guests order a drink with which the bartender is not familiar. Guests themselves may not be able to identify the ingredients in the drink they want to order, but rather may say things like, "It was red," or "I think it had a lemon liqueur in it," or "It tasted like a peach." In such situations, bartenders may need a drink reference source, or drink recipe file, to help them.

Traditional recipe files are in printed or book form, but today there are also Web-based recipe sources for bartenders. These sources are helpful, but rely on an Internet connection that may not be readily available to bartenders or may not be fast enough to service customers promptly. In addition, some smartphone app developers are creating automated drink recipe files.

Drink Assembly

With thousands of drink variations and hundreds of potential ingredients, the actual making or assembly of mixed drinks may seem confusing to beginners. However, there are only a few categories of mixed drinks, and once these are known, mixology becomes much easier.

The basic drink categories include highballs, stirred drinks, shaken cocktails, and blender drinks. All these mixed beverages have certain similarities:

- They contain a major alcoholic ingredient, most often a spirit.
- They have one or more complementary ingredients, which can be alcoholic or nonalcoholic.
- They have additional ingredients that add color and flavor.
- They may contain a fruit or vegetable garnish.

In assembling any mixed drink, bartenders must know a variety of things included in the drink's standardized recipe:

- The amount of major ingredient required
- The proportion of other ingredients added to the major ingredient
- The type and size glass to use (see chapter 7)
- The use and placement of the garnish

There are four basic ways mixed drinks can be assembled:

- *Build-mixing*, in which a beverage is made by layering (adding one at a time) the individual drink ingredients to the glass in which the drink will be served.

- *Stir-mixing*, in which the ingredients are stirred with ice, and then poured through a strainer into a chilled serving glass.

- *Shake-mixing*, in which ingredients are placed in a container and are shaken either by hand or in a mechanical mixer. Shaking is best for drinks that contain ingredients that are heavy and do not blend easily.

- *Blend-mixing*, involving the use of an electric blender to make a **blender drink**. Blending is most often used for drinks that have ice or solid food as part of the recipe. For some drinks blending can also be used in place of shaking.

HIGHBALLS

More than one-half the drinks sold in the average bar are **highballs**. A highball is the broad name given to the family of mixed drinks that are composed of a spirit and a larger proportion of a nonalcoholic mixer. These are served in special "highball" glasses that typically hold 6 to 10 fluid ounces. Popular examples include gin and tonic, Scotch and soda, rum and cola, and whiskey and cola. Bartenders follow basics steps in the assembly of these drinks:

1. Fill a highball glass two-thirds full with ice.

2. Pour the appropriate amount of liquor, typically 1.5 to 2.0 ounces.

3. Pour in the mixer to within ½ to 1 inch of the top of the glass.

4. Stir if noncarbonated. Carbonated drinks self-mix.

5. Garnish if called for. Add a stir stick or straw.

STIRRED COCKTAILS

Manhattans, martinis, and gimlets are in the stirred cocktail group. There are two types of stirred cocktails: *straight up* is made in a shaker with ice and is transferred to a glass without the ice; *on the rocks* is mixed in the service glass with ice, or stirred in a shaker and then transferred to an ice-filled glass.

Bartenders follow basics steps in the assembly of these drinks:

1. Use a shaker glass filled one-third full with ice.

2. Add the supplemental ingredients by starting with ingredients used in the smallest amounts.

3. Add the proper amount of primary liquor ingredient.

4. Stir well in one direction about 8 to 12 times, letting the ice in the shaker cool the drink.

5. Use a strainer and pour the mixture into a chilled cocktail glass. Garnish as per the standardized recipe.

SHAKEN COCKTAILS

Shaken cocktails are the showiest of mixed drinks. Shaken cocktails are similar to stirred cocktails, but use a shaking motion to combine the ingredients. Drink components are poured over ice into a cocktail shaker, the shaker is covered and vigorously shaken, and the resulting mixture is strained into a glass of an appropriate size and shape (*Exhibit 6.13*). When preparing cocktails that contain syrups, fruit juices, or dairy, shaking is generally preferred over stirring. The more aggressive mixing action better combines these ingredients. Shaken cocktails include whiskey sours, daiquiris, and pink ladies.

Exhibit 6.13

Bartenders follow basics steps in the assembly of these drinks:

1. Use a shaker filled one-third to one-half full with ice.

2. Add the measured ingredients to the shaker.

3. Put the metal cap on the shaker and shake vigorously at least 10 times.

4. Remove the cap and strain the drink into a chilled glass.

5. Add the garnish.

In some cases, bartenders will use a blender to provide a very high level of mixing not attainable merely by shaking. If a blender is used to create a blender drink, care must be taken to blend ingredients for the right amount of time, since over- or underblending can reduce the quality of the drink. If a blender is used, the blender speed is usually on the "high" setting. The blender cup should be washed, rinsed, and sanitized immediately after the drink is served, and it should be stored in an inverted position.

STRAIGHT DRINKS

For some clientele, the enjoyment of drinking certain alcoholic beverages comes from drinking them straight or straight up. This means that the beverage is poured into a small glass or "shot" glass, and sipped or consumed all at one time. Many beverage managers have found success in offering flavored spirits as shooters in a shot glass, or as tooters as they are called when served in a test-tube-like drinking glass. Once reserved for college students and those bent on becoming intoxicated, shooters are now an accepted way of consuming some popular tequilas and many of the flavored liquors and liqueurs springing up on the market.

SUMMARY

1. **Explain the relationship between spirit distillation and proof.**

   Distillation is the process by which the alcohol content of a beverage is increased. Because the boiling point of water is 212°F (100°C) and alcohol boils at 173°F (78.3°C), a distiller can boil a liquid mixture containing alcohol at a temperature above 172°F (77.8°) but below 212° (100°C). The alcohol will vaporize, can be captured, and added back in greater concentration, thus raising the level of alcohol in the beverage. A unit of proof equals one-half of 1 percent of alcohol. Thus, if a spirit product is 80 proof, it contains 40 percent alcohol. The distillation process allows a spirit maker to precisely control the amount of alcohol in the product being made. The distillation process makes control of proof possible.

2. **Identify the seven major spirit types.**

   The seven major spirit types are vodka, gin, rum, tequila, whiskey, brandy, and liqueurs. Vodka is a neutral white spirit made from grain or potatoes. Gin is a white spirit flavored with juniper berries. Rum is the white or brown spirit that results from the distillation of sugarcane, whereas tequila is a Mexican spirit made from the blue agave plant. Whiskey, or whisky, is a family of brown spirits distilled from grain beverages and aged in wood. Brandy is the distillation of a fruit-based spirit, but most commonly grape juice. Liqueurs consist of a large number of flavored spirits that have been sweetened with sugar.

3. **Explain the importance of standardized recipes to profitable drink production.**

Standardized drink recipes provide consistency for customers because each drink served will look and taste the same and will consistently provide the same value to customers. Standardized recipes also allow managers to know their product costs in advance. A format for standardized drink recipes should be developed to indicate all information necessary to prepare a drink including ingredients, quantity of ingredients, preparation methods, garnish if any, and glassware to be used.

4. **Describe how standardized drink recipes are developed.**

To create standardized drink recipes for use in a restaurant or foodservice operation, managers first choose the recipes they will use and then standardize the amount of alcohol to be included in the drink. Next, managers calculate the cost of the drink to help establish an appropriate selling price. They also review the recipe for any potential food safety or sanitation-related issues. Finally, they standardize the drink's method of production and presentation and record it for their bartender's future use. If specialty drinks are to be added to the menu, these may include a taste and appearance test, with those drinks scoring highest on the test being placed on the menu.

5. **Explain the importance of standardized drink recipes to serving alcohol responsibly.**

It is always illegal to serve an intoxicated guest. Beverage servers must carefully monitor the number of drinks served to guests since the number of drinks consumed is one important factor that has a direct impact on a guest's blood alcohol level (BAC). The use of standardized drink recipes permits servers to know exactly how many standard (1.5-fluid-ounce portions of an 80-proof spirit) drinks a guest has consumed in a given time period. This information is essential to monitoring a guest's potential BAC level and the responsible service of alcohol.

6. **Identify and state the purpose of each of the major ingredients in a mixed drink.**

The key ingredients in most mixed drinks are spirits, mixers, garnish, and ice. The spirit used gives the drink its flavor. Spirits may be well brands or call brands. Well brands should be consistent with the image the operation seeks to portray to guests. Call brands should be served exactly as requested. Good-quality mixers are an essential part of many drinks. They should be made from fresh ingredients if prepared by the operation, or purchased from suppliers with a reputation for high quality. Garnishes "top off" the drink and add to guests' enjoyment. Like mixers, garnishes should be fresh, be of high quality, and be appropriate for the drink they will enhance. The quality of the water used to make the ice will directly impact the flavor of the drink. As a result, only quality ice should be served.

APPLICATION EXERCISE

Recipe costing is an important part of every manager's job. Apply what you know to find the per-drink cost for each of the two recipes listed. Round your answer to the nearest penny.

Recipe #1
DRINK CATEGORY: VODKA
DRINK RECIPE: GERRY'S JUST PEACHY (HOUSE SPECIALTY DRINK)

Ingredient	Amount	Purchase Unit	Cost per Purchase Unit	Cost per Fluid Ounce or Piece	Ingredient Cost
Peach vodka	2 oz	750 ml	$9.75	$	$
Raspberry liqueur	1 oz	1 L	8.95	$	$
Cranberry juice	3 oz	1 gal	2.75	$	$
Tahiti lime	½ lime	1 dozen	6.00	$	$
			Total Cost	$	$

Recipe #2
DRINK CATEGORY: RUM
DRINK RECIPE: RUM SPRINTER

Ingredient	Amount	Purchase Unit	Cost per Purchase Unit	Cost per Fluid Ounce or Piece	Ingredient Cost
Spiced rum	¾ oz	1 L	$14.20	$	$
Blackberry liqueur	¼ oz	750 ml	7.95	$	$
Crème de bananes	½ oz	750 ml	8.75	$	$
Orange juice	4 oz	1 gal	3.99	$	$
			Total Cost	$	$

REVIEW YOUR LEARNING

Select the best answer for each question.

1. What is the process that allows a spirit maker to precisely control the amount of alcohol in the product being made?

   A. Steeping

   B. Maceration

   C. Fermentation

   D. Distillation

2. What is the alcohol content of a 90-proof spirit?

   A. 35%

   B. 45%

   C. 55%

   D. 65%

3. How many fluid ounces of 80-proof spirit are contained in one standard mixed drink?

   A. 0.5 oz

   B. 1.0 oz

   C. 1.5 oz

   D. 2.0 oz

4. What is the name for a spirit drink ordered shaken or stirred with ice, then strained from the ice and served by itself?

   A. Neat

   B. Blended

   C. Straight up

   D. On the rocks

5. What makes one martini drink drier than another?

   A. The shape of the ice cubes

   B. The amount of tonic in the drink

   C. The use of Dutch versus English gin

   D. The amount of vermouth in each drink

6. What type of spirit is Cognac?

   A. Brandy

   B. Whiskey

   C. Scotch

   D. Liqueur

7. Which type of whisky has a smoky taste as result of its exposure to smoke from peat fires?

   A. Canadian

   B. Bourbon

   C. Scotch

   D. Rye

8. A bar's standardized drink recipe calls for a total of 3 fluid ounces of 80-proof spirit to make a Long Island iced tea. How many standard drinks are contained in this recipe?

   A. 1.5

   B. 2.0

   C. 2.5

   D. 3.0

9. What is the likely result if a bartender consistently underpours when preparing mixed drinks?

   A. Dissatisfied guests

   B. Product shortages

   C. Increased operating costs

   D. Increased guest satisfaction

10. In addition to ice, what three ingredients form the basis for most mixed drinks?

    A. Alcohol, juice, and garnish

    B. Alcohol, cola, and fruit

    C. Alcohol, mixer, and garnish

    D. Alcohol, mixer, and fruit

7

Bar Management

CHAPTER LEARNING OBJECTIVES

After completing this chapter, you should be able to:

- Summarize the importance of proper facility design, layout, décor, and atmosphere to successful beverage operations.

- Explain the three major types of drink production systems used in beverage operations.

- Describe the kind of equipment and tools needed for beverage operations.

- Identify the 10 major types of bar glassware and their usage.

- Discuss how to select, orient, and train bar staff.

- Explain the two purposes of effective bar staff scheduling.

KEY TERMS

assisted drink production system, p. 170

automated drink production system, p. 170

beverage-control system, p. 158

call-in (employee), p. 184

centralized storage area, p. 158

décor, p. 156

drink tab, p. 162

jigger, p. 170

labor cost percentage, p. 181

manual drink production system, p. 170

no-show (employee), p. 184

par stock, p. 158

point of sale (POS) system, p. 160

public areas, p. 157

public bar, p. 161

service bar, p. 160

wine steward, p. 175

CASE STUDY

"Excuse me, Miss!" a well-dressed man barked at Paula as she hurried back toward the bar at the Gaslight Marquise Club. It was a Friday night and the club was full to capacity. Paula was nearly overwhelmed trying to keep up with her assigned tables. It wasn't helping any that Trey, the new bartender, was having trouble keeping up with the drink requests submitted by the servers. Drink orders were taking forever and the servers, and customers, were getting frustrated.

Paula turned to the man seated with a group of three others. "Look, I know you're not our server," he began, "and it's clear you're very busy, but we ordered our drinks over 15 minutes ago and haven't seen our server since. Fifteen minutes for one round of beers? That's way too long!"

Paula glanced around the bar. She saw Tina, the server assigned to this man's section, waiting at the bar pickup station, where it was clear Trey was falling further and further behind. Paula had worked at the club for four years. She had seen it this busy before, but normally on nights like this, there were two more servers and another bartender on the schedule.

"Look," said the customer, clearly agitated, "if it's going to take this long to get our drinks, we'll just go somewhere else. But before we go, I want to talk to the manager!"

1. Do you think the slow service received by the customers at the Gaslight bar is the fault of the employees? Of the manager?

2. Assume you were the manager. What would you say to this customer when he complains to you?

THE BAR

The layout and design of a bar, as well as the bar's general décor and atmosphere, are extremely important to its successful operation and its profitability. **Décor** is the style of furnishings and decorative items that give an operation its character. The service staff members rely on a well-designed bar for efficient service, while the types of customers who choose to patronize an establishment also depend on the atmosphere, or image, created by the facility.

Exhibit 7.1

Layout and Design

Layout and design are critical components of beverage operations. They contribute to the efficiency of the operation and help create an environment that appeals to guests. Design determines the theme, style, layout, color scheme, furnishings, and even lighting. Whether a bar is sleek and modern, old world, or decorated according to a theme (such as nautical, Polynesian, 1920s, or an almost infinitely long list of other possibilities), the layout, along with décor, sets the bar's mood (*Exhibit 7.1*).

Designing a bar and beverage facility is complex and challenging. It takes extensive research to learn about the needs and desires of guests and what products and services they seek. If the bar is part of a larger restaurant or foodservice operation, planners must evaluate the entire facility in which the bar will be located. They do so to ensure that the bar will complement the rest of the operation both aesthetically and functionally.

Design and layout decisions are made early in the planning stages of any operation. They must be constantly monitored to assess how well they are working. Design involves more than surface décor and the mood that it sets. Design is the end result of many details, including décor and layout. Proper design enables a good workflow and the blending of the operation's needs with guest satisfaction. The key to good design is to keep all the components in balance.

ELEMENTS OF LAYOUT AND DESIGN

Well-planned layouts contain groups of guest sections and employee workstations strategically placed to enable guest enjoyment and work efficiency goals to be met at the same time. Sections are linked together by pathways designed so employees will have the space needed to do their jobs effectively. Layouts are partly determined by the amount of square footage in the facility. They also depend on the shapes of the areas, the positions of entryways and exits, and the relationship of the bar(s) to areas of other activities such as foodservice, dancing, and other entertainment offerings.

The activities planned for the facility along with the furnishings and equipment necessary to carry them out also affect the layout. Practical matters such as the location of plumbing, electrical wiring, ventilation, and other concerns must be considered. In addition, health, safety, and fire code requirements are critical and must be addressed early in the planning process.

Good layouts play up the strategic elements of the bar. For example, an island bar in the center of the guest area may be appropriate for a bar catering to young professionals where the bar is the center stage around which people mingle. In a family-style restaurant, a bar might be more appropriately positioned off to the side in a less noticeable location.

The following basic principles are important in the layout and design of the beverage operation:

A CUSTOMER-ORIENTED PERSPECTIVE IS IMPORTANT All public areas, those areas within normal view of the guests, must be designed with the guests in mind. The beverage operation's guests buy a "total experience," including food and beverages, service, atmosphere, and cleanliness. Therefore, all public areas should be designed to please the guests. Since the guest is also buying service, features that enable fast and efficient service must be considered as well. Bartenders must have properly designed workstations that enable them to quickly perform their work and that do not require them to leave the area to record sales or to travel to remote storage areas. Servers must be able to quickly order, pick up, and deliver drinks.

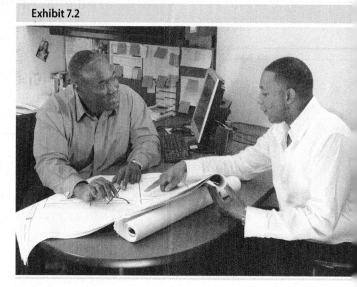

Exhibit 7.2

THE ENTIRE FACILITY SHOULD BE DESIGNED AT THE SAME TIME
Although this design principle might appear to be obvious, it is sometimes ignored. Planners must consider the beverage operation at the same time as they plan all other foodservice spaces. It is not effective to allocate foodservice space that is required and "let the beverage operation have the remainder." Rather, both food and beverage spaces must be planned together (*Exhibit 7.2*).

THE CONSIDERATION OF REVENUE AND PRODUCT CONTROLS IS ESSENTIAL When designing or remodeling the beverage facility, designers must consider the type of beverage-control system that will be used. A **beverage-control system** consists of the computer hardware and software used to manage an operation's automated drink sales. This means controlling products as well as the revenue they generate. Although a great number of choices are available, basic principles of physical operation remain the same. Most managers agree that it is easier to design a beverage-control system when there are few physical constraints. It is much more difficult when control system designs must work around physical constraints. For example, if the layout of a room is such that it is difficult or impossible for bartenders and servers to share needed POS data entry terminals, the production of drinks may be slowed.

DESIGNING FOR OPERATIONAL EFFICIENCY

In addition to drink preparation areas, most facilities must also provide both centralized and behind-bar storage areas. The **centralized storage area** is used to store all alcoholic beverages from the time they are received until they are issued to the bar. It should be designed with security in mind; that is, unauthorized employees should not be able to enter the beverage storage area. Generally, space should be adequate to store a maximum of two to four weeks' supply of liquor. Wine storage must be secure, and requirements for temperature, humidity, and lighting must be met (see chapter 8).

The location of the centralized beverage storage area is generally not critical to an efficient beverage-control system. Replenishing par stock levels is typically done before the shift starts, when business is slow. **Par stock** is the amount of a product that should be readily available to bartenders at all times. For example, if the average usage of a particular spirit product is two bottles per day, the par stock of that item may be set by management at three or even four bottles to ensure that bartenders do not run out of it in the middle of their shifts.

Behind-bar storage must be adequate to store all the par levels of liquors, wines, beers, mixers, and other ingredients and supplies that will be used during busy shifts. The adequacy of behind-bar storage areas has a direct impact on efficiency. Since behind-bar space is often at a premium, storage for draft beer and soft drinks can be at a remote site with dispensing lines, pumping equipment, and other related equipment items housed in nonpublic spaces. If a large number of draft beers are offered, extensive refrigerated storage areas for these items must be considered.

From a product-control perspective, behind-bar storage areas must be adequate in size, easily locked, and close to (if not within) the bartenders' work centers, so bartenders do not need to waste time in the middle of a rush to secure additional supplies. In addition to alcoholic beverages, a sufficient quantity of other items is typically stored in the immediate bar area. These items include disposable products such as straws, napkins, and stir sticks.

Refrigerated storage may be necessary for drink mixes, such as Bloody Mary mix and mixes for exotic drinks made with dairy products or fruit juices, fruit and vegetables for garnishes, and fruit for drinks such as strawberry daiquiris. Ice cream and other frozen mixes require specialized product storage space.

Glassware availability is another essential design-related issue. Since space behind the bar is generally limited, the proper supply of glassware must be available for immediate use before a bartender's shift begins. In addition, adequate equipment is necessary to properly wash, rinse, and sanitize glassware. Even when plans call for most glasses to be washed elsewhere, some arrangements for behind-bar glass washing are generally necessary. Managers should consult with local or state health authorities to review beverage facility designs to ensure that sanitation requirements are met.

To provide extra storage space, glass racks that are suspended from the ceiling are popular in many operations since they can be incorporated into the facility's décor. Shelving and countertops may also be used. In some operations, glasses needed for lounge service are given to bartenders by beverage servers at the time beverage orders are placed. This reduces glass storage needs behind the bar. In all cases, however, it is the manager's job to make sure that there is adequate space to store soiled, clean, and drying glassware.

DESIGNING FOR EMPLOYEE PRODUCTIVITY

Drink production areas are typically referred to simply as "the bar," and they can be designed in a variety of ways. Larger operations require more bar space whereas smaller operations require less. In all cases, however, the bar area should be designed to optimize employee productivity.

Most bars are designed to allow more than one bartender to work comfortably during busy periods. However, the bar should be designed so that one bartender can also comfortably operate it during slower periods. For control purposes, the goals of bar design are twofold: The bar design must promote high employee-productivity levels and it must take into account beverage production and revenue control procedures.

Workstation design directly affects bartender productivity. With the right design, bartenders can work quickly and more economically. Bartenders should be able to perform related activities in one place. For example, if they need to prepare garnishes, they should have space to store and clean fresh fruit and vegetables and to prepare and store garnishes until they are used. If fresh produce is supplied by and prepared in the kitchen prior to the beginning of bartenders' shifts, only a storage area may be required. If this garnish preparation assistance is not provided, a larger bar preparation area including space for cutting boards may be necessary.

There must be space for preparing ordered drinks. This means having glassware at hand and close to needed ice, liquor, mixes, and garnishes. This space must be near the beverage pickup area and close to the **point of sale (POS) system**. A bar's POS system records and stores a bar's sales, product usage, and other important operating information.

Typically, an effective bar layout consists of workstations and common areas. The workstations can be set up for public bar sales to guests seated at the bar. They also can be designed as **service bars**, the areas at which service staff pick up drinks to deliver to customers. In most cases, service bars do not deal directly with guests. Bartenders in service bars handle the needs of servers for supplying beverages to lounge, dining area, or banquet guests. Common areas include space for bartenders to perform shared tasks such as washing glasses or preparing garnishes.

The arrangement of bar components varies with the needs of the facility. If there is no foodservice and few seating places other than at the bar, the service bar will be small or nonexistent. Large facilities may have one or many separate service bars to handle the more diverse needs of the operation.

Lighting, work counter height, and workspace design are some of the areas planners must consider. Although muted lighting often works well in guest areas, brighter lighting is needed in beverage preparation areas. Work counters in beverage areas should be about 34 inches high so that bartenders can work more productively. There must be enough space so that the required number of employees can work comfortably.

Product flow must be considered and backtracking must be minimized. Unfortunately, some beverage workstations have been designed so that the bartender goes one way to get a required bottle, another way to enter revenue information, and reverses direction to serve drinks. Effectively designed bars help bartenders be more productive by eliminating unnecessary trips.

Conveniently located space is needed for all tools bartenders require (including portion control devices, drink recipe sources, cutting boards, blenders, knives, mixing spoons, and strainers). The work area must be comfortable. Heat from undercounter dishwashers, refrigeration compressors, and inadequate ventilation can hamper bartenders' productivity.

Proper lighting of the drink order or pickup area is important so that servers can easily identify drink orders and perform their required record-keeping tasks. Space and adequate lighting for processing credit and debit card payments must also be considered.

Exhibit 7.3 shows an example of a well-designed bar that incorporates the elements discussed.

SERVICE-RELATED DESIGN CONCERNS

The layout and design of bars will vary based on the type of beverage service provided to guests. The two ways of getting drinks from bartenders to guests, either directly from the bartender or indirectly through servers, differ.

DIRECT SERVICE: BARTENDER TO GUEST Direct bartender to guest service requires design considerations to provide bartenders ample space to work effectively behind the public bar. The **public bar** is the bar over which bartenders directly serve guests. Often, the physical length of the public bar is determined by the need for a specific number of seats or standing spaces in front of the bar, as permitted by local laws. The number of drinks served over the bar is generally determined by its length, and this is influenced by the number of workstations behind it. Each working bartender typically performs some direct beverage service.

Exhibit 7.3

SAMPLE BAR LAYOUT

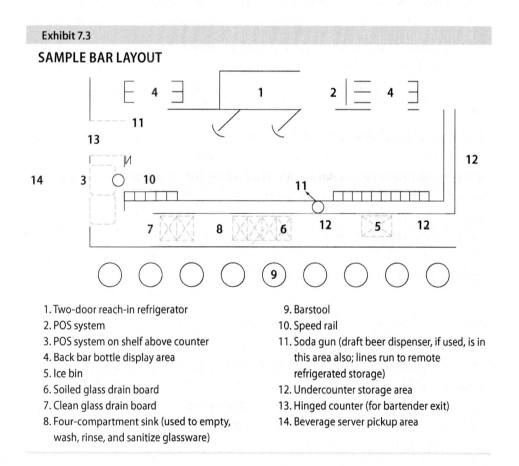

1. Two-door reach-in refrigerator
2. POS system
3. POS system on shelf above counter
4. Back bar bottle display area
5. Ice bin
6. Soiled glass drain board
7. Clean glass drain board
8. Four-compartment sink (used to empty, wash, rinse, and sanitize glassware)
9. Barstool
10. Speed rail
11. Soda gun (draft beer dispenser, if used, is in this area also; lines run to remote refrigerated storage)
12. Undercounter storage area
13. Hinged counter (for bartender exit)
14. Beverage server pickup area

IF YOU'RE NOT NOTICED, YOU LOSE:

As a consultant, I was working with a 40-year-old, upper-positioned, continental-style family-owned restaurant near Dallas, Texas. The family's next generation (two brothers) had taken over, so they were remodeling and repositioning the restaurant for a new generation. They hired me to lead their concept and project. We remodeled, tested, and made menu changes while remaining open. The outside of the building was white stucco with a European dress and finish.

When it came time to paint the outside of the building, they used a special primer before applying the final color. The primer was pink. Then it rained for over three weeks straight. As a result the pink color remained on the building for close to a month. During that month, revenue increased by over 120 percent! People came in saying that they had driven past the building for 20 years, but they had never "seen it" before. Because the building was now highly visible, revenue increased greatly, without one other marketing effort. Since then, I've never looked at the exterior of a restaurant or bar the same. Visibility is money: use signs, flags (movement), colors, or any treatment you can to move eyes to your business!

INDIRECT SERVICE: BARTENDER TO SERVER TO GUEST Indirect beverage service can take place at dining-room tables, service bars, at the service stations of public bars, and at public bars without assigned service workstations. If an operation is to provide excellent service to its guests, its service areas and traffic patterns must be designed with the following factors in mind:

- The pickup station must be conveniently located for server access. As the distance of the bar from guest seating areas increases, service time also increases.

- The service bar workstation should be compact, separate, and designed to optimize bartender productivity since in larger operations that is where most of the drinks are prepared.

- To make beverage serving easier, space must be available for servers to place and pick up orders. When server pickup areas are crowded with guests, this task becomes difficult. The actual space for beverage pickup must be large enough to place drinks that have been prepared for several servers on cocktail trays. An efficient, productive bartender is immediately slowed down if there is not adequate space to place all drinks that have been prepared.

- Space must also be available to store items that servers may need including glasses, ice, garnishes, disposable supplies, and service towels.

- During slow periods there may not be a beverage server present. In this case, the bartender may be required to serve drinks to guests seated at tables in the lounge. Easy access from the drink production area at the bar to the guest seating areas is important.

In an operation that also serves food, the beverage staff may need to interact with restaurant or foodservice servers to transfer drink tabs. A **drink tab** is a guest's running total of charges for drinks that have been served but not yet paid for. For that reason, the location of the bar relative to the dining area is important. Also, it is unwise for guests who desire only food to be made to walk through the lounge, or for bar-only guests to be required to pass through the dining room. However, it is important that entry areas, checkrooms, and restrooms are convenient for all guests.

Décor and Atmosphere

Layout and design of a bar are important elements that help ensure prompt service and make the guests feel welcome. In addition, the décor and atmosphere in a beverage facility can impact the demographics of the guests. It can also affect how frequently those guests come to the bar and how long they stay. In most cases, guests do not come to a bar simply to drink. Some come to socialize or to relax. Some come for business, while others come for leisure. Different bars attract different customers. A quiet, darkly lit, romantic facility attracts different customers than a bright sports bar with large-screen TVs and pool tables.

In all cases, the décor and atmosphere should welcome guests. All facilities should be clean, properly lighted, and comfortable. It is the manager's job to ensure the operation is inviting to guests. When an operation's physical facility looks shabby or dirty, guests will likely assume the worst about how the business is operated. In addition, when facilities are not professionally maintained injuries can occur. The operation may not be able to defend against a charge of negligence from an injured person. Basic facility concerns in a beverage operation include seating, flooring, and lighting.

SEATING

Seating involves the tables, chairs, and booths in the operation. The look and style of seating greatly impacts the feelings guests have when they enter a beverage operation (*Exhibit 7.4*). Soft, plush, and oversized chairs indicate opulence and high style. Wooden barstools and chairs may indicate casual comfort. In all cases, seating areas must be kept clean and be inspected on a regular basis. An especially annoying maintenance issue for guests involves table leveling. Tables that are not level with the floor make consuming beverages difficult. They are also a safety hazard. With a proper inspection program, there is no excuse for wobbly tables or for the need of foreign objects such as matchbooks or folded paper to be placed under them. Quality tables are built with individual leg levelers. These levelers should be properly used to ensure table stability.

Exhibit 7.4

Bar tabletops may be made of a variety of materials including tile, metal, wood, wood laminates, glass, and synthetic plastics. Maintenance of tabletops involves ensuring that they are not cracked, ragged-edged, or broken and therefore capable of creating a safety hazard. In addition, they must be regularly cleaned and sanitized to prevent the growth of bacteria and to maximize the aesthetic appeal of the table when guests are seated.

Chairs must be regularly inspected to ensure that they are safe. Loose or wobbly chairs must be repaired or replaced immediately. Guests come in a variety of sizes and chairs should be maintained to support the maximum weight likely to be encountered. In most cases, bar chairs are built to have a seat height between 18 to 20 inches from the floor. These should be purchased and maintained to "fit" with the operation's table heights. This is generally 27 to 30 inches for regular tables at which guests are seated and 40 to 42 inches for stand-up cocktail-style tables.

Booths are a popular form of bar seating. They should be inspected just as often as regular tables and chairs; however, because of the special stresses placed on booth seating surfaces when guests "slide" into them, fabric and vinyl booth seat coverings should be carefully inspected for signs of wear and tear. When detected, these should be promptly repaired or replaced. If not maintained, small stress point damages and punctures can develop into larger problems that will ultimately cause unsightly rips and tears in booth seating materials.

FLOORING

The flooring in a beverage operation serves an aesthetic purpose as well as a functional one. A facility's choice of flooring material goes a long way toward establishing the décor, theme, and ambience sought by the bar's interior design. While floors can be made out of virtually any material, the three most popular flooring types are wood, carpet, and ceramic tile. Each flooring material has its strengths and drawbacks, and each must be properly maintained.

WOOD Wood has been used as a flooring material for centuries. It is valued for its good looks, ease of cleaning, and durability. Today, wood material used for flooring is specially treated at the factory with polyurethane or acrylic urethane. This treatment provides an attractive appearance and a more durable finish than is achieved when wood planking for a floor is merely varnished. Depending on the type of wood used and how that wood has been finished when manufactured or upon installation, typical routine maintenance tasks involve sweeping and cleaning to avoid damaging the wood's finish. Properly maintained wood floors will last for years and provide a rich, warm look to the bar. In most communities, the use of wood flooring in back-of-house bar production areas is prohibited because wood is often slippery when wet. Also, wood floors may be difficult to clean properly because they are not resistant to spillage.

CARPET Carpet as a floor covering adds warmth and is soft under the feet. Carpet provides a quieter surface than wood and helps absorb sounds from a bar seating area. Besides its feel underfoot, carpets are popular choices for bar areas because of the wide range of colors and patterns that are available. In addition, carpeting can be purchased in a wide range of prices. Installation costs are also lower than for wood or ceramic tile. As a result, even the most modest bar facility design budgets can include attractive and durable carpet.

Carpets can be easily maintained with frequent vacuuming, spot cleaning as needed, and regularly scheduled shampooing. Carpet has the added advantage of hiding minor irregularities in the floor that it covers. For example, if minor shifting of a building results in uneven flooring in some places, these defects can frequently be covered with carpet in a way that is aesthetically pleasing and that is still safe for guests and employees who must walk in these areas. Like wood, in most communities the use of carpet in drink production areas is prohibited because carpet would absorb spills and thus be difficult to clean properly.

CERAMIC TILE When properly installed, a ceramic tile floor will outlast nearly any other floor covering product created for the same use. It is impervious to water, and it is the nearly unanimous choice of building engineers and designers for use in restrooms and drink preparation areas. It is durable, stain and odor resistant, does not absorb spills, and can be easily cleaned with common soaps or detergents and water. Ceramic tile will not dent or split like wood floors and will not cut or tear as can carpet. Like carpet, ceramic tile comes in a large array of colors and patterns. Two disadvantages of ceramic tile, however, are the very high installation costs and the tendency of tile to become slippery when wet. Ceramic tile is so durable that it can be cleaned using high-pressure steam. As a result, in most communities ceramic tile is the only flooring material allowed for use in beverage production areas.

Of course, beverage operations can be successful with wood, carpet, or tile floors. The choice of material depends on the décor and atmosphere of the establishment, as well as the budget allotted to installation and maintenance. Each of these materials, however, must be well maintained according to an appropriate cleaning and maintenance schedule.

LIGHTING

The right lighting can make a dramatic impact on the ambience of a restaurant or foodservice operation. Lighting is an essential part of setting the mood. Too dim a lighting level may make it hard to read menus and see the food a diner has been served. Too much light can make a room excessively harsh looking and, as a result, make guests feel uncomfortable.

Lighting in an establishment can take many forms:

- Natural sunlight
- Table lamps and candles
- Wall-mounted (sconce) lights
- Ceiling-mounted lights: exposed
- Ceiling-mounted lights: recessed
- Chandeliers
- Pendent (drop-down) lights

The management of lighting in a beverage facility consists primarily of keeping fixtures clean and light bulbs operational. Care must be taken when

WHAT'S THE FOOTPRINT?

CFL is short for *compact fluorescent light*. This type of light bulb uses less energy and lasts longer than more traditional incandescent light bulbs. CFLs use about one-fourth the energy of traditional bulbs. Because they use less energy to produce the same amount of light, operations using them experience lower energy costs. And because CFLs use less electricity to produce the same amount of light, they reduce the amount of electricity that must be produced, and that reduces the amount of pollution produced.

cleaning light fixtures. In the best of situations, the cleaning will occur with the power to the lights turned off. When that is not possible, it is important that cleaning tools and procedures be appropriate for working with live electricity. This is likely to entail dusting, not washing, the fixtures and lights.

BAR EQUIPMENT AND SUPPLIES

To ensure that an operation is able to deliver to the standards it sets, managers must ensure that bartenders and servers have the right equipment, tools, and supplies to do their job correctly. There are various considerations that go into choosing and maintaining the right beverage equipment, bar tools, and glassware for an operation.

Beverage Equipment

When designing the bar operation, consider the type and amount of beverage equipment that will be needed. Quality bar and beverage equipment is costly, but buying quality products is a good long-term investment. Quality products work better and maintain their appearance longer. Equipment breakdowns are costly in both time and money. They also can cause guest service delays and result in poor-quality drinks, which can ultimately create negative guest impressions of the operation.

Quality products cannot be judged by price alone. The indicators of quality products include performance, technical considerations, ease of use, aesthetics, warranties, and the availability of convenient service when needed. Several factors should be considered in planning any equipment purchases such as need, cost, performance, safety and sanitation, and construction.

NEED

It is necessary to cost-justify the need for every item of beverage equipment being considered for purchase. Equipment should have the proper capacity and be suited to the tasks performed in the operation. Where possible, high-cost items such as refrigerated units and glass-washing sinks or machines should be located so that two or more bartenders may use them. This reduces capital equipment costs significantly and reduces space needs.

COST

Some managers carefully consider the up-front purchase costs of equipment but do not keep in mind other costs associated with the purchase:

- Installation
- Cleaning

- Maintenance
- Repair
- Training
- Need for special supplies
- Financing
- Insurance
- Operating costs

When purchase decisions are made, all associated costs must be identified and considered.

PERFORMANCE

Performance is measured by the extent to which the equipment performs the tasks for which it was purchased. Does the blender prepare drinks within necessary time limitations? In the required quantity? Is the refrigerated unit sufficiently large to handle one shift's needs? Does the glass-washing equipment system produce the number of clean glasses needed, when they are needed? Manufacturers' and suppliers' claims about equipment performance can often be checked by asking managers of other operations who already own similar equipment.

SAFETY AND SANITATION

Some managers fail to think about safety when beverage equipment is purchased. However, it is easy to imagine protruding, sharp edges on equipment and shelves, poorly designed or constructed ice bins, and sinks and counter shelving units that can puncture, catch clothing, or otherwise create safety hazards. It is especially important that electrical equipment be properly installed and grounded. Beverage equipment must always be sanitary and easy to clean. Maintaining basic sanitation can be difficult. For example, when galvanized metal is used for refrigerator interiors or when steel surfaces overlap it can make proper cleaning difficult. Other examples include sink basins and ice bins that are not designed to be easily cleaned.

CONSTRUCTION

Beverage equipment must be durable because beverage personnel do not always handle equipment carefully and most items are in constant use. Shortcuts in construction, including substituting low-quality materials and poor craftsmanship, may reduce prices but seldom produce good long-term investments. Careful study of equipment specification information provided by manufacturers helps ensure the purchase of quality products.

Manager's Memo

Beverage equipment is purchased only once or very infrequently, unlike beverage products and supplies that are ordered regularly. Equipment represents a long-term investment. When considering equipment purchases, thoughtful managers address important questions:

- Will the product do what we need it to do?
- Will the product save time or money?
- Can the time and cost savings be justified?
- What is the impact on the operation if the product breaks down?
- How much maintenance is required?
- Are repair and maintenance services available at a reasonable price and in a reasonable time?

WHAT'S THE FOOTPRINT?

Refrigerated units with glass fronts save energy by reducing "hunting" time. Hunting time is the amount of time it takes to locate specific items in facilities where multiple units are in use.

Modern glass-front refrigerators can also monitor room temperatures and the product load levels inside them. They respond to load changes by reducing run time and energy usage when loads are light and increasing them when the refrigerator is full. Auto sensors reduce run times on these machines. They also reduce maintenance costs and extend equipment life because the machine's compressors run only as often and as long as needed.

Exhibit 7.5

While the specific equipment needs of a bar can vary, most managers will purchase key pieces:

• Refrigerators

• Ice machines

• Glass-washing sinks and equipment

• Drink production equipment

REFRIGERATORS

One or more refrigerated units are required behind most bars. They are used to store bottled and draft beer, cream, juice and drink mixes, vegetable and fruit garnishes, chilled wines, and other miscellaneous items. A multipurpose unit, either chest-type or front opening, is often used, and must have enough space to hold most items needed for at least one busy shift. In many instances, because of space considerations, case and keg beer must be stored in remote refrigerated units, along with draft beer hooked to dispensing lines running to the bar.

There are key operational considerations when selecting refrigerated equipment:

• The size of the unit is important. It must be adequate for the operation.

• The direction in which doors open should be correct for the location. Both right and left door swings are available.

• Interior lighting is useful if the behind-bar area is not adequately lighted.

• Shelving should be adjustable.

• Doors that can be locked are desirable.

• Interior and exterior components of units should be easy to clean.

• When units are visible to the public, they should be designed and color-coordinated with the facility's décor.

• Units not on enclosed bases must be on legs tall enough to permit sweeping and mopping under them.

• Units should meet the standards for sanitation and ease of cleaning established by NSF International.

ICE MACHINES

Large ice machines are not generally located in the immediate behind-bar area. However, units must be placed reasonably close to the area so that ice supplies can be easily transported to the behind-bar ice bins or other ice holders as needed (*Exhibit 7.5*).

There are key operational considerations when selecting ice machines:

• The capacity must be correct for the operation. If an ice machine is selected that cannot provide ice for an entire shift, managers may have to rely on "backup" ice that is either prepared ahead of time and stored, or purchased from suppliers. The size of the bins that hold the ice must also be adequate.

- When units will not be in public view, less expensive exterior finishes can be considered.

- Insulated ice storage bins may reduce melting of cubes in storage if units must be placed in high-temperature areas.

- The best units allow ice to be removed easily from the storage bins.

- Machines must meet all standards established by NSF International.

The importance of reliable ice machines cannot be overemphasized. Overworked or undependable ice machines are costly in many ways. In addition to choosing quality machines, some managers use service contracts that guarantee an uninterrupted ice supply. With these contracts, the service company or machine distributor guarantees that the machine will supply ice, or it will be responsible to pay for or deliver bags of ice until the machine is repaired.

GLASSWARE-WASHING SINKS AND EQUIPMENT

Stainless-steel sinks should be used for manual glassware washing and they must meet local health department codes. When glassware washing takes place behind the bar, a three- or four-compartment sink is most frequently required. Separate sink compartments are used for dumping ice and remaining liquids from the glassware, while the others are for washing, rinsing, and sanitizing glassware. When choosing glassware-washing sinks and equipment there are additional concerns that managers must consider:

- NSF International standards must be met.

- Use of chemicals instead of heat for sanitizing glassware reduces equipment costs and is often the most labor-effective.

- Drain boards for both soiled and clean items should be long enough to hold normal numbers of soiled glassware prior to washing, and clean glassware before they are used or put into storage.

- Proper working height is important. Drain tables that are approximately 34 inches in working height with a sink depth of approximately 12 inches may be most comfortable for employees of average height.

- Since the sink is one of the largest units to be installed in the behind-bar area, its dimensions and location should be assessed early in the planning process.

- Undercounter glassware-washing machines are sometimes used in high-volume bar operations. If used, they should be commercial units that meet NSF International standards.

THINK ABOUT IT . . .

Some customers think that bartenders who use jiggers are going out of their way to ensure no "extra" alcohol is served, reducing the value of the drink. How would you manage this perception by customers?

DRINK PRODUCTION EQUIPMENT

Essentially, three approaches are used to produce drinks in a commercial beverage operation. Drinks may be produced manually, using assistance, or using automation.

MANUAL DRINK PRODUCTION In a **manual drink production system**, skilled bartenders make each drink themselves. In this system, all bartenders must be properly trained to prepare many drinks. Bartenders follow the property's standard recipes (see chapter 6) whenever they prepare a drink. They use a measuring tool such as a **jigger**, a small shot glass–type tool used to accurately measure the amount of alcohol served in drinks, to ensure portion control. In most cases, jiggers have lines that indicate the quantity of spirits they hold in exactly the same way that food measuring spoons indicate the quantities they hold. Common sizes range from 0.5 ounce to 2 ounces.

When producing a drink manually, the bartender holds the jigger, in sight of the customer if seated at the bar, and pours until the alcoholic beverage reaches the appropriate line. Then the jigger's contents are poured into the proper glassware. This method is accurate and helps ensure that beverage costs are in line with plans and that the drinks will be of the same consistent quality and taste. It also assists in the property's efforts to serve alcoholic beverages responsibly because a count of the standard drinks billed to the customer indicates the total quantity of alcohol the customer has consumed.

ASSISTED DRINK PRODUCTION Equipment that does some or almost all of the work that bartenders normally perform has been available for many years. In an **assisted drink production system**, bartenders use metered pour spouts to help control beverage quantity in the drinks they produce.

A pouring spout inserted in the top of the bottle allows only a specified amount of alcohol to be dispensed each time the bottle is inverted. For example, if a manager decides to use a 1.5-ounce portion, a 1.5-ounce pour spout can be purchased and used so only this amount can be poured without inverting the bottle again to pour a second portion.

Pour spouts are available at a variety of prices as well as volume amounts and can be used for wine as well as spirits. Some pour spouts monitor simple portion size; other more advanced systems interface with automated beverage production systems. These systems calculate product usage and compute expected revenue levels and product cost percentages.

AUTOMATED DRINK PRODUCTION In an **automated drink production system**, all or nearly all of a drink's production is performed by machine. The use of automated drink systems reduces opportunities for bartenders to give away free drinks because the system keeps a record of the number of drinks produced, the amount of alcohol of each type dispensed, and the revenue value of the drinks. There are other possible benefits of an automated beverage dispensing system:

- The elimination of over- or underpouring
- Reduced spillage
- A reduction in drink pricing errors
- Accurate record keeping for all products sold
- Fewer bartender errors
- Less need for bartender supervision
- Lower and more consistent product costs
- Reduced cost per product ounce when purchasing because spirits can be purchased in larger containers
- Reduced legal liability potential because the amount of alcohol in each drink is tightly controlled

There are essentially two types of automated equipment systems: metered systems and fully automated ones. A metered automated system delivers selected beverages via a "gun" similar to that often used for soft drinks, a stationary head, a spout strip, or other device. It serves a portion-controlled amount of beverage product, and it simultaneously "counts" the number of portions of each beverage served. The bartender then adds mixers like soda or tonic. This type of system can be, but does not have to be, tied into the operation's POS system. This integration allows the POS system to record and store the number of drinks sold and revenues generated as well as other important sales data.

In a fully-automated system, a piece of dispensing equipment performs the same tasks as in the metered system, but additionally prepares preprogrammed drink selections by automatically adding mixers. Some systems can also make drinks containing two or more liquors or juices. These systems are more expensive than metered systems. This type of equipment is most often electronically connected to the operation's POS system and may even need to have a sale fully recorded in the POS system before it will dispense a drink. See more information about this in chapter 9.

Despite their many control advantages, some managers hesitate to purchase automated drink production systems for a variety of reasons:

- If equipment breaks down, it creates an awkward situation with untrained bartenders producing drinks manually until the operation can get the equipment fixed. In addition, it can be difficult to hand pour from larger bottles that were purchased for use with automated equipment.
- Guests seeing the equipment in use may feel that they are receiving a smaller portion or lower-quality drink than ordered. This may affect both sales and guest attitudes.

- Since it is difficult to objectively evaluate the payback period, it is hard to determine the "worth" of the equipment.

- With some types of equipment, experienced and trained bartenders are still needed to prepare certain drinks.

- Some bartenders have negative attitudes toward automated beverage equipment.

The philosophy and type of operation determine the feasibility of using automated beverage equipment. Today, many beverage professionals agree that there is a place for this equipment in the industry and expect automated systems to become more prevalent. Some general concerns are important when this equipment is selected:

- The equipment must produce products of the type and quality needed by the operation. Although automated equipment is compatible with most operations, some facilities that stress high levels of bartender–guest interaction may not have an interest in it.

- Managers must not decide to use this equipment because "everybody does" or because of a salesperson's recommendations. The equipment must be considered from a cost, compatibility, and operational perspective.

- Managers must analyze their operations to calculate existing costs and potential savings. It is not wise to take the word of others about savings or to accept national cost, loss, or savings averages. It is necessary to study information pertaining to the specific facility.

- Equipment costs must be assessed at the same time potential savings are estimated. It is necessary to know how many years it will take the reduced costs and increased revenue to equal the cost of the equipment including maintenance and repair.

- Supervision and control are needed even with automated systems. Dishonest employees can try to cheat even when sophisticated control systems are in place. Also, theft of revenue is possible in areas not placed under automated control.

- If purchased for an existing facility, the proposed equipment must fit into existing operations. Employees must be able to adapt to it, and the equipment must be compatible with what the operation's guests want.

Bar Tools

In addition to drink production systems, many small tools and utensils are essential or simply make bartending easier (*Exhibit 7.6*). Some of the most common of these are listed in *Exhibit 7.7*.

Exhibit 7.6

Exhibit 7.7

BAR TOOLS REQUIRED FOR DRINK MAKING

- Bar spoons
- Cocktail picks
- Fruit tongs
- Ice picks and crushers
- Pitchers
- Serrated knives
- Sugar or salt bowls

- Bar towels
- Cocktail shaker glasses
- Garnish containers
- Ice scoops and tongs
- Portion tools (jiggers and shot glasses)
- Speed pourers

- Wooden muddlers (mixers)
- Blenders
- Corkscrews
- Glass mats
- Juice squeezers
- Recipe book, cards, files, or access in POS system

- Storage containers
- Can and bottle openers
- Cutting boards
- Glass salters
- Mixing glasses
- Salt shakers
- Strainers

Glassware

Drinks are served in glasses. Managers can select from hundreds of different styles and sizes of glasses when they plan how drinks should be served, and their choices are important. For example, champagne served in a frosted beer mug will produce a poor-tasting glass of champagne and an unhappy guest. Managers can choose from many types of glassware, but the use of some types is more popular or more traditional than others. These are the 10 most popular glassware types and sizes used in bars (see *Exhibit 7.8*):

Exhibit 7.8

THE 10 MOST POPULAR GLASSWARE TYPES

Wine Glasses
Used for
Wine

Champagne Flute
Used for
Champagne

Snifter
Used for
Brandy

Beer Pilsner or Mug
Used for
Beer

Collins Glass
Used for
Larger Mixed Drinks

Martini Glass
Used for
Martinis

High Ball Glass
Used for
Mixed Drinks

Rocks Glass
Used for
Smaller Mixed Drinks
Shots of Alcohol
Over Ice

Shot Glass
Used for
Shots of Alcohol

Irish Coffee Glass
Used for
Coffee or Hot
Alcoholic Drinks

- **Wine Glass (4 to 12 ounces):** Red wines are typically served in larger glasses to allow drinkers to enjoy the wine's bouquet. White wines are generally served in smaller glasses so they can retain the wine's cooler serving temperatures. Dessert wine glasses may be even smaller than those used for white wines.

- **Champagne Flute (6 to 8 ounces):** The long stem of this glass is designed to be grasped by the fingers to keep the drinker's hand from transferring the higher body temperature to the cold contents of the glass. The tall shape of the glass helps prevent the drink from going flat too quickly. It also lets bubbles rise more slowly, maintaining the product's fine taste and giving the best visual effect of the drink's carbonation.

- **Snifter (16 to 18 ounces):** These glasses are popular for brandy or Cognac so they are often called brandy snifters. The large bowl maximizes the surface area of the beverage and allows the drink to be gently swirled to release the maximum amount of bouquet. Typically the brandy is poured to the widest part of the glass. The large surface area allows the aroma of the contents to rise and be concentrated at the narrow mouth for maximum effect.

- **Beer Pilsner or Mug (12 to 16 ounces):** Many managers consider the pilsner-style glass as the best for beer, and it has a narrow, footed base that expands outward toward the top. Other managers prefer mugs or steins of various sizes and shapes.

- **Collins Glass (6 to 16 ounces):** This popular shaped all-purpose glass is used for mixed drinks, water, soft drinks, juice, or other nonalcoholic beverages.

- **Martini Glass (4 to 6 ounces):** The classic martini glass has straight edges expanding outward from the stem at approximately a 60-degree angle. Also known as a martini saucer, this glass is sometimes used to serve margaritas and other smaller-portioned frozen drinks.

- **Highball Glass (8 to 14 ounces):** The highball glass is popular because highball cocktails are popular (see chapter 6). Tall and slender, it displays a variety of colorful cocktails very well.

- **Rocks Glass (8 to 10 ounces):** A rocks glass is short, heavy for its size, wide-rimmed, and is essential for any bar. It is also known in some operations as an "old-fashioned" or "lowball" glass. Often, cocktails with whiskey as the base ingredient are served in glasses of this type.

- **Shot Glass (2 to 2.5 ounces):** This glass is used for many types of spirits that are served "straight up," or without ice. While some sipping drinks are served in this glass, it is used most often for drinks designed to be swallowed in a single gulp, or shot.

- **Irish Coffee Glass (6 to 16 ounces):** This tempered clear glass mug attractively displays hot drinks including Irish coffee, regular coffee, cider, tea, or other served-hot beverages.

Numerous other glasses of various shapes and sizes are available. These include those used for cordials, shooters, margaritas, hurricanes, piña coladas, mai tais, and frozen and on-the-rocks daiquiris. The right glassware can help increase drink sales, makes drinks look and taste more appealing, and gives a good impression to customers. Most important, *clean* glassware is essential to guest satisfaction. As a result, managers should monitor mechanical or manual glass-cleaning procedures in the bar carefully and often.

BAR STAFFING

Design, layout, and interior decoration help create an establishment's atmosphere. The proper equipment and supplies are needed to produce quality products. It is really the operation's staff, however, that contribute most to making an operation successful. When employees are professional, efficient, and courteous, guests will keep coming back. Staff members who are inattentive, careless, or rude have a negative effect on an operation's ability to meet its sales and profit goals.

Staff needs are unique to each beverage operation. In small, owner-operated bars, one or two people perform most personnel functions. Larger operations typically have several categories of employees who must interact to accomplish their tasks. When managers, bartenders, beverage servers, receptionists, cashiers, food servers, chefs, and wine stewards (those who assist guests in selecting wines) are part of an operation, the facility must be designed to accommodate their training and workspace needs.

Managers cannot operate their bar and beverage facilities without the help of knowledgeable and skilled employees. Managers need employees who are motivated and open-minded and who enjoy working with people. While previous beverage experience is often helpful, many managers do not consider this to be a crucial employee selection factor. Job knowledge and skills can be taught. Instead, managers often look for characteristics such as attitude, desire, honesty, and stability.

OPEN FOR BUSINESS — KEEPING IT SAFE

Many bars wash their glassware manually. To do it properly, a three-compartment sink is needed and the following steps are used:

1. Discard drink remains from glasses before washing.

2. Clean glasses in the first sink using a detergent solution and hot water of at least 110°F (43°C). Scrub glasses with a brush and replace the detergent when the suds are done or the water is dirty.

3. Rinse items in the second sink filled with clean water. Replace rinse water when it becomes cloudy or dirty.

4. Immerse the item in an approved sanitizing solution in the third sink for the required amount of time. The sanitizing solution must be at the correct temperature and concentration. Use a test kit to check the concentration of the sanitizing solution.

5. Allow glasses to air dry upside down on perforated mats that permit water drainage and air circulation.

6. Never dry the inside or outside of a glass with a cloth.

Responsibilities of Beverage Personnel

Beverage operations vary in the number and types of personnel they need to operate successfully. In addition to the manager, bar operations typically employ workers in several positions:

- *Bartenders* primarily prepare and may serve alcoholic beverages to guests.

- *Beverage servers* primarily serve but may pour selected alcoholic beverages such as wines for guests.

- *Wine stewards* are trained primarily in assisting guests in the selection of wines.

Sample job descriptions for each of these positions are given in *Exhibits 7.9* to *7.11.*

Exhibit 7.9

Sample Job Description for a Bartender

Job title: Bartender

Reports to: Operation manager or beverage manager

Responsibilities:

The bartender must meet the following responsibilities:
- Adhere to company policies and procedures to ensure that all tasks are performed in a correct and efficient manner.
- Maintain a clean and well-organized bar.
- Keep up-to-date with current industry trends.

Job Tasks:

The bartender is responsible for the following job tasks that should be done according to the goals, policies, and standard operating procedures of the organization:
- Prepare drinks according to standardized recipes.
- Stock the bar before opening and as needed to maintain par stock.
- Follow all control systems.
- Take inventory of bar supplies as requested by the manager or assistant manager.
- Prepare garnishes.
- Record all bar and beverage revenues.
- Handle cash and other payments according to procedures outlined by company policies.
- Close the register.
- Keep all equipment, fixtures, and areas in public and nonpublic spaces clean and free of hazards at all times.
- Clean and sanitize all bar and beverage equipment.
- Communicate effectively with all other facility personnel and guests.
- Perform any additional tasks as assigned by management.

Exhibit 7.10

Sample Job Description for a Beverage Server

Job title: Beverage server

Reports to: Operation manager, beverage manager, or service supervisor

Responsibilities:

The beverage server must meet the following responsibilities:
- Adhere to company policies and procedures to ensure that all tasks are performed in a correct and efficient manner.
- Keep up-to-date with industry trends.

Job Tasks:

The beverage server is responsible for the following tasks that should be done according to the goals, policies, and procedures of the organization:
- Take guests' beverage orders, give beverage orders to bartender, and serve beverages to guests.
- Use POS equipment correctly.
- Handle cash and charges according to procedures outlined by company policies.
- Keep service areas clean and free of hazards at all times.
- Follow all control systems.
- Communicate effectively with all other facility personnel and guests.
- Perform any additional tasks as assigned by management.

Exhibit 7.11

Sample Job Description for a Wine Steward

Job title: Wine steward

Reports to: Operation manager, food and beverage manager, dining-room manager, or service supervisor

Responsibilities:

The wine steward must meet the following responsibilities:
- Adhere to company policies and procedures to ensure that all tasks are performed in a correct and efficient manner.
- Keep up-to-date with industry trends.

Job Tasks:

The wine steward is responsible for the following tasks that should be done according to the goals, policies, and procedures of the organization:
- Answer guests' questions about wines.
- Take guests' wine orders.
- Procure wine and serve it to guests.
- Add wine charges to guests' checks.
- Assist management with wine purchasing decisions.
- Keep wine inventory in optimum condition.
- Plan and conduct wine selection training sessions with management.
- Follow all control systems.
- Communicate effectively with all other facility personnel and guests.
- Perform any additional tasks as assigned by management.

Staff Recruitment and Selection

Some managers working in large restaurant or foodservice establishments or hotels may have a human resources department to help recruit staff members. Typically, however, managers in smaller establishments and most stand-alone bar operations do not have access to this assistance. Regardless as to whether a human resources professional or a manager performs the task, the same basic procedures for staff recruitment and selection should be used. Steps helpful in recruitment and selection include the following:

• Be sure that job descriptions that identify tasks required for the position are up-to-date.

• Announce vacancies through sources that have proven effective in the past. These sources may include newspaper advertisements, word-of-mouth communication, Internet job posting sites, recruitment campaigns with friends and relatives of current employees, and interaction with the placement services in local colleges and universities. Experienced managers also look for opportunities for recruitment from within because existing employees might desire promotions or transfers to vacant positions.

• Applicants should complete a job application form. The application should be kept simple and should require only information judged necessary for considering job suitability. Extreme care must be taken to ensure that there are no violations of federal, state, or local laws concerning age, race, or other discriminatory practices in hiring.

• Conduct a preliminary interview to determine basic information about the applicant. Before this, managers study the application form and resume, if provided. They preplan interview questions to ask and how to interpret responses to the questions. During the interview, managers encourage the applicants to ask their own questions to help ensure that the applicant knows about the organization and the position for which the application is being made.

• Conduct selection tests, if applicable. For example, an experienced bartender should know the ingredients in common drinks and might be able to describe basic characteristics of selected wines. An experienced beverage server should know how to carry a tray of drinks and might role-play dialogue for common guest interaction situations.

• Ensure that all legal concerns are addressed and that all legitimate applicants have been given fair consideration.

• Make the employment decision. The best managers notify those applicants who will not be employed as well as those who are.

Orientation and Training

Once selected, employees must be oriented and trained. First impressions do count! In many operations, the vast majority of all employee turnover occurs within the first several months of employment. To minimize the chances of this happening, managers concentrate on selecting the right staff member and then helping the new employee quickly establish himself or herself within the organization. Managers employ a variety of strategies as they plan effective employee orientation programs:

- They plan for the orientation in advance. Any forms that must be completed, such as tax and insurance forms, are compiled and ready for the new staff member's arrival. Managers anticipate questions new employees may have and are ready to provide answers to these questions.

Exhibit 7.12

- Managers or their designee meet personally with the new employee. Documents such as the employee handbook; all relevant work policies, such as attendance, absenteeism, and tardiness; and the employee's job description are reviewed (*Exhibit 7.12*). Managers discuss details about compensation (when and how employees are paid) and benefits that are available to the new worker.

- Employees are given a tour of the entire facility and are introduced to their new coworkers along the way.

- Employees are assigned a mentor. Managers designate an experienced employee to serve as a contact person for the new staff member so that someone will always be available to answer basic questions and to provide assistance at the time it is needed.

Effective orientation is the first step in an effective training program. Recall from chapter 3 that training is an important part of the growth and development of all employees. Many personnel problems result from improper training. If not properly trained, new employees learn by imitating the behavior of experienced employees. This process can perpetuate bad habits or ineffective processes. Managers and their operation always benefit from the effective training of each employee.

The job description indicates the most important tasks required for a position. These tasks should be the focus of new staff training. Employees must be able to perform all tasks required by the job description. Use the process outlined in chapter 3 to tailor a training program to the specific tasks in a given employee's job description.

THINK ABOUT IT . . .

Bartenders, servers, and managers must be trained to learn the signs of intoxication. What other employees do you think should be trained in this area? Why?

Manager's Memo

As discussed in earlier chapters, bartenders and servers must not serve alcohol to intoxicated guests. Managers should train all of their bartenders and service staff to start counting drinks when customers place their order and continue counting until they leave the operation. In bar areas, a tab can be left in front of the customer or in a convenient back-of-bar location so bartenders and servers can monitor it. Servers can keep a drink tally on the back of the customer check for customers in the dining room.

Unfortunately, counting drinks can be difficult, if not impossible, in some situations such as stand-up receptions where customers move around and are served at different locations by different servers. Then servers must be trained to rely on observation to spot possible intoxication.

Remember that training is not a one-time event that happens in the first weeks of a new employee's tenure. Training never ends. Employees must be coached to provide reinforcement when tasks are done correctly. Managers must also provide feedback and corrective action when a change in work procedures is required. Training programs need to be evaluated regularly. Employees who complete training programs should be able to meet the company's standards of work performance. If standards are not being met, managers need to analyze the training to determine if improvements are needed. Continually monitoring training enables managers to operate successful beverage facilities staffed with skilled, capable employees who have positive attitudes toward guests.

Scheduling

Scheduling employees is an important management task. A properly prepared schedule has two primary purposes:

- To ensure that the correct number of employees are available to provide guests with prompt, efficient service and properly prepared products
- To ensure labor costs meet management's pre-established budget goals

How well managers schedule their employees affects a variety of crucial operational areas:

- The quality of products and services provided to guests
- The employees' level of job satisfaction
- The operation's profitability
- The perception that the manager's own boss has of his or her ability to manage effectively

The process of scheduling staff has come a long way in the past 20 years. Today, managers can choose from a variety of inexpensive software tools to create the actual employee schedule. The advantages of using these programs are many and include the ability to preload important employee data such as requested days off, prearranged vacations, maximum allowable hours to be worked, restrictions on when those hours can be worked (if any), employee time preferences, and numerous additional factors identified as important by management.

The manner in which the schedule is presented and distributed to staff will vary according to the individual needs of the operation. However, all effective employee schedules should include key information:

- The dates covered by the schedule
- The day of the week covered by the schedule
- Employees' first and last names
- Scheduled days to work
- Scheduled days off

- Scheduled start time, designated by a.m. and p.m.

- Scheduled stop time, designated by a.m. and p.m.

- Total schedule period hours to be worked

- On and off days for salaried personnel

- The date the schedule was prepared

- The individual who has prepared and approved the schedule

DEVELOPING THE SCHEDULE

Regardless of whether managers develop the employee schedule manually or use available software, several principles should be used:

1. **Begin with Forecasted Volume:** Managers must begin with an accurate forecast of anticipated business volume, using either the number of guests served or the revenue dollars to be generated. This forecasted volume provides a budget for the manager to work within.

2. **Develop a Productivity Target and Schedule to Meet It:** Effective managers always have the target productivity measurement in mind as they build schedules. For example, if the measurement used is a labor cost percentage, a commonly used measure of productivity that expresses labor costs as a percentage of revenue achieved, managers can compute the anticipated percentage that would result from the schedule. The forecasted labor percentage will match the actual labor cost percentage if the operation attains its forecasted revenue volume.

3. **Schedule for the Needs of Guests First and Employees Second:** Typically, employees have strong feelings about when they want to work and for how long. A manager's job is to ensure that employees are available when they are needed and not just when employees "prefer" to work. Never let the operation be understaffed or overstaffed because of employee preferences.

4. **Avoid Scheduling Overtime Whenever Possible:** Overtime pay is expensive. In some cases overtime may be unavoidable as scheduled employees are absent from work, as revenue volume levels unexpectedly increase, or as extra work must be completed. In all cases, however, an employee schedule should not be developed with "built-in" overtime. If it does, this almost always indicates that the manager has failed to develop an effective staff with enough flexibility to address normal fluctuations in business operations.

MANAGER'S MATH

The labor cost percentage is one of the restaurant and foodservice industry's most commonly used measures of labor productivity. Labor cost percentage is calculated using the following formula:

Labor cost ÷ Total revenue ÷ Labor cost percentage

Calculate the labor cost percentage achieved by the Taco Town restaurant for each day it operated last week. Also calculate the labor cost percentage achieved for the entire week.

TACO TOWN: LAST WEEK

Date	Cost of Labor	Total Revenue	Labor Cost %
Monday	$1,400	$3,800	%
Tuesday	1,800	5,400	
Wednesday	1,900	4,900	
Thursday	2,000	6,800	
Friday	2,500	10,400	
Saturday	2,800	12,600	
Sunday	1,100	3,400	
Week total	$	$	%

(Answers: Monday 37%; Tuesday 33%; Wednesday 39%; Thursday 29%; Friday 24%; Saturday 22%; Sunday 32; Week total cost of labor, $13,500; Week total revenue, $47,300; Week total labor cost 29%)

THINK ABOUT IT . . .

Some managers like to schedule as few employees as necessary based on the estimated customer count. Others prefer to slightly overschedule to ensure that customer demand is met. Which method do you prefer? Why?

RESTAURANT TECHNOLOGY

Advanced technology has changed the options available for managers who wish to distribute employee schedules. These same managers may wish to quickly distribute changes to their original schedule made necessary by changes in volume forecasts, employee illnesses, or employee terminations.

Increasingly, managers create and distribute employee work schedules via email. Because emails can be retrieved via computer, tablet, or smartphone, employees can easily retrieve real-time updated schedules. This communication approach allows employers to make schedule changes as needed and get key information out to affected employees immediately.

5. **Where Possible, Use Part-Time Employees for Peak Volume Periods:** In most beverage operations there are peak periods of volume and slower periods. For example, in some operations the hours between 9:00 p.m. and 11:30 p.m. may be very busy. As a result, additional staff, particularly in beverage server positions, may be needed. Historically, managers have enlarged their staffs during these peak periods with part-time employees. This is a sound idea for most managers; however, it is important to recognize that the total number of hours worked per week is important for many employees seeking to meet their personal financial goals. Good managers are sensitive to this, and they hire only as many part-time employees as can be reasonably assured sufficient hours to make their part-time jobs desirable.

6. **Consider and Grant Employee Schedule Requests Whenever Possible:** Managers face a variety of challenges. One is balancing the personal needs of employees with the operation's scheduling needs. Employees typically request earned or vacation time off, preferred days off, and special days off for personal time. While the operation's scheduling needs must be primary in the manager's schedule planning, the wise manager accommodates legitimate employee work schedule requests whenever possible. This must be done in a fair way, and there should be a system by which each employee has a reasonable chance for requests to be granted.

7. **Be Fair When Scheduling Preferred Time Periods:** In many operations the workweek consists of some shifts that are less desirable than others. For example, Friday and Saturday nights might be busier than shifts earlier in the week. As a result, it is likely that beverage employees working busier shifts will receive greater tip income than those working at other times. Managers should ensure that, given the skill level of employees and the scheduling policies in effect, the most desirable work shifts are assigned in a fair and equitable manner.

8. **Communicate Scheduling Decisions in a Timely Manner:** For most employees, their weekly work schedule dictates a significant portion of their personal lives. Time for shopping, doing personal errands, visiting friends, and traveling are all dependent, in large measure, on their work schedules. It is important that managers complete and communicate work schedules in a timely manner.

MANAGING THE SCHEDULE

Once the manager has developed the schedule, it should be distributed quickly and accurately. In many operations, schedules are posted in one or more central areas of the property. In other cases, managers include the schedule along with paychecks. Increasingly, managers email schedules or post them in secured areas on the Internet. *Exhibit 7.13* is an example of an employee schedule created for an establishment with a large bar area.

Exhibit 7.13

EMPLOYEE SCHEDULE FOR THE BLACKWELL STEAK AND SEAFOOD HOUSE (2/23–3/1)

Server	1 Monday 2/23	2 Tuesday 2/24	3 Wednesday 2/25	4 Thursday 2/26	5 Friday 2/27	6 Saturday 2/28	7 Sunday 3/1
Sofianna	3–10 p.m.		3–10 p.m.	5–10 p.m.	3–10 p.m.	3–10 p.m.	
Vanessa	4–11 p.m.	4–11 p.m.	4–11 p.m.	5–10 p.m.			4–11 p.m.
Scarlett	6–11 p.m.	7–11 p.m.	7–11 p.m.	5–10 p.m.	7–11 p.m.		
Jackson	6–11 p.m.	7–11 p.m.	7–11 p.m.		7–11 p.m.	4–11 p.m.	
William		3–10 p.m.		3–10 p.m.	3–10 p.m.	5–11 p.m.	5–11 p.m.
Joseph			6–10 p.m.	6–10 p.m.	5–10 p.m.	5–10 p.m.	5–10 p.m.
Herodina					7–11 p.m.	7–11 p.m.	7–11 p.m.

Host							
Amanda	4–11 p.m.		4–11 p.m.		6–10 p.m.	6–10 p.m.	4–11 p.m.
Daniel		4–11 p.m.		4–11 p.m.	4–11 p.m.	4–11 p.m.	6–10 p.m.

Bus Person							
Damien	4–10 p.m.	4–10 p.m.	4–10 p.m.	4–10 p.m.	4–10 p.m.		
Nate	5–11 p.m.				5–11 p.m.	5–11 p.m.	5–11 p.m.
Jeremy		5–11 p.m.	5–11 p.m.	5–11 p.m.		6–10 p.m.	6–10 p.m.

Dish Washer							
Stephanie	3–11 p.m.	3–11 p.m.	3–11 p.m.	3–11 p.m.	3–11 p.m.		
Kellie	5 p.m.–12 a.m.	5 p.m.–12 a.m.	5 p.m.–12 a.m.			3–11 p.m.	3–11 p.m.
Lacey				5 p.m.–12 a.m.	5 p.m.–12 a.m.	5 p.m.–12 a.m.	5 p.m.–12 a.m.

Bartender							
Heather	4–10 p.m.	4–10 p.m.	4–10 p.m.		4–10 p.m.	4–10 p.m.	
Peggy		5–11 p.m.		5–11 p.m.	5–11 p.m.		4–10 p.m.
Alberto	5–11 p.m.		5–11 p.m.	4–10 p.m.		5–11 p.m.	5–11 p.m.

Cook							
Bethany	1–9 p.m.	1–9 p.m.			1–9 p.m.	1–9 p.m.	2–10 p.m.
Karla	2–10 p.m.			2–10 p.m.	2–10 p.m.	1–9 p.m.	2–10 p.m.
Frankie	4 p.m.–12 a.m.	4 p.m.–12 a.m.	4 p.m.–12 a.m.	4 p.m.–12 a.m.	4 p.m.–12 a.m.		
Scott	4 p.m.–12 a.m.	4 p.m.–12 a.m.	4 p.m.–12 a.m.	4 p.m.–12 a.m.	4 p.m.–12 a.m.		
Joshua		5–11 p.m.	1–9 p.m.		5–11 p.m.	5–11 p.m.	5–11 p.m.
Barry			5–11 p.m.	1–9 p.m.		5–11 p.m.	1–9 p.m.

Date Prepared: 2/16   **Prepared By:** Allisha

Manager's Memo

Experienced managers know it is sometimes easier to develop what seems to be a fair time-off policy than to apply it. Employees do have traumatic or important events that occur in their personal lives and, sometimes, these events are more important to them than their job.

As a result, employees may need to violate a time-off policy, but for very good reasons known only to themselves or their managers. In these cases, managers should seek fairness to all as they balance the needs of their operations with the needs of their employees.

Sometimes, alterations to the schedule must be made. These changes should be quickly communicated to the affected employees. Managers should monitor schedules carefully and adjust them as needed in response to specific situations that can arise:

- Significant increases or decreases in forecasted business volumes.
- Unanticipated voluntary and involuntary employee separations.
- Employee call-ins, the industry term used to describe employees who, on a day they are scheduled to work, notify managers that they will not be working. This is sometimes referred to as a "call-off."
- Employee no-shows, the industry term used to describe employees who, on a day they are scheduled to work, do not notify managers that they will not be working, and then do not report for their assigned shift.

Those responsible for planning and then managing schedules should be careful not to take advantage of their best employees. For example, if the operation is busiest on the weekends, the best employees should not be scheduled to work every weekend unless they prefer this schedule. In other words, they should not be "punished" for being good at their jobs. Neither should any single employee or group of employees be given any unfair preference in scheduling.

SUMMARY

1. **Summarize the importance of proper facility design, layout, décor, and atmosphere to successful beverage operations.**

   Facility layout and design is crucial to the success of a beverage operation. A facility's overall design directly affects the type of guests who will choose the operation as well as how well those guests are served. It is important that the facility be designed with guests' needs foremost in mind. The design and layout should also allow for efficiency in the operation of the facility. Adequate workspace and storage needs must be considered. Additionally, employee productivity is directly affected by an operation's design, as is the quality of guest services provided. Seating, flooring, and lighting are important considerations that add to an establishment's décor and atmosphere.

2. **Explain the three major types of drink production systems used in beverage operations.**

   The three major types of drink production systems are manual, assisted, and automated. In a manual system bartenders prepare each drink by hand using tools such as jiggers to control the amount of alcohol in each drink. In an assisted system, pour spouts that fit on bottle tops and dispense predetermined amounts of alcohol each time they are inverted control the amount of alcohol in each drink. In an automated system, either a part (metered system) or all (fully automated system) of drink production is performed by machine to control the amount of alcohol in each drink.

3. **Describe the kind of equipment and tools needed for beverage operations.**

Equipment and tool needs may vary by establishment, but most managers will purchase several key pieces of equipment, including refrigerators, ice machines, glass-washing sinks and equipment, and drink production equipment. Managers consider a variety of criteria for each purchase. Drink production equipment can be manual, assisted, or automated. In addition, managers use a variety of small bar tools and utensils in drink production.

4. **Identify the 10 major types of bar glassware and their usage.**

The 10 most popular glass types are the highball glass, used to serve a variety of highballs; the rocks glass, also known as an "old-fashioned" or "lowball" glass used to serve cocktails with whiskey as the base ingredient; wine glasses used for red, white, and dessert wines; shot glasses for many types of spirits that are served straight up or as shots; beer glasses in pilsner, mug, or stein forms; champagne flutes for serving carbonated wines; snifters for serving Cognac and brandy; martini glasses for martinis and other similar cocktails; Collins glasses for serving mixed drinks, water, soft drinks, and juice; and Irish coffee mugs, made of clear tempered glass and used for serving hot beverages.

5. **Discuss how to select, orient, and train bar staff.**

Managers cannot operate beverage facilities without the help of knowledgeable and skilled employees. Managers must choose employees who are motivated and open-minded, and who enjoy working with people. While previous beverage experience may be important, attitude, desire, honesty, and stability are more so. Once selected, employees must be oriented and trained. In many operations the vast majority of all employee turnover occurs within the first several months of employment. To minimize the chances of this happening, managers concentrate on selecting the right staff member, helping the new employee become oriented to the operation, and teaching all new employees what they must know to do a good job.

6. **Explain the two purposes of effective bar staff scheduling.**

The two primary purposes of effective bar employee scheduling are to ensure the correct number of employees to provide guests with prompt, efficient service and to ensure the amount spent on labor is in keeping with management's pre-established budget goals. How well managers schedule employees affects a variety of crucial operational areas, including the quality of products and services provided to guests and employees' level of job satisfaction. A manager's own performance is often judged by how well their employee schedules achieve the two primary purposes of effective scheduling.

APPLICATION EXERCISE

The sanitizing of manually washed glassware is essential to the safe service of alcoholic beverages. Write a one-page standard operating procedure (SOP) for manually sanitizing glassware that meets your local health code requirements. Health code requirements can be found online and in the National Restaurant Association's ServSafe Coursebook. In your SOP, address the following issues:

1. The importance of properly sanitizing glassware

2. The proper way to prepare a sink for use in sanitizing glassware

3. How to know the proper concentration of sanitizer to be used

4. How to know the proper water temperature for sanitizing glassware

5. How to know the amount of time the glassware should remain immersed in the sanitizing solution

6. When to change the sanitizing solution

REVIEW YOUR LEARNING

Select the best answer for each question.

1. **What is the industry standard height from the floor for chair seats?**
   A. 16 to 18 in.
   B. 18 to 20 in.
   C. 20 to 22 in.
   D. 22 to 24 in.

2. **Which flooring type is the nearly unanimous choice of building engineers and designers for use in restaurant and foodservice restrooms and drink preparation areas?**
   A. Wood
   B. Carpet
   C. Ceramic tile
   D. Poured concrete

3. **What is the recommend height for bartender's work counters?**
   A. 24 in.
   B. 34 in.
   C. 44 in.
   D. 54 in.

4. **When managers select an automated drink production system**
   A. bartenders free-pour drinks automatically when the drinks are ordered.
   B. bartenders automatically use metered pour spouts to help control beverage dispensing.
   C. all or nearly all of a drink's production is performed automatically by machine.
   D. all employees are automatically informed when they must work together to increase drink production.

5. **Which glass type would be best for serving Cognac?**
   A. Flute
   B. Rocks
   C. Snifter
   D. Highball

6. **Which glass type would be best for serving a carbonated white wine?**
   A. Highball
   B. Collins
   C. Pilsner
   D. Flute

7. **At what temperature should wash water used for manual glassware cleaning be maintained?**
   A. 100°F (38°C)
   B. 110°F (43°C)
   C. 140°F (60°C)
   D. 165°F (74°C)

8. **When should managers encourage job applicants to ask specific questions about the jobs for which they are applying?**
   A. When the applicant fills out the application form
   B. At the time the applicant is selected for the job
   C. During the preliminary job interview
   D. On the applicant's first day of work

9. **What is the primary role of a wine steward?**
   A. Choose the wine glasses used in an operation
   B. Create dining-room employee schedules
   C. Make house wines and wash wine glasses
   D. Answer guests' questions about wines

10. **What are the two primary purposes of effective employee schedules?**
   A. Optimize guest service and maximize the ability to meet financial objectives
   B. Optimize guest service and reduce the number of hours worked by employees
   C. Meet financial objectives and increase the number of hours worked by employees
   D. Provide adequate guest service and maximize the number of hours worked by employees

FIELD PROJECT

As a beverage manager, you will hire beverage servers. Develop a list of five pre-employment questions you think would be most important to ask your prospective servers before they are hired.

Before preparing your questions you will need to do one of the following:

- *If you are 21 years of age*, visit a local beverage operation that offers waitstaff service. Ask your server what questions he or she would ask if hiring prospective servers.

- *If you are under 21 years of age*, visit a local restaurant or foodservice operation and ask if the manager will share with you key questions he or she asks prospective employees who will be hired to serve food items. Use that information to help you formulate your own beverage server–related questions.

8

Purchasing, Receiving, Storing, and Issuing

INSIDE THIS CHAPTER

- Professional Beverage Management Practices
- Beverage Inventory Assessment
- Purchasing Beverages
- Receiving Beverages
- Storing Beverages
- Issuing Beverages

CHAPTER LEARNING OBJECTIVES

After completing this chapter, you should be able to:

- Explain the difference between physical and perpetual inventory systems.

- List the two key objectives of an effective beverage purchasing program.

- Explain the purpose of effective beverage receiving and storage practices.

- Describe the purpose of an issue requisition.

- Explain how to calculate an inventory turnover rate.

KEY TERMS

average inventory, p. 207

capital, p. 197

cash flow, p. 197

control state, p. 194

cost of goods sold (COGS), p. 207

first in, first out (FIFO), p. 193

inventory turnover rate, p. 207

last in, first out (LIFO), p. 193

lead time, p. 198

license state, p. 194

order point, p. 198

perpetual inventory, p. 192

physical inventory, p. 191

rotation, p. 201

safety level, p. 198

CASE STUDY

"How can you run out of my favorite gin?", demanded the customer.

Marco, the bartender at the Votive Restaurant, tried to explain. "We really don't sell much of that brand. It looks like we forgot to restock it and we ran out. I can get you another brand."

Marco knew this guest, who was usually friendly and tipped well. But not today.

"Young man," grumbled the customer, getting up to leave, "if I wanted bad gin, I would have gone somewhere else. I came here because you usually have the best bar selection in town."

"This happens way too often," thought Marco. "Last week we ran out of a premium vodka. And the week before that, we ran out of our most popular draft beer."

Both times some customers got mad, and it showed up in lower tips. Marco wondered why the manager couldn't keep the right products in the right amounts on hand at the right time.

1. How do you think the lack of popular beverages affects the customers and the employees of an establishment?

2. What will happen in an establishment if it continually runs out of the beverage brands or products its customers prefer?

PROFESSIONAL BEVERAGE MANAGEMENT PRACTICES

Managers face a variety of challenges in securing and maintaining the products needed to serve drinks. They must consider which beverage products to buy. They must also consider the amount of beverage products needed to meet customer demand. After placing orders, managers must ensure that beverage products are properly received. The receiving process entails matching the products ordered with those delivered. It also means ensuring that the products have arrived in good condition. After the product is delivered, managers must safely store products, issuing them from storage as needed.

The entire process of managing beverage products in storage involves several separate tasks:

- Inventory assessment
- Purchasing
- Receiving
- Storing
- Issuing

BEVERAGE INVENTORY ASSESSMENT

Managers seeking to understand beverage purchasing, receiving, storing, and issuing must begin by first understanding beverage inventory procedures. Most operations will have several inventories. These inventories include alcoholic beverages, glassware and dishes, food items, nonalcoholic beverages, and cleaning and office supplies. An operation's inventory accounts for both the amount and the value of the products held in the operation. These inventory levels are also known in the industry as the amount "on hand."

The quantity of products on hand impacts decisions about when and how much more to purchase. Beverage managers should assess their inventory levels on a regular basis. The frequency of inventory assessment will vary based on the size of an operation. It will also depend on the operation's volume level. All beverage operations will benefit from a regular assessment of inventory, because the inventory process allows managers to make several key decisions related to the following:

- Maintaining product quality
- Determining what to buy
- Determining how much to buy

- Determining when to buy
- Determining costs
- Reducing theft

Restaurant and foodservice professionals often use two basic systems as they manage the products held in inventory: physical inventory and perpetual inventory.

Physical Inventory

Managers typically assess the amount of products they have on hand by taking a physical inventory. In a physical inventory system, managers count and record the amounts of each product in storage. Typically, they also determine the value of the products held in inventory. In some operations, managers require that two people, working together, take the physical inventory. They do this to help ensure accuracy and to reduce control problems, such as theft.

Exhibit 8.1 shows a physical inventory form that identifies the information typically collected for each inventoried item.

Note that seven bottles of Old Hoshler whiskey were in the beverage storeroom when the manager took the inventory count. Each bottle has a purchase price of $17.50. This was known because the cost per bottle was recorded when the product was delivered. Therefore, the total inventory cost of this product is $122.50:

$$7 \quad \times \quad \$17.50 \quad = \quad \$122.50$$

Total bottles   Cost per bottle   Cost price

Exhibit 8.1
PHYSICAL INVENTORY FORM

Item	Purchase Unit	No. of Units in Inventory	Purchase Price	Total Cost
Old Hoshler Whiskey	Bottle (750 ml)	7	$ 17.50	$ 122.50
Joliet Gin	Bottle (1 L)	4	22.75	91.00
Total				$ 213.50

Exhibit 8.2

When managers complete a physical beverage inventory, they know the amounts and value of all products on hand. This information will be needed prior to determining what, if any, new products must be ordered.

Some nonbeverage items used in a bar may be inventoried regularly to determine when they must be reordered. Examples include fruit, juices, and dairy products (*Exhibit 8.2*). A physical beverage inventory should be taken as often as is needed to assist managers in their purchasing tasks. It is normally taken at least once per month to determine the dollar value of beverage products on hand. This inventory is typically taken on the last day of the month or accounting period and information from it is used to prepare the cost of beverages sold portion of the operation's profit and loss statement (see chapter 9).

Perpetual Inventory System

A **perpetual inventory** system is a *continuous* count of the number of items in inventory. The amounts of product in a perpetual inventory system are not continually determined by a physical count, but by keeping a running total of purchases, or deposits, and usage, or withdrawals. Actual physical inventory counts are, however, taken periodically to ensure the accuracy of the perpetual inventory system. The key advantage of a perpetual inventory system is that the managers always know the quantity of products that should be available.

Managers use a perpetual inventory system just like a checkbook. With a checkbook, as money is deposited in the bank, the balance on the account goes up. Likewise, as products are delivered to the storeroom, the perpetual inventory record increases. Conversely, as money is withdrawn from the bank, the balance in the bank decreases. The same is true for the inventory. As products are issued for use, the quantity of product in storage decreases. When their record keeping is good, managers know the quantity of beverage products that should be in inventory all the time.

Exhibit 8.3 shows the typical format for a perpetual inventory form.

Exhibit 8.3

PERPETUAL INVENTORY FORM

Item: Old Hatter Scotch (750 ml)

Date	No. of Purchase Units		Balance
	In	Out	
			7
9/15	—	5	2
9/16	12	4	10

Notice that there were 7 bottles of Old Hatter Scotch available at the beginning of the inventory period. On the first date of 9/15, 5 bottles were issued, so only 2 bottles should have remained in inventory.

7	–	5	=	2
Bottles beginning inventory		**Bottles issued on 9/15**		**Bottles remaining**

On the next day, 12 bottles were purchased and 4 bottles were issued. There was then a net balance of 10 bottles.

2	+	12	–	4	=	10
Bottles beginning inventory		**Bottles purchased on 9/16**		**Bottles issued on 9/16**		**Bottles remaining**

When using a perpetual inventory system, the manager should spot-check the number of bottles in the storage area periodically. This ensures that the number of bottles on hand actually equals the balance indicated on the perpetual inventory form.

Note that it is necessary to keep track of the quantity only, not the cost, of products available in a perpetual inventory system. That is because a perpetual inventory system cannot be relied on to provide actual inventory and cost data used to prepare an operation's financial summaries. Eliminating the need to collect unnecessary information helps reduce the time required for the perpetual inventory process. This makes the procedure more attractive to busy beverage managers.

Use of a perpetual inventory system allows the beverage manager to better control beverage products. When verified with a regularly scheduled physical count, the beverage manager knows whether there is a discrepancy between recorded information and physical count. As a result, he or she is able to take corrective action on a timely basis.

Calculating Inventory Values

Managers should also know the value of the products they have in inventory. Recall from *Exhibit 8.1* that a physical inventory form includes a space for recording the value of products in inventory. Establishing the value of an inventory is more complex than it first appears. That is so because there are four basic ways that values of beverage inventories can be assigned:

- **FIFO:** The first in, first out (FIFO) method assumes that products are withdrawn from inventory in the order in which they are received and entered into storage. Therefore, the products that remain in storage are judged to be the most recently purchased items. The value of inventory becomes the cost of the most recently purchased products.

- **LIFO:** The last in, first out (LIFO) method assumes the reverse of the FIFO method: The products most recently purchased are used first. The value of inventory is represented by the unit cost of items in inventory the longest.

RESTAURANT TECHNOLOGY

Computerized systems are available to help with inventory counts and to help establish inventory values. For example, optical scanners can be used to read bar codes on bottles of products held in storage. Managers simply use the scanner to "count" each bottle and the program uses current prices paid for products to calculate total inventory values.

Technology-driven approaches provide fast and accurate methods to determine inventory values. As a result, technology is increasingly used to replace the manual inventory systems currently deployed in many establishments.

- **Actual cost:** This method of inventory valuation considers the actual price paid for each product in inventory. The inventory value is the sum of the actual unit costs.
- **Weighted average:** This method of inventory valuation considers the quantity of each product purchased at different unit prices. The inventory value is priced on the basis of average prices paid for each product, and the average price is weighted according to the number of products purchased at each price.

Managers choose one valuation system when taking a physical inventory and should use that same system consistently. This is because there are tax implications and restrictions on changing inventory valuation methods. Normally, the beverage manager, working with another responsible employee, will determine the quantities and values of inventoried items. In small operations the manager-owner, working alone, may conduct inventory counts and assess product values.

PURCHASING BEVERAGES

Purchasing involves the series of activities that begin when beverage and supply needs are determined and ends after these items are sold or used by the operation. This definition is broader than the common idea that purchasing simply means buying. Professional beverage purchasers must determine what they need to buy, how much to buy, and when to buy it.

Buying alcoholic beverages is very different from buying food products. Unlike with food products, government regulations often affect sources of alcoholic beverage supply. States can be either **control states** or **license states**. In control, or monopoly, states the state is the sole supplier of liquor. All individuals and retail establishments must purchase liquor directly from state stores. In license states, the state frequently licenses wholesalers, distributors, and sometimes manufacturers to sell alcoholic beverages.

Liquor purchasing is considerably more complex in license states than in control states. Wholesalers do not carry all brands in all quantities. Distributors usually have exclusive sales authority over certain brands. Some manufacturers have their own distribution networks.

These distribution networks can differ greatly. One beverage manufacturer may have its own distribution system, while another may give exclusive territorial rights to certain distributors. Still other manufacturers sell only to wholesalers. The end result of these different distribution networks is that no single supplier carries a complete selection of all available brands and items. For this reason, purchasers must order from several supply sources.

The pricing of beverage products sold to restaurant and foodservice operations is also different from food products. Because of the strict control imposed by government alcoholic beverage agencies, there is often very little flexibility in their purchase price. Strict minimum wholesale price requirements severely limit discounting in some states. In addition to pricing control, many states impose strict payment and credit controls.

In some states the matter of credit is not negotiable. State regulations vary from allowing no credit to extending 30-day credit with requirements about the manner of repayment. Even in states where suppliers are allowed a choice within the state's requirements, many suppliers require prompt payment and short terms. The usual credit term is 30 days. Failure to pay on time in certain states is punishable by fines and even loss of a liquor license.

Regardless of the manner in which beverages are sold in a state, a manager's relationship with suppliers must be professional at all times. Buyers may be offered cash, attendance at holiday parties, or other gifts to increase a supplier's business. In all cases, managers must be ethical in their purchasing activities.

Managers responsible for purchasing must identify and obtain the products that allow their organization to meet the wants and needs of their customers. The process is never-ending because customers' preferences change, new product alternatives are continually introduced, and ensuring quality is always a concern. When purchasing beverage products, managers have two primary concerns: what and how much to buy.

What to Buy

The beverage products that managers should purchase depend on the type of operation and the characteristics of an operation's target customers. Managers need to consider who the guests are and what needs they have. They must also consider products that complement the facility's décor and theme. Managers assessing what to buy must make many decisions:

- What are the regulations that govern the types of beverages an operation may sell?
- What are the profit goals for the operation?
- What alcoholic beverages should be offered? Distilled spirits? Beer? Wine?
- If spirits are offered: How broad should the selection be? What is the desired quality of well liquors? What proof liquors should be sold?
- If beer is offered: Will draft beer be stocked? How many brands? What bottled and canned brands should be carried?
- If wines are sold: What should be the extent of the selection?
- Will house wines be offered? If so, what quality should they be? Will they be sold only by the glass? Carafe?

Popular beverages should always be available, and bars should be stocked to provide a reasonable assortment of drinks. Upscale tastes will mean a wider range of offerings; more modest demands will usually result in a less extensive number of offerings.

Managers must carefully consider if they can afford to stock seldom requested beverages. A product that sells infrequently represents money that could have been more profitably used elsewhere. However, many establishments do carry a certain number of slow-moving items that are stocked as a favor to regular guests. Depending on their operations, beverage buyers may make different purchasing decisions regarding beers, wines, and spirits.

BEER ON DRAFT, BOTTLED, OR CANNED

Keg beer typically has a higher profit margin than canned or bottled beer. However, keg beer is not pasteurized and is more fragile. There must be adequate refrigeration space for beer kegs, and beer lines and taps must be cleaned frequently. If keg beer is stocked, it must be in response to a demand that ensures sufficient turnover to warrant the investment in equipment and maintenance. Most bar and beverage facilities offer several of the most popular canned and bottled beers. In recent years, buyers have also had to consider a variety of imports and low-calorie and nonalcoholic products.

WINE

Wine selection can be more complicated than choosing other alcoholic beverages. A good wine list can be assembled from well-known, well-regarded products from both domestic and foreign wineries. Purchasing lesser-known wines requires in-depth knowledge of product offerings, what constitutes value, and a feeling for what customers want to buy. When an extensive wine list is desired, some operations hire wine list consultants to help make purchasing recommendations.

Exhibit 8.4

SPIRITS

The spirit selection that should be offered varies greatly by establishment. Some bar and beverage facilities are completely stocked and it is a source of pride to them that almost every drink request can be filled (*Exhibit 8.4*). Other establishments go to the other extreme and restrict guest choices by offering very limited spirit selections.

Managers select their well brands and call brands based on what they know about their guests' preferences and on market conditions. Quality and value relative to the price charged the guest are major factors in determining which well brands to buy. Other important factors include supplier prices, discounts, terms, services, product reputation, and product availability. The operation's concept and needs and brands used by competitors are additional concerns. Suggestions from knowledgeable spirit consultants including supplier representatives can be of great value.

Since most establishments cannot offer every possible call liquor, managers must make good brand decisions. Generally, they attempt to stock appropriate well brands and those call brands most frequently requested by their guests. Also, they monitor inventory levels carefully so that brands that have lost popularity can be used up and deleted from the purchasing list.

How Much to Buy

Managers must be concerned about buying too much or too little as they make beverage purchasing decisions. Most operations serve the same types of products on a regular basis, so specific product needs do not change rapidly. However, the quantity of beverages needed can change because of different estimates of the number of customers to be served.

Managers typically use different procedures to determine purchase quantities for different products. Highly perishable items such as dairy products used in mixes and fruit or vegetables used for garnishes, for example, are most often purchased in quantities that will be used over a several-day period. Draft beer may be purchased to be used in a week or less. Spirits can be purchased for several months' usage. Some wines may be purchased with the intent that they will be held for many years.

Problems can occur when beverage products are not purchased in the right amounts. For example, problems can arise when an excessive quantity is purchased:

- The purchase ties up **capital**, or the amount of the owner's money invested in the business, that could be used for other purposes.
- The purchase impacts **cash flow**, or the amount of money needed to pay bills when due.
- More space must be available to store products.
- There is an increased risk of product theft, damage, or destruction.
- Quality deterioration may occur with perishable products.
- Handling costs increase. For example, additional time is required to receive and store products and conduct inventory counts.

Inadequate purchase quantities can also create serious problems caused by the inability to meet guests' drink requests and those guests' resulting disappointments. The actual amount of products needed is the primary

THINK ABOUT IT . . .

Vendors are usually experts in the products they provide, and their assistance can provide real value to managers. What types of information might vendors provide to managers to help them make beverage purchasing decisions?

consideration when deciding how much to buy, but there are other important considerations:

- **Minimum orders:** Some vendors may specify a minimum dollar value of products for delivery. Most wine vendors, for example, would not deliver only one bottle of wine.

- **Anticipated increases or decreases in product prices:** When product prices are increasing, products may be purchased in larger-than-normal quantities. When prices are decreasing, buyers may purchase in smaller quantities to take advantage of lower prices when future purchases are made.

- **Promotions:** Larger quantities may be purchased when, for example, vendors or manufacturers offer promotional discounts to introduce new products or to quickly sell products they wish to stop offering in the future.

- **The amount of time between deliveries:** When the time between deliveries is longer, purchase amounts must be larger. When the time between deliveries is shorter, purchase amounts can be smaller.

Determining what to buy is essential, but knowing exactly how much to buy is just as critical. The amount of product purchased should be based on a carefully planned system of ordering. This way the operation neither ties up excessive amounts of cash in inventory, nor fails to have products and supplies available to meet guest demand.

Experienced beverage managers review purchase, inventory, and sales records to estimate the amount of products that will be used within a specified time period. Proper inventory levels can then be set for each type of beer, wine, or spirit based on these records.

Also, managers should consider lead time, expressed in purchase units, to allow for the amount of product used between the time of ordering and delivery. The manager must also establish a safety level, a minimum inventory level below which inventory should not fall to allow for greater than anticipated sales or longer than anticipated delivery times. The order point or minimum inventory level is the estimated number of units used between the order and delivery dates, or lead time, plus the number of units required to maintain the safety level.

The actual number of units to order at the order point is based on estimated future usage. For example, if deliveries are weekly, the number of units to order is the number to be used in the coming week plus any units required to bring the inventory to its desired safety level. See chapter 9 to learn about forecasting beverage usage.

To illustrate, assume an operation needs five cases of house wine in inventory at all times to avoid running out. Five cases is the safety level. The operation uses two cases between the time an order is placed and the time it is received. With these facts known, managers can calculate the order point.

5 cases   **+**   **2 cases**   **=**   **7 cases**

Safety level   **Lead time**   **Order point**

In this example, house wine should be ordered when inventory levels are at seven cases.

When determining how much to buy, several factors can impact a manager's decision. He or she must consider the operation's needs in these situations:

- When vendors are not dependable

- When the operation is in a remote location and delivery delays are common

- When market situations cause unpredictable conditions that affect product availability, and the potential for back-orders of some items

RECEIVING BEVERAGES

It does little good to make smart purchasing decisions unless there is follow-through at the time of product receiving. It is necessary to ensure that products that are ordered are, in fact, received. Most suppliers are ethical, but they are all human. Human error can cause extensive and costly loses to beverage operations that do not consistently and effectively check to ensure that there are no problems at the time beverages are delivered. To properly prepare for receiving beverages, managers take specific actions:

- Provide adequate space for receiving.

- Provide needed receiving equipment such as carts and dollies.

- Establish allowable delivery periods and communicate these to vendors.

- Identify and train receiving personnel.

- Develop a records system for recording the acceptance of delivered products.

The list of issues that can occur when products are received is seemingly endless. It is important for the beverage manager to first design a receiving system that incorporates basic control principles, and second to consistently ensure that these procedures are practiced.

Exhibit 8.5 shows the key aspects of an effective receiving system.

Exhibit 8.5
OVERVIEW OF THE RECEIVING PROCESS

Check Against Purchase Orders

Check Against Delivery Invoices

Accept Products

Move to Storage Area(s)

Complete Receiving Tasks and Records

Checking Against Purchase Orders

To properly oversee beverage product deliveries the beverage manager, or those who are responsible for product receiving, must know the specifics of each order. This becomes easier when written purchase orders, not verbal phone orders, are in use. Written purchase orders can then be checked to ensure that the products being received meet the specifics of the purchase order.

A copy of the purchase order or purchase record that was agreed on at the time of purchasing should be available in the receiving area. Personnel with receiving responsibilities will then know what to expect, including the following:

- Which supplier will be delivering?
- What day is the delivery expected?
- What products are coming in?
- In what volume or quantity will they arrive?
- What is the size of the purchase unit?
- What is the agreed-on price?
- What quality is expected?

By checking the quantity and quality of products delivered against purchase orders, receiving personnel can ensure that they do not accept items that were not ordered or are in damaged condition. They also must not sign delivery invoices if only partial or no delivery of expected items occurs. Finally, they must accept only items of proper brand and quality.

Checking Against Delivery Invoices

The delivery invoice provided by the vendor becomes important after products have been checked against written purchase orders (*Exhibit 8.6*). The delivery invoice will be the basis on which payment claims from the supplier will be made. It is critical that all items on the delivery invoice are received in the correct quantity and at the correct prices. If there are no problems with the delivery invoice, it can be signed. One copy must be routed by the receiver to the appropriate beverage or other manager for later verification with other information at times of payment processing. If there are rejections of products or variations between ordered and delivered items that should result in corrections or alternations to the invoice, a written record of that fact must be made. For example, if items on the invoice are not delivered in the correct quantity or quality, a note should be included on the invoice.

Exhibit 8.6

Accepting Products

After the previous steps have been carefully and correctly completed, the delivery invoice should be signed to note acceptance of the product. Typically, beverage products become the property of the beverage operation at this point.

Sometimes delivery personnel exert pressure on receiving staff to speed up the receiving process. It does take time to count and complete proper product inspection. However, receiving staff must invest the time necessary to do their jobs well. It is for this reason that managers often state that no deliveries are to be made during specified time periods. If, for example, all employees are busy during lunch, they will not have time to correctly complete the receiving process and so no deliveries should be accepted then.

THINK ABOUT IT . . .

Sometimes delivery persons want to rush the receiving staff and make adjustment later, if needed. What would your policy be if delivery personnel tried to rush your receiving staff?

Moving to Storage Area(s)

After completing the receiving process, staff should move products to the proper storage area(s). At this stage, managers should enforce several important storage principles:

- Movement of product to inventory areas should be undertaken by beverage employees, not by delivery personnel. There is an increased chance of theft when nonbeverage delivery staff members are allowed into beverage storage areas containing large quantities of expensive and theft-prone products.

- Prompt removal to storage areas reduces the chance for theft when products are left in unprotected delivery areas.

- Spoilage becomes less of an issue when products are moved from delivery areas to storage areas maintained at the correct storage temperatures.

Completing Receiving Tasks and Records

Large operations may use a special receiving report to provide a record of products received. They may also create a record of product transfers from receiving to storage areas if different staff members perform these tasks.

When products are placed in storage, many managers require staff to mark the date of delivery on the incoming products. They also must require that products be rotated. Rotation is the process used to ensure the use of the oldest products first by placing all incoming products behind or under those items already in inventory.

If a perpetual inventory system is in use, these records are updated at the time products are placed in storage. Finally, receiving records can, with invoices attached, be used as an authorizing source for payment of the products that have been received. These records, including the signed delivery invoice, should be submitted to the appropriate person for payment immediately or on at least a daily basis.

Managers should minimize opportunities for employee and supplier theft when receiving and placing products into storage. The complete receiving system should be designed for security. To help guard against theft, experienced managers incorporate several key strategies into the receiving process:

- The person responsible for purchasing should not also do the receiving, unless the owner or manager performs both of those duties.

- Selected staff members should be trained to receive and should always perform this task.

- Product delivery should be made at nonbusy times so that receiving personnel have the opportunity to complete all required tasks.

- Deliveries should be made to a specified area of the beverage operation.

- Products should be immediately moved to storage after the receiving process is complete.

- Nonbeverage personnel should not be allowed in back-of-house areas including storage spaces.

- The outside door to storage areas should be kept locked when not in use.

STORING BEVERAGES

After purchasing and receiving beverage products, managers most often must store products until the products are issued to the bar area. Just as purchasing involves more than calling in an order and receiving requires more than putting things in the storeroom, so must the beverage manager be concerned about proper storage and issuing practices.

A beverage operation's financial goals are directly affected by storage practices. If products are stored correctly, all of the products that are purchased will be used to generate revenue. However, if products are not properly stored they can be broken, damaged, or stolen. Any of those outcomes will result in increased costs. When products are purchased and paid for but then not used, more products will have to be purchased at additional cost to generate the same amount of revenue.

Product quality and cost concerns must be addressed when managers plan storage procedures. If this is not done, all of the efforts to maintain quality and cost standards when products were purchased and received will have been wasted. Fortunately, the best storage procedures do not require excessive time or costs to implement and maintain.

Most beverage products are relatively nonperishable. Unlike perishable food products such as dairy items and produce, most properly stored beverages can be held for long periods of time without this concern. Managers must, however, implement procedures to keep products secure, to maintain quality, and to provide information necessary for accounting systems. Each of these concerns is addressed separately.

THINK ABOUT IT . . .

In some operations, storage areas are kept unlocked during the workday when employees are present and locked when the operation is closed. Does this practice make sense to you? Why or why not?

Keeping Inventory Secure

Security at the time of beverage storage requires managers to address several important questions:

- How much product should be available?
- How much product is available?
- What procedures are needed to keep unauthorized personnel from gaining access to storage areas?

Managers use a variety of procedures to help reduce the possibility of product theft while it is in storage:

- Access to storage areas should be limited to the fewest possible number of staff members needing this access.
- Keep storage areas locked when possible. In some operations, beverage storage areas are always locked except during times when products are issued (*Exhibit 8.7*).
- Use separate and locked refrigerated storage areas for beverage products. If possible, separate wines that need to be chilled, for example, from other refrigerated products. In some cases, one compartment of a reach-in refrigerator can be used for this purpose. Or alternatively, a lockable shelving unit within a walk-in refrigerator can be used.
- Practice effective inventory control procedures. It is critical that the manager know the amount of each product that is—and should be— available in storage areas.
- If beverage products must be issued during the shift, a manager or supervisor should be the one to do this, if possible. Not only does this practice encourage effective issuing, but it also helps maintain control over door keys and access to storage areas.
- Storage areas must be effectively designed. Doors and walls must extend to the ceiling; windows are unnecessary. Storage area alarm systems should be considered.
- Use other control practices, if needed. Some operations, for example, keep the most expensive items locked in areas within lockable storage areas. Closed-circuit television systems and motion detectors are also used in some operations.

Retaining Product Quality

Beverage products should remain in storage areas for the shortest reasonable amount of time possible. However, it is still necessary to practice effective storage strategies to retain product quality during storage. These

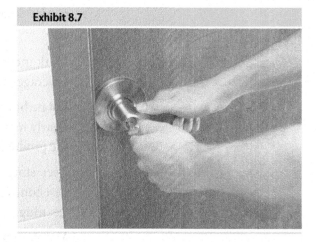

Exhibit 8.7

KEEPING IT SAFE

Storeroom safety procedures protect products and employees. There are several keys to keeping storage areas safe:

- Provide employees with wheeled carts or dollies, if possible, to minimize injury due to lifting and carrying heavy loads.
- Keep storage areas neat and free of clutter and trip hazards.
- Place all items in an orderly fashion on shelving with heavier items placed near the bottom and lighter items on top.
- Wipe up any spills immediately. Place warning signs near any wet floor areas.
- Repair damaged flooring areas immediately.
- Provide adequate lighting for all storage area tasks.
- Train employees to walk carefully when carrying items into or out of storage areas.

are practices that help maintain product quality when beverages are in storage:

- Mark incoming products. Put the date of delivery on cases or bottles of beverage products.

- Rotate beverage products. With the date of entry into storage areas clearly marked on the bottle or case, it becomes possible to ensure that the products in inventory the longest are issued first.

- Keep storage areas clean. Routine cleaning is important; so are regular pest control efforts. Maintain effective lighting so that the results of cleaning programs can be easily inspected.

- Maintain product-specific storage temperatures for beers, wines, and spirits.

BEER STORAGE

Beer has the shortest storage life of any alcoholic beverage. Canned and bottled beer may generally be stored at temperatures between 40°F and 70°F (4.5°C and 21°C). However, all but the strongest beers should not be stored for longer than three to four months. Beers with ABVs above 8 percent can be stored and aged for longer time periods. Most beers kept in storage too long will lose their flavor and their aroma. In addition, unpasteurized beer should be refrigerated at all times and all beer should be kept out of direct sunlight.

Beer bottles should be stored upright to avoid leakage. Beer cans packaged in cases may be stacked. All bottles and cans should be stored in a way that minimizes the chance for dirt and dust to come into contact with the beer containers. Keg beers should be stored in a manner that allows for easy keg movement and for ease in tapping. Beer storage areas should also allow for easy product rotation and ease of taking inventory.

WINE STORAGE

The most important factor in wine storage is even temperature. Temperature fluctuation in wine storage areas should be avoided. There is no single best temperature for storing wines. Rather there are a range of acceptable temperatures that vary based on the length of time the wine is expected to be held in storage.

Many wine experts agree that wines are best served at cellar temperature, generally considered to be between 65°F and 70°F (18°C and 21°C). The best temperatures for long-term storage of five or more years for red wines is lower, usually between 55°F and 60°F (13°C and 16°C).

For shorter-term red wine storage of less than five years, and for storing white wines, temperatures up to 70°F (21°C) are acceptable. It is not advisable to store any wine in areas where temperatures exceed this level. White wines may be stored under refrigeration temperatures of approximately 41°F (5°C) for several months with no loss of quality.

In addition to proper temperature control, managers must ensure humidity control in wine storage areas. If the humidity level is too high, meaning the air is too damp, molds may grow and damage labels, foil wrappings, and corks. If humidity levels are too low, corks may dry out and cause leakage. Humidity levels between 50 and 70 percent are best for most wines. Air-conditioned storage areas generally can provide proper temperature and humidity control.

Exhibit 8.8

Sunlight is the enemy of proper wine storage. While most wines are stored in colored glass to minimize the effects of light (*Exhibit 8.8*), care must still be taken to keep wines out of direct sunlight. Bottles of still and sparkling wines should be stored on their sides so that wine is always in full contact with the bottle's cork. This contact with the wine keeps the cork moist and expanded, and prevents it from drying out and causing wine spoilage.

Fortified wines and any spirits closed with cork should be stored upright as the higher alcohol content of these products can, over time, damage the corks and cause leakage. Wines and spirits closed with plastic or metal stoppers or screw caps may also be stored upright. Wine products in cases should be stored off the floor to permit air circulation and prevent mold.

SPIRITS STORAGE

In general, spirits may be stored for several years at common dry storage temperatures between 50°F and 70°F (10°C and 21°C). Bottles should be stored upright with their labels facing out for ease of taking inventory. Spirits storage areas should be kept clean and secure.

OTHER PRODUCT STORAGE

In addition to dry storage areas for bar supplies such as extra glassware, carbonated beverages, napkins, straws and the like, bars most often will require additional refrigerator and freezer storage areas. Storage for refrigerated items must include adequate space for fruit and vegetables for garnishes, mixers, and dairy products such as milk and cream. Freezer storage is needed for ice creams and sherbets as well as some concentrated drink mixes.

ISSUING BEVERAGES

Issuing is the process of moving products from storage rooms to drink production and service areas. The correct quantity of products must be issued to meet estimated guest demand. This process must be carefully controlled to minimize product misuse and so managers can match issues of items with the amount of revenues they should produce.

Importance of Effective Issuing

Should there be some relationship between the quantity of drinks sold by the operation and the quantity of products removed from storage areas? Of course there should be, and effective issuing practices best ensure that this happens.

Some managers allow any employee who needs something from storage to retrieve what is needed at any time. When this tactic is used, every employee is really in charge of issuing. For example, bartenders obtain spirit products, dining-room servers may retrieve wines, and other employees may be permitted to enter storage areas to obtain additional glassware or other items. In each of these cases, the security of products is put at risk.

Beverage managers must do all that is practical to control beverage products at the time of issue. Beverage costs are increased if there is a lack of control in this process. Given the importance of security, it is difficult to justify the open-door policies that exist in some operations.

Beverage operations come in all sizes. Large operations may have a full-time receiving and issuing staff member whose duties involve only these two tasks. The vast majority of beverage operations, however, do not employ staff members with only receiving or storing duties. As a result, control at time of product issue in these organizations can become a challenge.

In most cases, beverages should be issued from product storage areas on a regular schedule. For example, bars can be stocked at the beginning of the day, end of the day, or between busy shifts. If regularly scheduled stocking of bars takes place, the number of emergency issues during busy bar shifts should be minimized.

Managers must ensure that their employees use basic procedures for issuing beverage products:

- Bottles should be issued on a bottle-for-bottle basis to reestablish production area par levels.

- The bartender readying the area for stocking can complete an issue requisition, but the beverage manager should then sign it prior to any product issuing. *Exhibit 8.9* shows a sample beverage issue requisition. Note that the bartender would fill out the first three columns of the

Manager's Memo

Although *cost of goods sold (COGS)* is the industry term for the amount of product used to generate revenue, a more accurate term might be *cost of goods gone (COGG)*! That is because there are a variety of situations in which goods (beverages) are gone, but not sold:

- When beverages are stolen from inventory, they are gone, but not sold!

- When beverage bottles are broken in storage the products they contained are gone, but not sold!

- When beverages are allowed to spoil or deteriorate in quality and must be discarded they are gone, but not sold!

- When beverages are deceitfully consumed by employees, they are gone, but not sold!

In all of these cases the products were purchased and thus must be added to the operation's costs, but they did not generate sales. For that reason all beverage products must be carefully handled, stored, and secured.

form. Either the storage area personnel or the manager fills out the remaining two columns. Once completed, beverage issue requisitions can be used for calculating daily beverage costs and for completing perpetual inventory records.

Exhibit 8.9

SAMPLE BEVERAGE ISSUE REQUISITION

Shift: _____ Tuesday p.m. _____ Date: _____ 5/7 _____

Beverage outlet: _____ Tiki Bar _____ Completed by: _____ S. Larson _____

Product	Number of Bottles	Bottle Size	Bottle Cost	Total Cost
Murphy's Dark Rum	2	750 ml	$12.50	$25.00
Herron Hill Vodka	1	1 L	10.75	10.75
Total	3			$35.75

Issued by: _____ K. Gray _____ Authorized by: _____ J. Belloit _____

Received by: _____ S. Larson _____

Inventory Turnover Rate

One way to better manage the size of a beverage inventory is to calculate the **inventory turnover rate**: the number of times each accounting period, typically a month, that the quantity of beverages in inventory must be purchased to generate the beverage revenue for that time period.

Inventory turnover rates measure the frequency with which beverages are ordered and sold. The formula for the inventory turnover rate is:

$$\text{Cost of goods sold (COGS)} \div \text{Average amount in inventory} = \text{Inventory turnover rate}$$

The **cost of goods sold (COGS)** is the cost to purchase the beverage products that generated beverage revenue within a specific time period. The calculations required to determine COGS are addressed in detail in chapter 9. **Average inventory** is the value, or amount, of products in inventory at the beginning of the period plus the amount of inventory at the end of the period, divided by two. Recall from the start of the chapter that there are multiple methods for determining inventory value.

THINK ABOUT IT . . .

How important do you think taking inventory is from the view of most employees who may be asked to assist in the task? If you were a manager, would you tell employees why the counting of inventory is so important? Why or why not?

To illustrate how to calculate an inventory turnover rate, assume a manager conducts a physical inventory of the beverage products in all storage areas on the first day of every month using the physical inventory system procedures addressed earlier in this chapter. This manager uses the LIFO valuation system. The manager determines the following from counts taken on July 1 and August 1. Remember that the beginning inventory of one month is also the ending inventory of the previous month, so the August 1 inventory is both the end of month inventory for July and the beginning of the month inventory for August:

Cost of beverage inventory on July 1 (beginning of July) = $39,500

Cost of beverage inventory on August 1 (end of July) = $37,500

Beverage cost (COGS) for the month = $88,000*

In this example, the beverage inventory turnover rate is calculated as follows:

$88,000	÷	([**$39,500**	+	**$37,500**]	÷	2)	=	**2.3 (rounded)**
Beverage		**Beginning**		**Ending**				**Inventory**
Cost (COGS)		**Inventory**		**Inventory**				**Turnover Rate**

If the inventory turns over approximately 2.3 times per month, the beverage products in inventory will last about 13 days (30 days in an average month ÷ 2.3 inventory turns = 13 days).

It is difficult to state what the "ideal" beverage inventory turnover rate should be. In those operations that hold a large number of slow selling but expensive wines in inventory, the monthly inventory turnover rates may be quite low, as little as 2 to 4 times per month. In those operations without extensive wine or spirits holdings, inventory turnover rates of 10 or more are common. It is important to note that the inventory turnover rate for a specific month may not, by itself, be especially helpful to the manager. Noting changes in inventory turnover rates from one time period to another, however, can be very helpful.

The ideal inventory turnover rates will vary by operation. Managers need to determine the ideal cost needed to ensure that all inventory is always available. These decisions are based on concerns about the challenges faced if too little or too much inventory is on hand at all times.

Regardless of the target established for the operation, the managers should note the changes between inventory turnover rates each time the inventory turnover rate is calculated. Managers need to ask why the inventory turnover rate is increasing or decreasing. What are the implications? What is the desired trend that the inventory turnover rate should take? The answers to these and related questions can help better control the beverage inventory and the costs of managing it.

To increase the usefulness of the calculation, some beverage managers calculate a separate inventory turnover rate for beers, wines, and spirits. Others combine all beverages into a single calculation.

*The calculation of the formula for determining COGS is addressed in detail in chapter 9.

OPEN FOR BUSINESS

MANAGER'S MATH

Roberta is the manager of the Logjam Steakhouse. She has calculated the following information about her operation:

Cost of beverage inventory at beginning of month: $18,250

Cost of beverage inventory at end of month: $17,550

Beverage COGS for the month: $89,500

What is her beverage inventory turnover rate for the month?

(Answer: 5)

SUMMARY

1. **Explain the difference between physical and perpetual inventory systems.**

   In a physical inventory system, managers count the number and record the amounts of each product in inventory. Typically, they also determine the monetary value of the products at the same time. The key advantage of a physical inventory system is its accuracy.

   A perpetual inventory system is a continuous count of the number of items in inventory. Managers determine the perpetual inventory by first establishing the actual amount of product on hand. Then they add to that number all purchased units and subtract all issued units. The key advantage of a perpetual inventory system is that the managers always know the quantity of product that should be available in inventory.

2. **List the two key objectives of an effective beverage purchasing program.**

   When purchasing beverage products, managers have two primary concerns: what to buy and how much to buy. Buying the wrong products can damage the operation's ability to properly serve its target market. Buying too much ties up capital, impacts cash flow, and requires additional storage space. It also increases the risk of theft and quality deterioration. Buying too little can create product outages that impact drink production and lead to disappointed customers.

3. **Explain the purpose of effective beverage receiving and storage practices.**

   The purpose of proper receiving practices is to ensure products ordered are delivered in the amount and quality indicated on the purchase order. In addition, the price of products delivered is verified at the time they are received and any variations in price are noted in writing. The purpose of proper storage is to ensure the security and quality of products stored until they are needed. Storage areas should always must be maintained at the proper temperature to ensure product quality, and locked to ensure product security.

4. **Describe the purpose of an issue requisition.**

   Effective issuing helps ensure that products removed from storage generate the expected amount of revenue. Issue requisitions provide a written record of the products that have been moved from storage areas to drink production or service areas. Bartenders complete issue requisitions as they ready their areas for stocking. Managers approve requisitions prior to any product issuing. The requisition document can be used to calculate daily beverage costs. Issue requisitions can also serve as the source of information used in updating perpetual inventory records.

5. **Explain how to calculate an inventory turnover rate.**

Inventory turnover rates measure the frequency with which beverages are ordered and sold. The formula for the inventory turnover rate is Cost of goods sold ÷ Average amount in inventory. The cost of goods sold (COGS) in the formula is the cost to purchase the beverage products that generated beverage revenue. The average inventory in the formula is the monetary value, or amount, of all products in inventory at the beginning of the period plus the amount of inventory at the end of the period, divided by two. Effective managers routinely calculate and monitor changes in their inventory turnover rates.

APPLICATION EXERCISE

Managers use beverage issue requisitions to help monitor inventory levels and to calculate costs. Complete the inventory issue requisition that has been submitted by a bartender to help determine the value of products to be issued from inventory in response to this request from the bartender at the Surfer Pool Bar.

Shift: _____ P.M. _____   **Date:** _____ 5/11 _____

Beverage outlet: _____ Surfer Pool Bar _____   **Completed by:** _____ Peggy Richards _____

Product	Number of Bottles	Bottle Size	Bottle Cost	Total Cost
Peach Schnapps	4	1 L	$ 9.45	
Murphy's Rum	3	750 ml	11.15	
Joliet Gin	1	750 ml	19.85	
McClay's Scotch	1	750 ml	12.95	
Three Onions Vodka	2	1 L	23.15	

Issued by: _____   **Authorized by:** _____

Received by: _____

What is the total dollar value of beverage products requested by this requisition?

REVIEW YOUR LEARNING

Select the best answer for each question.

1. The amount of money needed to pay bills when they are due is called
   A. capital.
   B. revenue.
   C. cash flow.
   D. net income.

2. When beverage products are delivered, the vendor's delivery invoice should be compared with the
   A. credit memo.
   B. purchase order.
   C. purchase specification.
   D. purchase requisition.

3. Which document transfers product ownership from the vendor to the property?
   A. Credit memo
   B. Purchase order
   C. Delivery invoice
   D. Purchase requisition

4. What is the formula that managers use to determine the order point of an inventory item?
   A. Lead time + Usage rate
   B. Lead time + Safety level
   C. Safety level + Usage rate
   D. Safety level + Vendor minimum

5. Which inventory value system is in use when products are valued at the cost of the most recently received products?
   A. LIFO
   B. FIFO
   C. FILO
   D. FFFO

6. What is the recommended range for humidity levels in wine storage areas?
   A. 0 to 20%
   B. 30 to 50%
   C. 50 to 70%
   D. 70 to 90%

7. What is the formula used to calculate average inventory?
   A. Purchases + Beginning inventory = Average inventory
   B. (Beginning inventory + Ending inventory) × 2 = Average inventory
   C. (Beginning inventory + Ending inventory) ÷ 2 = Average inventory
   D. (Beginning inventory + Purchases) − Ending inventory = Average inventory

8. A beverage operation's inventory turnover rate is 3. Approximately how many days will the beverage products in inventory last?
   A. 6
   B. 8
   C. 10
   D. 12

9. What document authorizes an employee to remove products from storage?
   A. Issue requisition
   B. Storage removal claim
   C. Deduction authorization request
   D. Inventory adjustment record

10. Assume a beginning inventory of $24,000 and ending inventory of $26,000. Assume Beverage Cost (COGS) of $100,000 for the same period. What was the inventory turnover rate for the period?
    A. 2
    B. 3
    C. 4
    D. 5

9

Controlling Bar Costs

INSIDE THIS CHAPTER

- Forecasting Beverage Usage
- Calculating Beverage Cost of Goods Sold (COGS)
- Controlling Preproduction Beverage Product Costs
- Controlling Beverage Production and Revenue Loss

CHAPTER LEARNING OBJECTIVES

After completing this chapter, you should be able to:

- Explain how managers forecast beverage sales.

- Demonstrate the calculation of beverage cost of goods sold (COGS).

- State the formula for a beverage cost percentage, and explain its use.

- Summarize procedures managers use to control preproduction beverage product costs.

- Identify ways to prevent the theft of beverage products and revenue.

KEY TERMS

CASE STUDY

"What's wrong, Elias? You look upset," said Marin, one of the head bartenders at the Knight's Cap bar.

"It just doesn't make any sense," replied Elias, the bar manager.

"What doesn't make sense?" asked Marin.

"Well, I just got our financial statements for last month. Sales were way up compared to last year," said Elias.

"That makes sense to me," said Marin. "I've been working here for five years and I've never seen it so busy. Our Fridays and Saturdays are crazy busy. So what's wrong with doing so much better than last year?"

"That's just the problem," said Elias. "We aren't doing better. Our sales are way up, but not our profits. We actually made less money last month than we did in the same month a year ago."

1. What could cause an operation to have significantly increased sales but decreased profit levels?

2. Assume you own the Knight's Cap bar. What would you want Elias to do to identify this problem and correct it?

FORECASTING BEVERAGE USAGE

To control beverage costs and meet profit goals, managers must perform several important tasks. They must be able to forecast beverage sales accurately. Managers must develop standardized drink recipes and ensure that the staff consistently uses these recipes. Finally, managers must supervise beverage production and service to correct problems as necessary.

When managers can anticipate the expected number of guests, they can purchase the appropriate quantities of beverage products. They can also staff their operations properly. When all bartenders know the **standardized recipes**, managers can ensure the recipes are used each time a drink is prepared. Standardized recipes are instructions for preparing a food or beverage item that includes the type and amount of ingredients and how they are combined, as well as information about garnishing and serving. By carefully supervising drink production and service, managers can more easily correct problems as they occur.

Forecasting Guest Counts

To begin the bar cost control process, managers create a **sales forecast**. The sales forecast is an estimate of what an operation will sell in a specific future time period. A sales forecast can estimate the anticipated revenue in the time period. It can also estimate the specific products that will be sold. Some sales forecasts estimate both.

Making accurate sales forecasts is one of a manager's most critical skills. The importance of an accurate sales forecast to a manager can be illustrated by answering the key question, "How many guests will I serve next week, and what will they buy?" When a manager knows the answer to this question, he or she can stock the right products, in the right quantities, to meet the guests' needs.

Forecasting beverage sales is generally more difficult than forecasting food sales. In most operations, the number of different food items on the menu is fairly limited. As a result, after estimating the number of guests to be served, managers can easily estimate what guests will buy. The number of different drinks served in a beverage operation, however, can be extremely large. And if forecasts of specific product sales are not done properly, product shortages can occur, resulting in reduced guest satisfaction.

Fortunately, with practice managers can forecast beverage sales and usage very accurately. The more managers know about their guests' behavior, the better they are able to estimate future sales. Managers cannot, of course, predict their *exact* business volumes for a future period. They can, however, do the next best thing: realistically predict the future. To prepare an accurate forecast, managers look to the past, the present, and the future.

THE PAST

The past is one of the best indicators of the future. The further back managers can track historical customer counts, the better a manager's forecasts will be. Historical **customer counts** are the number of guests served in a specific time period. A manager with historical data for the past 50 weeks is more likely to make a better forecast than one with only 2 weeks of data. Today's POS (point-of-sales) systems can provide managers with historical data that include the following:

- Prior day's customer count
- Average achieved customer counts for any number of prior *same* days (for example, Sundays, Fridays, or Tuesdays)
- Prior week's customer count
- Average customer count for the prior two weeks or month
- Actual customer count for the same day for one or more prior years
- Average daily customer count in the same month for one or more prior years

THE PRESENT

Historical data should always be considered in conjunction with the most recent data available. To illustrate, assume a manager knows that, on an annual average, customer counts have increased 5 percent each month from the same period last year. However, in the last two months the increase has been closer to zero. This may mean that the increase trend has slowed or stopped completely. The manager would need to take this change into account when making his or her forecast. Good managers always modify historical trends by closely examining present conditions.

THE FUTURE

Evaluating future conditions helps estimate the impact on customer counts from future events. Examples include the opening of new competitive operations, special scheduled occurrences including sporting events and concerts, or other significant happenings. Local newspapers, trade or business associations, and the chamber of commerce are all possible sources of helpful information regarding upcoming events that could affect sales levels.

When managers have considered past, present, and future sales-related information, they are ready to estimate future guest counts. This estimate, in combination with information about what guests will buy, allows managers to accurately forecast beverage sales and usage.

MANAGER'S MATH

Lani is a bar manager who wants to estimate her beverage product usage for next week. Based on her historical records, Lani has estimated the percentage of drinks sold next week that will likely be beer, wine, or a spirit. Assume Lani has forecast that 1,500 drinks will be sold next week. Use the following information to answer the questions.

LANI'S OPERATION

Date: *Next week*

Number of drinks estimated to be sold: *1,500*

Product	Number of Drinks Estimated to Be Sold	% of Drinks Estimated to Be Sold
Beer		30%
Wine		15
Spirit		55
Total	1,500	100%

1. How many beers will likely be sold next week?

2. How many glasses of wine will likely be sold next week?

3. How many spirit-based drinks will likely be sold next week?

(*Answers: 1. Beer, 450; 2. Wine, 225; 3. Spirit, 825*)

The Forecasting Process

To best learn how to forecast beverage sales, managers must first understand the forecasting process. To illustrate how managers forecast beverage sales and product usage, assume a beverage operation typically serves 1,000 guests per week. The bar is located in a downtown area. The operation's typical customers are young professionals who frequent the bar after work and on weekends. Customers are evenly split between men and women. *Exhibit 9.1* shows part of the operation's sales history, or record of drinks sales, from last week. The manager obtains the sales history information from the operation's POS system.

Exhibit 9.1		
BAR SALES HISTORY		
Date: *Last week*	**Number of customers served:** *1,000*	
Product	**Number of Drinks Sold**	**% of Drinks Sold**
Beer	380	19.0%
Wine	625	31.3
Spirit	995	49.8
Total	**2,000**	**100%**

To better understand the use of a sales history, note that last week the bar served a total of 2,000 drinks to 1,000 customers. Beer sales equaled 380 beers, or 19 percent of the total drink sales. Wine sales equaled 625 glasses, or 31.3 percent of the total drink sales. Spirit drinks made up the largest percentage with 995 drinks sold and 49.8 percent of the total.

Using a sales history like the one in *Exhibit 9.1* gives managers a good idea of which beverage categories an operation's customers will choose for drinks. These managers, however, need even more information. This is because it is unlikely that any operation serves only one kind of beer, wine, and spirit.

Managers need to know which *specific* brand of beer, wine, or spirit their guests will choose. Also, when a specific product is sold in various forms, the manager must know how much of each of these options guests will choose. For example, a manager will want to track sales by form when the same brand of a popular beer is offered in bottles, in cans, and on draft.

Forecasting Beer Sales

Managers who forecast beer sales and usage want to know what percentage of guests will buy beer and which specific beer products they buy. Managers also need to know the brands that sell. They must also know the product container, such as bottle, can, or keg. *Exhibit 9.2* is an example of a detailed beer sales history. It details the sales of this operation's top beer brands, by serving forms, for one week.

The manager knows the percentage of sales for each beer type. Therefore, when the manager estimates the total beer sales for a given time period, he or she can also extrapolate the beer sales by brand and serving form. For example, a manager determines that his or her operation will sell 1,000 beers next week. Using the data in *Exhibit 9.2*, the manager can estimate the number of servings of Brand 1 (draft) he or she is likely to sell:

1,000	×	17.3%	=	173
Estimated		**% sales of**		**Estimated sales**
total beer sales		**Brand 1 (draft)**		**of Brand 1 (draft)**

Managers may monitor beer product sales manually. However, the operation's POS system (*Exhibit 9.3*) is often able to provide detailed sales histories. Regardless of the system in place, accurate sales histories help managers better estimate future sales. Beer sales histories should include both brand and serving method.

Forecasting Wine Sales

The forecasting of wine sales is similar to that of beer sales. In establishments that sell wine by the glass, managers must forecast for both bottle and by-the-glass sales.

FORECASTING BOTTLED WINE SALES

Managers forecast bottled wine sales in the same manner as they would beer sales. In many cases, a single wine will be offered in only one bottle size, usually 750 milliliters. In these cases, managers determine the percentage of wine sales contributed by a single wine using a wine sales history report that treats each bottled wine as a single menu item. That is, each type of bottled wine is listed individually on the sales history. When the same wine is offered in two or more bottle sizes, a more detailed sales history like the one presented in *Exhibit 9.2* is required.

Remember that some wines will be carried in inventory and offered for sale even though their sales levels will be quite low. This is the case, for example, with some very rare or expensive wines. This strategy is appropriate for those establishments that consider having an extensive wine list an important part of their marketing efforts. However, excessive product inventory should generally be avoided. When properly stored, bottled wine is not highly perishable but does take up storage space and can be a target of theft. For this reason, sales of slower moving product must be carefully estimated to avoid over-purchasing.

Exhibit 9.2

DETAILED BAR SALES HISTORY
Date: *One week*

Beer Sales Detail	Number Sold	% Sold
Brand 1 (draft)	121	17.3%
Brand 1 (bottles)	25	3.6
Brand 2 (draft)	34	4.9
Brand 2 (cans)	26	3.7
Brand 3 (draft)	150	21.4
Brand 3 (cans)	35	5.0
Brand 4 (draft)	61	8.7
Brand 4 (bottles)	55	7.9
Brand 5 (cans)	42	6.0
Brand 6 (draft)	151	21.6
Total	**700**	**100%**

Exhibit 9.3

FORECASTING WINE-BY-THE-GLASS SALES

Forecasting the sale of by-the-glass and house wine is also done in a manner similar to beer sales. Managers first determine the number of guests who will select wine. Then they use detailed sales histories to help predict future by-the-glass or house wines sales. If house wines are offered by the glass and by the carafe, these two serving forms must be monitored individually. If guests remain fairly consistent in their buying habits, managers can make a good estimate of future by-the-glass wine sales.

Forecasting Spirit Sales

Using sales histories, it is easy to track the number of guests who order a mixed drink. Unlike with beer or wine brands, however, it can be harder to track and forecast the specific spirit purchased. For example, three guests order a gin and tonic. One guest requests one of the operation's call brands whereas another guest requests a drink made with the well brand of gin. The third wants to experiment by trying a new kind of gin and wants to let the bartender decide which brand it will be. In each case, the sale was a gin and tonic.

As this example illustrates, a different method of sales forecasting is necessary for use in estimating spirit sales. There are several approaches managers may use. Depending on the degree of accuracy desired by the manager and the capability of the operation's POS system, drink forecasts could be made in a variety of ways:

- By spirit type (e.g., vodka, gin, rum)
- By the requested drink (e.g., screwdriver, gimlet, rum and cola)
- By the spirit's brand name (e.g., Joliet gin, Murphy's rum)

Each of these approaches to recording spirit sales has merit. Managers must choose the one that works best for their operations. It is important to recognize that unlike beers and wine, there are literally hundreds, or even thousands, of different drinks that can be made and sold in a single operation. A POS system must be used that has the capability of providing managers with sales histories that provide the accuracy they desire.

Every manager should determine the amount of accuracy he or she desires when forecasting future sales. Generally, more accuracy is better than less accuracy. At the same time, there must be a relationship between the time, money, and effort required to maintain a very detailed count of spirits sold and the cost-effectiveness of doing so.

Whether forecasting beer, wine, or spirit sales, accurate estimates are essential to operations. Remember that managers estimate future sales for several important reasons:

- To have the proper types of beverages on hand
- To have the proper amounts of products on hand
- To schedule the proper number of employees
- To create accurate revenue estimates
- To create accurate cost of goods sold (COGS) estimates

CALCULATING BEVERAGE COST OF GOODS SOLD (COGS)

Managers of every type of restaurant or foodservice operation are concerned about meeting financial goals. Managers of beverage operations want to make a specified amount of profit, and managers in private clubs, military, and other types of noncommercial foodservice operations want to make a profit, break even, or lose no more than a specified amount of money.

Regardless of the type of operation, the financial success of a beverage facility cannot be determined without knowing its cost of goods sold (COGS). Recall from chapter 8 that COGS for beverages is the cost to purchase the beverage products used to generate beverage revenue within a specific and defined time period.

Beverage managers should calculate their COGS on a regular basis, be it weekly, monthly, or annually. Most managers also calculate COGS when financial statements are prepared because beverage cost is needed for those documents. In all cases, managers calculate COGS for two reasons:

- To compare the planned costs for beverages with the actual costs of beverages. This comparison helps managers determine if any corrective actions are needed to bring future beverage costs in line with the costs estimate in the operating budget. The **operating budget** is a financial plan that estimates revenues and expenses for a specific time period.
- To obtain the cost information required for the **income statement**, the financial document that summarizes the operation's profitability for a specific period of time.

In addition, the accurate calculation of COGS is especially important because it then allows managers to calculate **beverage cost percentage**. This is the proportion of beverage revenue spent on the products that generated that revenue. It is also a key measure used to assess manager effectiveness.

Exhibit 9.4 shows the calculations necessary to compute the beverage COGS for the On the Shore Restaurant during January 2012. Note that the calculation of COGS requires specific information:

- Beginning beverage inventory
- Purchases
- Value of beverages available
- Ending beverage inventory
- Transfers

Each of these information categories will be addressed in detail. Understanding each is essential to the computation of an accurate COGS total.

Exhibit 9.4			
CALCULATION OF COST OF GOODS (BEVERAGES) SOLD: JANUARY 2012			
Line		**On the Shore Restaurant**	
(1)	Value of beverage inventory (Beginning of period: Jan. 1)	$83,575	
(2)	Value of beverage purchases (During January)	187,615	
(3)	Total value of beverages available (During January)		$271,190
(4)	Value of beverage inventory (End of period: January)		(89,540)
(5)	Unadjusted cost of goods sold (Beverages: January)		181,650
(6)		Add adjustments to cost of goods sold: beverages	
(7)	Transfers **from** kitchen		6,550
(8)		Deduct adjustments to cost of goods sold: beverages	
(9)	Transfers **to** kitchen	(13,075)	
(10)	Transfers **to** marketing costs	(3,750)	(16,825)
(11)	Cost of goods sold (Beverages: January)		$171,375

Beginning Inventory

Beginning inventory (*Exhibit 9.4, Line 1*) is the value of all beverage products available for sale at the start of an accounting period. In a newly opened operation, beginning beverage inventory is the value of all the beverage products on hand when the doors of the operation are first opened.

For ongoing establishments, beginning inventory for one period is identical to the closing inventory for the prior period. For example, the beginning inventory value of $83,575 on January 1 for the On the Shore restaurant would be identical to the closing inventory reported on the last day of December, the prior month.

Purchases

Purchases (*Exhibit 9.4, Line 2*) is the total amount paid to vendors for all beverage products bought during the time period for which COGS is being calculated. In the example of the On the Shore operation, $187,615 is the sum total of all beverage product invoices that were paid in the month of January.

It is important to recognize that all checks for beverage payments written within the month are included in this total. It does not matter if the check was or was not cashed by the vendor by the end of the month. The fact that the payment was made in the month of January dictates that the amount be included in the month's beverage purchases total.

Value of Beverages Available

The value of beverages available for sale shown in *Exhibit 9.4, Line 3* represents the amount of product available for sale at the beginning of the accounting ($83,575) plus the value of all products purchased during the period ($187,615). In the On the Shore example, the total value of beverages available for sale is $271,190:

$83,575	+	$187,615	=	$271,190
Value of beverage inventory		Value of beverage purchases		Total value of beverages available

Ending Inventory

Ending inventory, also called closing inventory, shown in *Exhibit 9.4, Line 4*, is the value of the beverage inventory at the end of the accounting period. In the On the Shore example, the ending inventory is $89,540.

Recall from chapter 8 that the ending inventory is calculated by multiplying the number of product units on hand by their costs; for instance, multiplying the number of cases, kegs, or bottles by their cost. It is established by carefully taking a complete physical inventory of all beverage products.

> ## Manager's Memo
>
> Beverage inventory includes all beers, wines, and spirits. In some cases, managers also inventory their nonalcoholic drink mixes and other drink ingredients if these are stored separately for "bar only" use.
>
> Glassware, napkins, stir sticks, and the like are not typically included in beverage inventory totals. However, the decision to include them or not must be made by the manager, and then followed consistently each time the inventory value is calculated.

Completing an accurate physical inventory of beverage products is an exacting process. This is because beverage inventory will likely be held in storerooms and in bar areas. As a result, much inventory will be held in bottles that are only partially full. While the bottles are not full, the value of their contents must still be established. This is because the formula for total inventory is as follows:

$$\text{Value of products in storage areas} + \text{Value of products in production (bar) areas} = \text{Total inventory}$$

Unopened containers of beer, wine, and spirits can be counted in both storage and bar areas. Opened containers in the bar area, however, must also be included in the inventory. In some operations, the majority of inventory may actually be held in back-of-bar areas rather than in designated storage areas, and much of this product, especially spirits, will include opened and only partially full bottles. Accurately establishing the monetary value of partially full bottles can be challenging. Managers responsible for doing it can choose from several approaches:

- Counting
- Measuring
- Weighing

COUNTING

Counting full bottles in storage areas is easy, but assessing the value of partial bottles held in drink production areas is more difficult. Some managers do so by using the tenths system. When used, this system requires that the person taking inventory assign a value of 10/10 to a full bottle, 5/10 to a half bottle, and so forth to represent the amount remaining in a partially full bottle. Then, when inventory value is established, the bottle's full price is multiplied by the amount remaining in the bottle to establish the value of the partial bottle.

For example, imagine that a bottle of liquor cost $16.00 and, when inventory is taken, it is judged to be 4/10 full. The bottle's value for the purpose of the inventory would be $6.40.

$16.00 bottle cost × 0.40 bottle = $6.40

While the tenths system is only an approximation of actual product value, many managers feel it is accurate enough for their purposes and it has the great advantage of being very quick and easy to use. Determining the value of the bottle's contents is expedited when the bottle price is marked on the bottle at the time of issue.

MEASURING

Some managers use a ruler placed next to the bottle to determine the amount contained in a partially full bottle. Dollar values are then assigned to each inch or portion of an inch, and that amount is used for inventory evaluation. This system is accurate if bottles are not oddly shaped, is fairly quick, and is considered by some to be an improvement over the tenths system.

WEIGHING

The weighing approach is the most accurate of all because it uses a scale to determine the amount of product in partially full bottles. Managers simply place each opened bottle on a scale to assess the quantity of product remaining in it. One challenge to this system is the fact that the weights of bottles, which vary, must be subtracted to arrive at their content's actual weight. Also, different liqueurs weigh different amounts, and thus each bottle must be weighed individually.

This system, although accurate, is time-consuming. Managers can determine the weights of empty bottles by weighing them or can download a smartphone application that uses the phone to read bar codes on bottles and matches them to the bottle's weights. With such an application, managers simply key in the total weight of the partially full bottles and the app subtracts the weight of the bottle and calculates the value of the bottle's contents.

Regardless of the partial bottle counting system used, it is essential that liquor inventories be taken when the operation is closed so that product amounts on hand do not change when the inventory is being taken. If automated drink systems are used, it is also important to provide an estimate of any significant amount of product contained in the lines of the drink-dispensing system. The system's manufacturer can provide information that can be helpful in making this estimate.

OPEN FOR BUSINESS

MANAGER'S MATH

Lawrence is taking inventory at Art's Bar. Calculate the inventory value of the products listed on the partial inventory sheet to answer the questions that follow.

ART'S BAR
Physical Inventory For: *This month*

Product	Cost per Bottle	In Storage	At Bar	Total on Hand	Total $ Value
Scotch Brand 1	$11.50	3	0.6		
Scotch Brand 2	$14.25	5	1.5		
Scotch Brand 3	$19.50	2	0.8		
Total					$

1. What quantity of Scotch Brand 1 is on hand?
2. What is the value of all Scotch Brand 2 on hand?
3. What is the total value of Scotch Brands 1, 2, and 3 on hand?

(Answers: 1. 3.6 bottles; 2. $92.63; 3. $188.63)

Exhibit 9.5

In many beverage operations, drink garnishes represent a significant expense and must be properly accounted for.

Unadjusted Cost of Goods Sold

Unadjusted cost of goods sold, shown in *Exhibit 9.4, Line 5*, is the amount of beginning inventory, plus the value of all purchases, minus the amount of ending inventory. In the On the Shore example, the unadjusted cost of goods sold is $181,650:

$83,575	+	$187,615	−	$89,540	=	$181,650
Value of beginning inventory		Value of purchases		Value of ending inventory		Unadjusted cost of goods sold

This amount would represent beverage COGS if no adjustments to improve accuracy were made. Some managers end their calculations at this point and consider the unadjusted cost of goods sold to be their beverage costs for the period. Other managers, however, want to more closely match product revenue with product costs, and they make additional accuracy-enhancing changes, or adjustments, to the unadjusted cost of goods sold figure. These adjustments to initial inventory values are called transfers and are of two types: transfers in and transfers out. Transfers result in increases or decreases in beverage expense to match product costs with the revenue generated by the product's sale. Increases in value are identified by standard numbers while decreases are achieved by subtraction using either brackets—for example, ($2,000)—or a minus sign—for example, −$2,000—to indicate the amount of the downward adjustment.

Transfers

To better understand why managers make transfer adjustments, shown in *Exhibit 9.4, Lines 7, 9, and 10*, consider a popular bar that is part of an establishment. One of this bar's best-selling drinks is a Bloody Mary, served with a generous garnish of celery stalk (*Exhibit 9.5*). In this case, the establishment's kitchen would most likely supply the bar with the large number of celery stalks needed.

The cost of the celery, however, is best charged against the revenue generated from drink sales, not the establishment's food sales. Transfers from a kitchen *to* the bar, shown in *Exhibit 9.4, Line 7*, typically include the cost of produce such as lemons, limes, and celery sticks used for garnishes; fruit juices and mixers; and ice cream used for specialty drinks.

Transfers of beverage costs *to* the kitchen, shown in *Exhibit 9.4, Line 9*, represent the cost of wine and beer used in cooking and liqueurs used for tableside dessert flambéing. These beverage transfers represent costs initially charged to the bar, but which are actually food, not beverage, costs.

Transfers from beverage costs to marketing costs, shown in *Exhibit 9.4, Line 10*, might include the cost of complimentary beverages provided to potential guests looking for a site for a future wedding or banquet and to dissatisfied customers who receive a comp beverage as a way of seeking to satisfy them.

Transfers to bar costs will result in increases, or additions to, beverage cost of goods sold. As a result, these costs are added to the unadjusted cost of goods sold. Transfers from the bar to other areas, such as the kitchen or marketing department, decrease the beverage cost of goods sold. As a result, these costs are subtracted from the unadjusted cost of goods sold.

Making transfers to beverage COGS is important for accuracy and helps managers and bar staff remember that the use of fruit juices, milk, cherries, lemons, limes, and the like do impact the total costs of bar operations. After all appropriate adjustments have been made, the cost of goods sold is determined:

$181,650	+	$6,550	−	$13,075	−	$3,750	=	$171,375
Unadjusted cost of goods sold		Transfers from kitchen		Transfers to kitchen		Transfers to marketing costs		Cost of goods sold

Beverage Cost Percentage

Recall from chapter 7 that a labor cost percentage is one of the restaurant and foodservice industry's most commonly used measures of labor productivity. Labor cost percentage is calculated using the following formula:

$$\text{Labor cost} \div \text{Total revenue} = \text{Labor cost percentage}$$

Similarly, beverage cost percentage is one of the most commonly used measures of efficiency in beverage usage. Beverage cost percentage is calculated using the following formula:

$$\text{Cost of goods sold (beverages)} \div \text{Beverage revenue} = \text{Beverage cost percentage}$$

For example, if the beverage revenue for the On the Shore restaurant for January 2012 was $684,940 and COGS beverage was $171,375, the beverage cost percentage for the month would be 25 percent:

$171,375	÷	$684,940	=	0.25
Cost of goods sold (beverages)		Beverage revenue		Beverage cost percentage

Commonly reported beverage cost percentages in the hospitality industry generally range from 15 to 35 percent. Note that there is no "best" beverage cost percentage. Each operation must establish its targeted beverage cost percentage. Actual beverage cost percentages, when accurately calculated, should be neither higher nor lower than the established target.

Beverage costs that are too far below target indicate customers are not getting the beverage value managers intended for them. Beverage cost percentages that are too high indicate product or revenue control problems that require the immediate attention of managers.

CONTROLLING PREPRODUCTION BEVERAGE PRODUCT COSTS

Wise beverage managers realize the importance of using effective control procedures from the time products are purchased until they are sold. Managers cannot assume that control systems are less important than "meeting and greeting" the guest, or other duties the manager might perform. Attention to detail in a variety of activities is essential to effectively control beverage product costs and to maximize profits for any beverage operation.

Control in Purchasing

Managers can exercise control in the purchasing process by implementing a number of control-related principles:

- Ensuring that purchases are made only in quantities necessary to build a predetermined par stock level
- Evaluating the final cost of deals and special discounts before large purchases are made
- Carefully considering customer acceptance and value before changing well brands
- Regularly examining par stock levels to determine if the levels should be adjusted due to changes in sales
- Carefully monitoring inventory turnover rates (see chapter 8) to meet desired standards
- Ensuring that managers, not sales representatives, determine the inventory needs of the operation
- Paying bills in a way that takes advantage of available discounts
- Making purchases in the largest bottle sizes practical because the cost per ounce of most products will be lower as bottle size increases

Control in Receiving

Managers can exercise cost control in the receiving process by implementing a number of control-related principles:

1. Accepting deliveries only at nonpeak business times
2. Assigning a receiver who has been trained to receive products properly
3. Checking incoming beverages against both the purchase order and delivery invoices for brand, quantity, and price information; refusing unacceptable items; and obtaining proper credits

4. Verifying invoice extensions

5. Marking bottle prices on bottles or cases when received

6. Moving items to safe and appropriate storage promptly

7. If possible, allocating different employees for purchasing and receiving activities

Control in Storing

Managers can exercise cost control in the storage process by implementing a number of control-related principles:

1. Locking storage areas and limiting access to authorized personnel, and controlling keys to beverage storage areas

2. Using a perpetual inventory system so the managers know the actual quantity of each beverage in storage, and taking physical inventories at least monthly to assess the accuracy of the perpetual inventory system

3. Shelving items according to inventory records and using bin numbers (see chapter 5) and cards to control wine inventory

4. Establishing, using, and changing par stock levels as needed, both in central storage and in bar storage areas, and maintaining proper storage temperatures, especially for beer and wine

5. Assigning record keeping to personnel other than bartenders

6. Checking employee bags before employee departure

7. Spot-checking inventory levels and records and investigating discrepancies

Control in Issuing

Managers can exercise cost control in the issuing process by implementing a number of control-related principles:

1. Requiring written issue requisitions to remove items from storage

2. Making issues to bars only in the amount needed to build bar supplies back up to par levels

3. Issuing full bottles only in return for empties, and then breaking empty bottles or otherwise making bottles unusable according to applicable laws

4. Issuing items at predesignated times only

5. Assigning the responsibility for issuing all products to the person in charge of storage

WHAT'S THE FOOTPRINT?

While some managers believe glass bottles containing liquor must be broken when empty, most states simply prohibit the reuse of alcohol bottles, even for the same brand of beverage. Recycling liquor bottles is usually possible and always good for the environment.

In most cases, managers do not need to break empty liquor bottles, but they must scratch, deface, or mutilate the label so that it cannot be used again. If recycled, empty liquor bottles must be stored in containers marked "For Recycling Only" and must typically be removed from the premises promptly, typically within 10 days to two weeks. For example, in Wisconsin bottles for recycling must be removed within 10 days.

Managers who wish to recycle should check with their local Alcoholic Beverage Control (ABC) commission office for further information about specific requirements in their own states.

CONTROLLING BEVERAGE PRODUCTION AND REVENUE LOSS

A beverage manager's control procedures do not stop even when products are carefully guarded during purchasing, receiving, storing, and issuing. Managers must ensure that beverage products are protected while they are used to make drinks. Managers must also protect the revenue generated. Drink preparation and revenue collection are very closely related. There are two principles for managers who are concerned about controlling costs during drink preparation and revenue. First, all drinks should be prepared according to their standardized recipes. Second, the proper amount of revenue should be collected for each drink sold.

The Manager's Role

The specific ways in which managers monitor and control production costs and revenue will vary somewhat based on the drink preparation and revenue collection system in their operations. In all beverage operations, however, drinks must be prepared and served to guests. Three basic methods are most commonly used:

- Service by bartenders
- Service by beverage servers
- Service by bartenders and servers

SERVICE BY BARTENDERS

Customers can place their orders directly with the bartender, who then produces the drink and serves it. This is a labor-efficient delivery system for drinks served at the bar, and it may also be useful for lounge service when there are few customers.

SERVICE BY BEVERAGE SERVERS

In some operations, beverage servers take customer orders, a bartender prepares them, and the servers deliver them to the customers. The server then collects the revenue from the customer. This service style is most common in dining situations and in many upscale bar or lounge settings.

SERVICE BY BARTENDERS AND SERVERS

In some operations, the bartender may serve customers at the bar and a server may serve drinks in the lounge area. This system is often used in establishments where guests can consume meals at the bar. Larger establishments with designated lounge and dining areas also commonly use this type of service. During slow periods, there may not be a beverage server present. Then the bartender serves drinks to customers at tables as well as at the bar.

THINK ABOUT IT . . .

What will happen to an operation's profitability if beverage products are wasted or stolen? What happens if the proper amount of revenue is not collected or if it is collected but then is stolen?

Preproduction Control

At the start of each operating shift, bartenders and servers receive their beginning cash bank. The cash bank is the amount of money issued to them for use during their shift. This bank should, of course, be counted to ensure it contains the correct amount of money. Most managers require this. In some cases, managers count the money in the bank in the employee's presence to ensure that the amount is correct. This is important because employees assume responsibility for their banks until their shifts have ended. In some operations, the beverage staff sign a daily form acknowledging this responsibility.

When their control systems require it, managers may also take POS system readings in the employee's presence to ensure that no entries have been made prior to the beginning of the shift. In most operations, bartenders also assess, under the manager's supervision, the opening bar par level inventory to be sure it is complete.

Recall that a par level inventory system requires that a specified number of beverage bottles be in bar workstations at all times. For example, based on production needs, the manager may establish a bar par level of four bottles of well vodka per workstation. This means that at any given time there should be four bottles of well vodka behind the bar. Since the bartenders will be responsible for these four bottles, it is necessary to ensure that the bottles are present at the beginning of the bartender's shift.

When the cash bank amount, the POS revenue readings, and the products in inventory have all been verified, managers can begin the production and revenue control process.

Control During Production

Exhibit 9.6

One challenge for managers is to ensure that no drink is prepared and served to a guest unless the sale is properly recorded. In some small-volume operations, bartenders and servers use management-issued and -numbered guest checks to record beverage sales prior to preparing and serving drinks (*Exhibit 9.6*). With this system only drink orders recorded on guest checks are to be filled, thus creating a record of drink sales. In other operations, guest orders are recorded in a POS system by the bartender or server prior to drink production.

In most operations, it is policy not to finalize the sales until actual payment has been received. Then, when guests pay for their charges, the sales are recorded as "final" according to the operation's approved procedures. All revenue from the sale is then deposited in the proper cash bank. This process is known as closing a guest's tab. Bartenders and servers record all revenues using their assigned numbers, keys, or codes in the POS so it is easy to determine the sales that each worker has made.

In the old days, beverage managers and bartenders were encouraged to mind their Ps and Qs (pints and quarts) to ensure they would receive all the money due to them for the products they sold. Today's managers have sophisticated POS systems that produce detailed sales reports. This means today's managers must mind their Xs, Zs, and more.

When managers take an "X" report, they are only "reading" the sales information in their POS systems. Managers can take these reports any time they are open without affecting the day's sales total in the POS system. For example, a manager may decide to take a report at the end of a shift or even every hour. When managers take a "Z" report, they are resetting the POS system's daily sales totals back to zero. Typically, when an operation closes for the day, managers run Z reports to get their final sales and revenue totals for that day.

Exhibit 9.7

Bartenders should, of course, use standardized recipes each time drinks are prepared. They should not give drinks to servers unless the drink's sale has been properly recorded or entered in the POS system. In operations using guest checks, before filling servers' drink requests bartenders use validation marks, frequently stamped on the check, to certify that all drinks recorded above the mark have already been served. Bartenders then return guest checks to servers along with the drinks ordered.

No matter which beverage service system is used, beverage managers have many duties to perform to assure the security of revenues that are collected. These duties depend on a property's standardized operating procedures and its POS system. In most beverage operations, managers have specific control responsibilities:

- **Issue guest checks, if used:** In some operations, managers provide bartenders and servers with numbered guest checks at the beginning of each shift, and retain records of the checks issued and to whom they were given. Personnel typically sign for these checks, and must account for all the checks they receive. Managers usually keep unissued checks and unused checks in a secured area of their offices.

- **Supervise personnel:** Managers monitor all drink production and service operations and make sure that personnel follow procedures properly.

- **Verify sales entry errors:** Bartenders or servers notify beverage managers or other assigned personnel of any sales entry problems. These can include equipment failures, errors in entering sales information, voided or canceled sales, or refunds. Managers should keep a record of these problems.

- **Supervise closing procedures:** The manager on duty signs out personnel at the end of their shifts, after accounting for revenue that has been collected. Managers ensure that sales entry equipment, whether cash register or POS, has been closed out properly, and that all required operating reports have been completed (*Exhibit 9.7*).

- **Secure all revenues:** Managers receive and secure all cash, checks, and payment vouchers according to the operation's policies and procedures.

- **Monitor and evaluate the revenue control system:** Managers regularly assess the revenue control system and evaluate how well it is working. They base their evaluations on operation's reports, from employee feedback, and from their own personal observations.

Preventing Employee Theft

Most professional bartenders and servers are honest. Some are not. Because of the few dishonest employees, managers must implement controls designed to prevent employee theft.

Because bartenders have the most access to product inventory and revenue, including cash, control systems must be used to monitor their performance. There are several ways bartenders can attempt to defraud an operation.

- **Underpouring drinks:** By underpouring alcohol by as little as a quarter ounce, bartenders can pocket the sale of the "extra" sixth drink without affecting the beverage cost percentage. This practice can be avoided by requiring the use of a shot glass or jigger for every pour and by never allowing free pouring. Some managers employ shoppers. These are personnel hired to secretly evaluate an operation to make sure that procedures are being followed. Sometimes called mystery shoppers, or secret shoppers, these individuals secretly observe beverage employees at work and then report their observations to managers for their review and possible corrective action.

- **Overpouring drinks:** Some bartenders will add more than the standard amount of alcohol in a drink and then charge for a regular drink in an effort to increase the size of the guest's tip. Overpouring will cause the overall beverage cost percentage to increase. However, in an operation with many bartenders, the actions of one staff member may be hard to detect. This is often an area that shoppers will assess.

- **Using personal bottles:** Bartenders can defraud an operation by bringing in their own supply of alcohol. When they do, they make drinks from liquor in their own bottles, and keep the revenue from the drinks made. In this way, the operation's liquor inventory has not been reduced, so a manager may think that no drink was prepared and sold. This can be prevented by marking bottles in inventory and making sure bottle markings or stamps are secure so employees cannot replace them with their own bottles.

- **Selling drinks for cash, but recording them as spilled, returned, or complimentary:** No drinks should be given out except as approved by management, and drinks should be discarded only with the manager's approval. Also, supervision is required for bartenders who report excessive spills or show other evidence of high pouring costs.

- **Diluting liquor and keeping income for extra sales:** Shoppers should be used to watch bartenders and investigate guest complaints about beverage quality. Managers should keep an eye out for cloudy gin or vodka, or lighter-than-normal brown liquor drinks that indicate that water has been added to bottles of spirits.

• **Substituting lower-quality well brands for call brands and then pocketing the extra cash:** This can be prevented by ensuring that all drinks are entered into sales and revenue records, and that the amount recorded and printed on guest checks equals the total charged to guests.

• **Undercharging:** This occurs when guests are charged lower than normal prices because they are friends or acquaintances of the bartender. Audits and shoppers can help spot undercharging.

• **Trading liquor with a cook for food items:** Managers must enforce all eating and drinking policies, and stay alert for signs of eating and drinking on the job, such as used plates and glasses in employee areas.

• **Bringing in smaller personal jiggers to aid in overpouring or underpouring:** The portion control tools used in bars should be checked regularly by managers.

• **Removing cash from cash drawer:** The revenue control system should ensure that managers know how much cash should be on hand. Bartenders should be accountable for shortages, if this practice is legal in the property's location. In busy operations, managers will replace the entire cash drawer with a new one during a shift so the bartender can keep working.

• **Borrowing from cash bank:** The amount of money in cash banks should be kept constant. Managers should check banks at the beginning and end of the shift and lock up banks when they are not being used.

• **Giving away drinks:** No complimentary drinks should be given without management's approval, and a sales record should be kept for every complimentary drink poured. The use of shoppers can be helpful in curbing this practice.

• **Ringing up sales on another bartender's key:** Separate cash banks to help prevent this practice. If the use of separate cash banks is not practical, records of shortages that occur when each bartender is working should be kept and regularly reviewed.

In addition to monitoring bartenders, it is also necessary for managers to monitor servers. Several methods can be used by dishonest servers to defraud an operation:

• **Obtaining beverages without entering sales in the revenue control system:** Guest checks must be presented to bartenders for every drink prepared. If electronic POS systems are in use, the appropriate entry should be required for every transaction.

• **Reusing guest checks:** Bartenders should retain all used checks and keep them secure.

• **Under-adding check or omitting items:** Sometimes this is practiced for friends or to influence the amount of tips. All sales and revenue records should be audited to check items, prices, and arithmetic.

- **Providing high-priced items to friends and recording the sales as lower-priced items:** Guest check audits help spot this practice.

- **Collecting revenue from guests but alleging they walked out without paying:** Close supervision of the service areas minimizes walkout problems. Records should be kept of all walkouts—by server—and reviewed for frequent occurrences.

- **Claiming lost guest checks (if used):** Lost check records should be kept and reviewed for frequency of occurrence.

- **Tampering with checks:** Original guest checks should not have erasures, and all drinks listed on checks should be paid for.

- **Falsely claiming returned beverages:** All beverage returns, including "mistakes," should be reported to managers as they occur.

Preventing Theft by Guests

Some guests, like some employees, will steal from beverage operations when given the opportunity. Managers must implement control systems to minimize customer theft. Several methods can be used by dishonest customers to defraud an operation.

- **Failing to note arithmetic errors in their favor:** To avoid this, personnel should use calculators, registers, or POS entries to total revenue charges.

- **Passing worthless checks or using stolen credit cards:** Servers should always follow all necessary authorization and processing steps and check IDs carefully.

- **Walking out without paying in full:** Personnel should be trained to notice when guests are preparing to leave and present payment requests promptly. If there are multiple checks, they should be attached or stapled together to avoid partial payments.

- **Using worthless currency or traveler's checks:** Personnel should be trained to spot counterfeit currency, especially large bills. Managers can help prevent traveler's check fraud by ensuring cashiers watch the customer sign the bottom signature line. The top signature area is signed at the time of purchase from the issuing bank. Cashiers should compare the two signatures to ensure that they match and match the signature on a required customer identification card.

- **Making false claims about incorrect change:** Currency given to personnel should be left on the register or tip tray until the guest is satisfied with the accuracy of the transaction.

- **After-departure denying of payment card charges:** Guests should be required to sign all debit, credit, or other payment card vouchers.

- **Altering of guest checks:** Pencils or erasable ink should never be used to write guest checks.

THINK ABOUT IT . . .

Managers once used hard-copy guest checks for recording drink sales. Today, most operations use POS systems. What role might hard-copy guest checks still play in a beverage operation?

Putting It All Together

An effective system for controlling product usage and revenue is based on the ability to compare the anticipated and actual dollars generated from product sales. Managers must construct their control systems so that approved procedures are consistently carried out by personnel. They also must ensure data collection results in useful information and employees understand their roles in making the system work. To assess the quality of their beverage control systems managers must ensure their systems include basic, but essential, features:

- Bartenders and servers serve beverages responsibly in every situation and to every customer.

- Bartenders use standardized recipes, glassware, portion size, and bar par levels.

- Bartenders use portion-control tools (jiggers, shot glasses, or other measuring tools).

- Managers properly supervise employees.

- Beverages served meet the operation's quality standards and are appealingly presented.

- Servers and bartenders follow policies regarding returned drinks.

- Managers enforce policies regarding complimentary drinks.

- Only management determines drink prices.

- Managers use an effective revenue control system. Revenue is received for all beverages served, and beverage revenue control procedures minimize abuses by personnel who prepare and serve beverages.

- Only management personnel read or assemble revenue totals.

- Shoppers who evaluate bartender performance and honesty are hired and used as needed.

SUMMARY

1. **Explain how managers forecast beverage sales.**

   When forecasting sales, managers seek to predict how many guests will be served and what those guests will buy. After forecasting the number of guests to be served, managers forecast beverage sales using sales history summaries and detailed sales histories. A sales history summary tells managers the proportion of guests who ordered a beer, wine, or spirit product. A detailed sales history provides additional information that is useful when a product brand is offered in various packaging forms. When they are forecasting spirit sales, managers may choose from several forecasting approaches. These include those based on spirit type, by the requested drink, or by the spirit's brand name.

2. **Demonstrate the calculation of beverage cost of goods sold (COGS).**

A manager's calculation of COGS for a time period is a multistep process that begins by adding the value of beginning inventory to purchases made in the time period. The resulting number is the value of goods available for sale. To that number, managers subtract the value of any transfers from the bar and add the value of transfers to the bar. The resulting final number is the cost of goods sold.

3. **State the formula for a beverage cost percentage, and explain its use.**

The formula used to calculate a beverage cost percentage is as follows:

$$\frac{\text{Beverage cost of goods sold}} {} \div \text{Beverage revenue} = \text{Beverage cost percentage}$$

Beverage costs that are below pre-established targets may indicate customers are not receiving the intended value. Beverage cost percentages that are too high may indicate product or revenue control issues managers should address. A beverage cost percentage is one measure of a manager's effectiveness in controlling beverage production costs.

4. **Summarize procedures managers use to control preproduction beverage product costs.**

Managers control preproduction beverage product costs by establishing control systems in four key areas: purchasing, receiving, storing, and issuing. In all cases the control systems in these areas must emphasize the protection of product quality and security. Wasted or spoiled products increase costs. Theft of product also increases costs. The manager must develop and monitor purchasing, receiving, storing, and issuing procedures designed to avoid both of these cost-increasing preproduction situations.

5. **Identify ways to prevent the theft of beverage products and revenue.**

Managers develop control systems to ensure that beverage products and the revenue they generate are protected when drinks are produced and served. Bartenders, service personnel, and even customers can be sources of product or revenue theft. In designing control systems, managers focus on a key principle: *No drink should be prepared and served to a guest unless the sale is properly recorded.* When product sales are recorded *prior* to drink production, managers can use sales data to analyze product costs and revenue generation. They can then make improvements in production methods or revenue security systems as needed.

APPLICATION EXERCISE

Honesty is one of a professional bartender's most important characteristics. Assume you were the manager of a soon-to-be-opened nightclub. Develop a series of three questions you would ask each bartender you interview for employment to assess his or her honesty.

Share your questions with a classmate. Ask him or her how they would feel if your questions were asked to them in a job interview.

Experienced managers know that some persons can be dishonest when they answer interview questions. How could you minimize the chances of that happening?

REVIEW YOUR LEARNING

Select the best answer for each question.

1. **From what source do managers obtain detailed sales history information for their operations?**
   A. Beverage invoices
   B. Sales forecasts
   C. POS systems
   D. Bartenders

2. **For which beverage product is it most important to monitor historical sales of brand and packaging forms?**
   A. Beer
   B. Wine
   C. Spirits
   D. Liqueurs

3. **Last week Nathan's beverage operation served 500 guests. Of these guests, 35% bought beer and 25% bought wine. The remaining guests bought spirits. What number of guests bought spirits?**
   A. 125
   B. 175
   C. 200
   D. 250

4. **What financial document summarizes an operation's profitability for a specific period of time?**
   A. Sales history
   B. Sales forecast
   C. Operating budget
   D. Income statement

5. **At Jack's beverage operation, ending inventory for October last year was $22,500. His purchases in October were $55,000. His sales in October were $220,000. What was Jack's beginning inventory for November last year?**
   A. $22,500
   B. $77,500
   C. $142,500
   D. $220,000

6. **How do managers determine the cash value of their ending inventory?**
   A. By using the beginning inventory of the previous month
   B. By taking a complete physical inventory of all beverage products
   C. By summing all beverage invoices paid in the month
   D. By using a perpetual inventory system

7. What is the formula used to calculate a beverage cost percentage?

   A. Beverage cost of goods sold + Beverage revenue = Beverage cost percentage

   B. Beverage cost of goods sold − Beverage revenue = Beverage cost percentage

   C. Beverage cost of goods sold ÷ Beverage revenue = Beverage cost percentage

   D. Beverage cost of goods sold × Beverage revenue = Beverage cost percentage

8. In February, Raoul's cost of goods sold was $15,000. Beverages sales for the same period were $60,000. What was Raoul's beverage cost percentage for February?

   A. 20%

   B. 25%

   C. 33%

   D. 40%

9. What is a cash bank?

   A. The amount of money in a cash drawer at the end of an employee's shift

   B. The total amount of cash on hand in all of an operation's on-site cash drawers

   C. The amount of money issued to employees for use during their shifts

   D. The total sales generated by a beverage operation in one day

10. What is a requirement for professional beverage shoppers?

   A. They must have previous bartender experience.

   B. They must have previous management experience.

   C. They must do their work anonymously.

   D. They must work only when employees know they will be present.

FIELD PROJECT

Shopper services can identify employees who are violating established operating policies and procedures. When the completed shopper's reports are shared with managers, changes to control systems may be in order. In other cases, the control system is being defrauded by dishonest employees.

Consider how you would respond if a shopper's report included the following findings:

1. A server was observed on two occasions giving free drinks to customers who appeared to be friends.

2. A bartender was observed selling a drink but not recording the drink's sale in the operation's POS system.

3. A bartender was observed selling a guest a large (24-ounce) draft beer, but charging for a smaller beer (12-ounce).

Would the length of time a beverage worker had been employed by your operation impact the actions you would take? What other factors would you consider before deciding which action to take?

10 Marketing Beverage Products Responsibly

INSIDE THIS CHAPTER

- **The Manager's Role in Beverage Marketing**
- **What Customers Want in a Beverage Operation**
- **Identifying the Target Market**
- **Marketing Plans**
- **Pricing as a Marketing Tool**
- **On-Premise Selling**
- **The Future of Beverage Management**

CHAPTER LEARNING OBJECTIVES

After completing this chapter, you should be able to:

- Describe the manager's primary goal in marketing a beverage operation.

- Explain the importance of identifying an operation's target market.

- State the purposes of a marketing plan, marketing budget, and marketing schedule.

- Describe the two primary drink-pricing methods used by beverage managers.

- Identify on-premise beverage selling opportunities available to managers.

KEY TERMS

contribution margin (CM), p. 255

demographics, p. 243

discretionary income, p. 252

lifestyle, p. 243

marketing, p. 240

marketing plan, p. 244

marketing schedule, p. 250

menu clip-on, p. 261

promotion, p. 263

psychographics, p. 243

table tent, p. 260

target market, p. 242

CASE STUDY

Carole and Latashia both operate bars downtown. They are competitors, but they became friends when they met at a responsible beverage service training session at the State Restaurant Association's annual convention. Carole stopped at Latashia's operation to say hello, and to do a friendly check on how things are going there.

"How do you do it?" asked Carole.

"Do what?" responded Latashia.

"Well," said Carol as she glanced around Latashia's busy bar, "we basically sell the same products at pretty much the same prices, and both our facilities are well maintained. But your place always seems so much busier than mine. I mean, I'm glad you're doing well. I just don't get what's holding back my operation."

1. Do you think the effectiveness of advertising and marketing programs could have a significant impact on the number of customers who visit a beverage operation? Why?

2. What do you think is the role of a beverage operation's manager in ensuring his or her business is good and is continually growing?

THE MANAGER'S ROLE IN BEVERAGE MARKETING

Even profitable bar and beverage operations with regular customers need to constantly attract new customers to thrive. Increasing sales and profits requires an ever-expanding customer base. Consequently, effective managers realize that their most important role is to obtain and retain an expanding customer base.

Everything that managers do should have a goal of attracting customers. When managers do their jobs well, employees benefit because their jobs are secure. Customers benefit because they receive true value for their expenditures. Owners benefit from strong returns on their investments. Managers benefit both from their own professional development and from gaining a sense of success and accomplishment. Communities also benefit because well-run beverage operations help contribute to the overall health of the business community and area's quality of life.

In the restaurant and foodservice business, marketing is the primary tool managers use to retain and expand their customer base. **Marketing** is the formal process of telling and showing customers how their needs and wants will be met by an operation.

Marketing focuses on the needs and wants of customers. Selling, however, is primarily an activity designed to convince others to pay for an establishment's food, beverages, or services and thus increase revenue, which is the sales levels achieved by an operation in a specified time period.

Some managers confuse the concepts of marketing and selling. They are not the same. Marketing focuses on the needs of customers whereas selling focuses on increasing the operation's revenue. Selling is business oriented, while marketing is customer oriented. The good news for managers is that meeting the needs of their customers always results in opportunities to sell to them.

Selling is actually the last step in a very long marketing process. This process begins with a series of marketing-related questions:

- Who are our likely customers?
- What do those customers most want to buy?
- What will we sell to them?
- When will we sell it?
- How will we sell it?
- How much will we charge for it?
- How will we let our likely customers know about us?

Marketing professionals know that answering such critical questions must happen before an operation can sell products to customers.

Manager's Memo

The best managers know that putting guests' needs and wants first makes it easier to sell to them. That's because when customers' needs and wants are met, those customers are happy to buy.

Managers who continually assess how their actions will affect their customers are known to be customer-centric or customer-focused. That is, they continually center or focus their thoughts on their customer's needs when making decisions.

Managers make decisions about what products should be served. They also decide what prices should be charged, and even who is hired to serve the items. These decisions all affect customers directly.

There are many books and articles about marketing for the purpose of increasing sales. These resources are excellent ways to learn about new methods and ideas. There are, however, some basic marketing concepts and techniques that all managers should understand. There are fundamental tasks that managers must accomplish if an operation is to expand the number of customers it serves:

- Informing customers what products and services are provided

- Demonstrating that the prices charged represent true value

- Encouraging sales in a responsible manner

- Delivering the products and services responsibly and as promised

THINK ABOUT IT ...

Food professionals encourage diners to order as many items as they wish. Beverage professionals only serve guests the number of drinks they can consume responsibly. What implications does this difference have on marketing alcoholic beverages?

WHAT CUSTOMERS WANT IN A BEVERAGE OPERATION

To create and implement an effective marketing strategy, it is important to understand the buying characteristics of customers. Trying to meet everyone's needs and wants is unrealistic. Attracting a young, professional, singles crowd requires different strategies than attracting older, retired couples. In addition to different types of guests, people go to beverage operations for different reasons. Many go to be with a familiar group. These guests want to feel comfortable with the social aspect of the establishment (*Exhibit 10.1*). Another group may consist of drop-in customers who are en route to another place, or are waiting to meet someone. Still others are those people who plan to have a drink and then dine later.

Exhibit 10.1

Management must decide which groups they will try to attract. Then it must develop marketing approaches that will appeal to that group. Remember, however, that regardless of facility location, economic status of consumers, or goals of the beverage operation, all consumers seek value for their money.

Many managers mistakenly believe that consumers value low price above all else. After all, one of the first questions a buyer asks any seller is, "How much?" Do not be deceived into thinking that low price is the only factor that drives customers to an establishment. Price is only one of several factors customers consider when making buying decisions. Customers today, as in the past, tend to value and buy based on one or more product characteristics:

- Quality products

- Quality service

- Cleanliness

- Price

Customers expect a certain level of product and service quality when they make a buying decision. When their expectations are exceeded, they perceive high levels of quality. When their expectations are not met, they perceive low levels of quality. Consider, for example, two consumers. One buys a beer for $1, the other pays $4.

In the first case, the guest waits 20 minutes before getting his beer. When it comes, it is warm, flat, and served in a visibly soiled pint glass. In the second case, the customer promptly receives a cold pint of sparkling fresh beer, served by a smiling server in a pleasant, clean environment and in a beer-clean glass. The first consumer, in his own mind, received no value for the expenditure. The second guest received a great value and will likely return.

Quality is remembered long after price is forgotten. Why? Because cheap and inferior products do not supply good value. Anything can be made cheaper, but not necessarily better. Value is the ideal blend of quality product, service, cleanliness, and price. It is not driven by price alone.

While price is important, it often gets too much attention. In many important buying decisions, such as choosing a doctor or buying a home, price is a factor in selection. However, in most cases price is not the most important one. People seem to know that it is not price but *what you get for the price* that matters.

It takes a great deal more than low prices to develop a long-term successful beverage facility. Customers want quality, or a high perceived value, in their purchases. Managers must stand behind their products and provide them at a fair price. Doing so will bring customers back.

IDENTIFYING THE TARGET MARKET

As part of analyzing a market environment, managers must accurately identify their customers. Once managers obtain detailed information about their customers, they can begin grouping them into categories, or target markets. A **target market** is made up of those potential customers whose specific needs and wants an operation seeks to meet. As noted, not all beverage guests want the same thing.

Segmenting a target market helps identify the people most likely to visit an operation. There are many ways to segment a market. Segmenting a market means to examine its unique components. One of the most common ways to segment the market is to do so based on its demographic and psychographic differences.

Demographic Variables

Beverage managers often segment their customers based on **demographics**. Demographics are statistical characteristics of the population. There are a large number of demographics used to segment customers:

- Age
- Education
- Ethnicity
- Geography
- Home ownership
- Household size
- Income level

- Nationality
- Occupation
- Race
- Religion
- Sexual orientation
- Spending patterns
- Stage in family life cycle

Analyzing the demographic variables of a target market can help managers better understand what target market guests seek in a beverage operation.

Psychographic Variables

Psychographics permit market segmentation based on differences in customers' social class, beliefs, attitudes, and other lifestyle factors.

Lifestyle is a term that most people understand but have a hard time defining. **Lifestyle** may be defined as the patterns in which people live and spend their time and money. This definition sees guests in terms of how and what they buy. In other words, the definition predicts differences in consumer behavior.

Behind the behaviors that encompass lifestyle lie a number of other complex factors related to consumers' personalities and values. Psychographics describe the human characteristics of customers.

Psychographics are used primarily to help segment markets, but they have other purposes. For example, psychographics can be useful when managers try to determine the answers to the following questions:

- What beverage marketing efforts would work best?
- How would marketing efforts best be communicated to the target market (e.g., radio, television, the Internet, and social media)?
- How will the target market likely respond to the marketing effort?

Psychographics are important when managers design advertising and promotional materials. The words or phrases used, the graphic images displayed, and even the background music used should be selected with the preferences of a specific target market in mind. Using psychographics effectively in marketing efforts results in selling efforts that have more impact, produce more sales, and yield more profits.

OPEN FOR BUSINESS

BY THE CUSTOMER/ FOR THE CUSTOMER

Tech-savvy customers are a relatively new psychographic group. Beverage managers who embrace emerging marketing technologies have powerful new tools for communicating with this group. Social media sites and sites with user-generated content like Facebook, Twitter, Yelp, and TripAdvisor are among the most popular sites with current tech-savvy customers.

Tomorrow, the names of the important social media sites may be the same or different. But it is clear that the number of tech-savvy consumers is growing. Tech-savvy managers should continually reach out to these customers in ways that fit into the guests' advanced technology lifestyles.

MARKETING PLANS

A **marketing plan** is a detailed listing of specific activities designed to reach the revenue goals of a beverage operation. A marketing plan is like a road map for the facility's marketing efforts. Developing a marketing plan is a formal process that involves answering a series of questions:

- What marketing activity should be undertaken?
- Who will do it?
- When will it be done?
- How much money will be needed to do it?
- How will the plan's results be measured?

Creating a Marketing Plan

Managers plan so that they can affect the future. When creating a marketing plan, managers want to influence the way their current and future customers view their operations. They also seek to influence how often customers will come to the facilities and what those guests will buy when they visit.

Effective marketing plans have five things in common:

- They are written.
- They are targeted.
- They are time-sensitive.
- They include cost estimates.
- They are customer-focused.

MARKETING PLANS ARE WRITTEN

A marketing plan should be a formal, written document. Remember that a marketing plan details what should be done, when it should be done, where it should be done, and who should do it. A manager cannot create an effective plan without carefully recording the decisions made in response to these important questions.

Managers are typically very busy, attending to many details. An operation's marketing plans must be committed to writing and reviewed regularly. Otherwise, it is too easy for a busy manager to forget when an important marketing activity should be done, or even who should do it.

MARKETING PLANS ARE TARGETED

A marketing plan may have several components, each of which addresses a different target market segment. For example, a bar may target one type of customer through the week and a different customer type on the weekends. Similarly, in a restaurant, certain marketing activities may be targeted at the restaurant's lounge customers, while slightly different activities will target the dining-room customers. On a Monday night an establishment may offer a wine special for those eating in its dining room, while at the same time offering promotions on pitchers of beer in its lounge in an effort to attract fans of Monday Night Football.

Managers must know their target market well. They must also recognize how segments of that market can be best addressed by specific and highly focused marketing activities. And these different activities should be incorporated into the marketing plan.

MARKETING PLANS ARE TIME-SENSITIVE

An effective marketing plan addresses a specific time period. This time period can be as long as a year or as short as a month. To monitor the marketing activities that should be undertaken, and to know when they should be started or completed, the marketing plan must outline specific time periods for completion. In some cases the time period identified for completing an activity will be critically important to its effectiveness.

For example, assume an establishment has a private room in addition to its regular seating area that it can use for small banquets and private parties (*Exhibit 10.2*). Many local businesses in the establishment's market area sponsor social events in December. The establishment's manager wants to offer a special "Holiday Party" package to maximize end-of-year revenue. This package will target smaller local companies and will include drinks and appetizers at one set price per party attendee.

Exhibit 10.2

Clearly, early December is too late to begin marketing these holiday parties. By that time, most business planners will have already made their party arrangements. In this example, midsummer or early fall would likely be the best time to contact potential customers about booking the special room for holiday events.

Any dollars committed to marketing activities are dollars that cannot be spent on other needs of the operation, including equipment, supplies, or staff. Some forms of marketing may be expensive, while others are not. In all cases, it is essential that managers thoroughly consider the estimated costs of each marketing activity. In some cases, managers can easily estimate costs. In other cases, the costs are harder to determine and the manager may need to work with prospective partners to determine the potential costs.

To illustrate, assume a manager decides to place an advertisement in a local magazine. The manager has determined that this magazine is widely read by the operation's target market. In this case, the manager should contact the magazine to determine the price of placing an ad prior to including that activity in a marketing plan.

The size of an operation's marketing budget will often vary based on the revenue it currently achieves, its revenue goals, and a variety of other factors. In all cases, however, the costs of the individual activities in the marketing plan must be known in advance so that the manager can stay within the operation's established marketing budget.

MARKETING PLANS ARE CUSTOMER-FOCUSED

Marketing is a means of communicating with customers. Therefore, marketing managers must continually keep customers foremost in mind. Effective managers know that each marketing activity should be chosen carefully and only after considering several factors:

- What message is to be communicated?
- How can that message best be delivered?
- What are the customers' desired responses?
- How can the customers' responses be monitored and assessed?

Experienced managers know that the assessment of marketing efforts can be challenging. To illustrate, assume an operation is experiencing increased sales. The operation's manager decides to place an ad on the radio. Sales continue to increase. It may be difficult, in this example, to know the precise impact on sales of the new radio ad. Despite that challenge, effective managers wishing to determine the impact of their marketing effort can use a variety of objective measures:

- Number of new customers served
- Total number of customers served
- Number of drinks sold

- Changes in number of drinks sold
- Changes (increases) in revenue
- Total revenue achieved

WHY CREATE A MARKETING PLAN?

Formal marketing plans help establishments in many ways. In spite of the benefits, some managers fail to create effective marketing plans. There are several reasons for this:

- **Lack of time:** Some managers claim to be too busy to plan their marketing activities.
- **Lack of budget:** Some managers think their marketing budgets are too small to require the organized planning of their marketing activities.
- **Inability to measure effectiveness:** Some managers believe there is no way to measure the effectiveness of their marketing activities. As a result, they consider formal marketing plans to be unnecessary.
- **Lack of knowledge:** Some managers are not comfortable making the decisions needed to create an effective marketing plan.

Of course, if managers are to achieve their revenue goals, then effective marketing is a must. Managers who cannot *find* the time to plan must *make* the time. Similarly, a small marketing budget or even the challenges of assessing the effectiveness of marketing activities are poor reasons for neglecting the planning process. In fact, a small marketing budget makes its effective use even more critical.

Lack of knowledge is the only good reason not to plan. By reading, studying, and seeking input from others, however, managers can learn what they need to know about marketing, market planning, and how to evaluate the effectiveness of their own marketing efforts.

The Beverage Marketing Budget

Because financial resources are limited, a manager's marketing plan must be based on a budget. Marketing budgets are established using one of four methods:

- Estimate of what the business can afford after other costs are paid
- Percentage of actual or forecasted revenue
- Amount spent on promotions by competitors
- Marketing plan objectives and the actions needed to achieve them

WHAT'S THE FOOTPRINT?

Increasingly, consumers are concerned about their impact on the environment. Some operations have responded to this by making eco-friendliness a significant part of their marketing efforts.

As customers increase their own awareness of green practices, expect them to also pay increased attention to the green practices of the operations they frequent. Managers targeting these eco-minded customers would do well to point out that they, too, are eco-minded! For example, some operations offer a 10 percent discount to bicycle riders. Others offer similar discounts to customers who walk or take public transportation to their operation. Other examples include hosting a tasting of a locally produced beverage product and marketing the operation's recycling efforts as they relate to bottles and cans.

The first two methods, what the business can afford and the percentage of revenue, are the simplest methods used to determine a marketing budget. In the first instance, a manager might develop the marketing budget by looking at revenue and costs from the previous year and projected revenue and costs for the year in question to gain a sense of how much could be spent in the coming year's marketing budget.

In the case of a marketing budget tied to a percentage of revenue, a manager would carefully forecast monthly sales, determine a monthly percentage for marketing, and sum the 12-month marketing amounts to arrive at the annual marketing budget. To use this approach, managers first do two things: collect data and forecast revenue.

DATA COLLECTION

Managers should not randomly choose the percentage amount of revenue they will spend on marketing. To establish an appropriate amount for marketing efforts, managers should collect data and information based on their estimates of how planned activities will affect future operating revenue and expense. Managers must also collect other important information, including pricing information from media outlets (e.g., radio, television, the Internet, or print), advertising agencies, and vendors selling promotional products and services. Knowing the fees that various marketing avenues may charge helps managers make plans and determine the amount of needed marketing resources. They then use that revenue forecast information to help them establish the amount of money that can be reserved for marketing.

To better understand this concept, consider the manager who wants to give away promotional T-shirts to guests who attend a special event at the bar. To effectively plan for this promotion, the manager must know several variables. These include total number of T-shirts needed, the costs to produce the shirts, and the time required to make and deliver them. These variables must be accounted for in the marketing budget and money must be reserved for these activities.

REVENUE FORECASTS

After estimating marketing costs and the effectiveness of planned marketing programs, funds available for marketing must be determined. For example, a manager could decide to designate 4.25 percent of total revenue for the marketing budget. The manager would follow three steps:

1. Forecast monthly sales.

2. Determine the monthly percentage for marketing.

3. Add the 12-month marketing amounts to arrive at the annual marketing budget.

Exhibit 10.3
MARKETING BUDGET WORKSHEET

Month	Revenue Forecast	Marketing Budget @ 4.25% of Revenue
January	$ 100,000	$ 4,250
February	110,000	4,675
March	125,000	5,313
April	140,000	5,950
May	145,000	6,163
June	150,000	6,375
July	150,000	6,375
August	155,000	6,588
September	120,000	5,100
October	114,000	4,845
November	111,000	4,718
December	130,000	5,525
Total	$1,550,000	$65,875

To illustrate, consider the manager whose revenue forecast for the next 12 months is presented in the marketing budget worksheet in *Exhibit 10.3*.

In this example, the annual marketing budget would be $65,875. However, note that the annual budget may or may not be spent equally over the year. Managers detail the decisions about how and when to spend money from the marketing budget in the marketing plan. The plan includes developing specific marketing activities according to a marketing calendar.

Budgets based on what the business can afford or based on a percentage of revenue are both rather easy to calculate. However, in both cases, if sales decrease, the marketing budget shrinks. Such budget reductions are generally badly timed, as the need to promote an establishment is even greater during periods of declining sales.

Basing a marketing budget on the amount competitors spend on their promotions is also relatively simple, although obtaining accurate information needed to do so may be difficult. In some cases managers can get an idea of this figure by researching industry averages. However, a savvy manager is aware that the information used by competitors to determine marketing budgets may not apply to his or her establishment.

The final method, basing a marketing budget on the estimated cost of achieving a marketing plan's specific objectives, helps keep marketing efforts goal-focused. This method is a good one to use. It is also the most complex method because it requires the creation of a separate marketing plan and budget for each individual marketing initiative and activity.

OPEN FOR BUSINESS — MANAGER'S MATH

Assume that your beverage operation is creating its annual marketing budget. As part of the process you are forecasting revenue levels and designating 2.5 percent for marketing. Consider the data and then answer the questions that follow.

Month	Revenue Forecast	Marketing Budget @ 2.5% of Revenue
January	$ 90,000	$2,250
February	85,000	
March	100,000	2,500
Total		

1. How much money from February sales will be reserved for marketing?

2. What is the total revenue forecast for the 3-month period?

3. What will be the total amount of money reserved for marketing from the revenue generated in January, February, and March if the revenue forecast is correct?

(Answers: 1. $2,125; 2. $275,000; 3. $6,875)

Good managers look for ways to stretch their marketing budgets. The use of social media is a new way to do just that. Social media use is no fad. Social media sites have become one of the best ways for managers to talk to their customers at little cost.

All commercial, and even some noncommercial, beverage operations should consider how social media sites can assist their marketing efforts. The popularity of individual sites can change and the type of customer using a specific site can vary, but every beverage manager should link his or her own Web site with the most popular social media sites.

The Beverage Marketing Schedule

A typical marketing plan includes a variety of marketing tasks and activities. Consider, for example, a marketing plan that calls for advertising a bar's special Mardi Gras party in the local newspaper. If this task is to be completed in a timely manner, someone must be responsible for it. Contacting the newspaper, assisting in the creation of the ad, and approving the final invoice are all tasks someone must complete if the marketing activity is to be successful.

In many cases, the manager is responsible for undertaking all of the marketing tasks. Whether the manager does the tasks or delegates them to another employee, the manager must identify who should be responsible for each activity in the marketing plan. To do so, the manager creates a marketing schedule. A **marketing schedule** contains three key pieces of information about an operation's marketing activities:

- What is to be done?
- When will it be done?
- Who will do it?

This portion of the marketing plan need not be complicated. *Exhibit 10.4* provides an example of a form that can be used to build an establishment's beverage operation marketing activities schedule.

A marketing activities schedule can be thought of as a "to-do" list for marketing. The advantage of the schedule is that it clearly states what is to be done, by when, and by whom. Completion of the marketing budget and marketing schedule gives managers all they need to begin implementing their marketing plans.

Exhibit 10.4

SAMPLE MARKETING SCHEDULE

Marketing Objective	Supporting Marketing Activity	Date to Be Started	Date to Be Completed	Assigned To
Increase attendance at Valentine's Day winetasting event by 100 customers above prior year	Initiate radio advertising campaign	January 15	February 14	Beverage manager
Plan Mardi Gras party; new event with target of 50 customers in year one	Use social media for announcements	February 1	March 1	Establishment manager and beverage manager

PRICING AS A MARKETING TOOL

The prices that a beverage operation charges are an important part of its marketing strategy. Therefore, managers must understand basic pricing concepts. Managers can use beverage prices to build customer loyalty while providing their operations with the revenue needed to make a profit. The ability to price menu items properly is another of a manager's most important skills.

Buyers must have both a willingness and an ability to buy. When prices are too high, buyers are less *willing* to buy, and more customers are *unable* to buy. If prices are too low, however, a business may not generate enough revenue to pay its expenses and make a profit. Prices must be set very carefully.

First, managers should understand that price is both a noun and a verb. Thus, the price (noun) of a drink may be $6.50. To price (verb) a drink is the act of determining what to charge for the drink.

Second, managers must understand that pricing is both a science and an art. The science of pricing requires managers to use math skills to calculate costs and arrive at suggested selling prices. The art of pricing requires managers to recognize that, in the minds of customers, prices are subjective. Not every customer will respond to a specific item's price in exactly the same way.

Managers responsible for setting drink prices must keep key pricing principles in mind:

1. **Prices act as signs to buyers:** When prices are low, they deliver a "buy" signal to customers, who can now better afford the items they want and are willing to pay for. When prices are too high, they can discourage customers from buying.

2. **Prices must reflect real costs:** Proper pricing recognizes that managers must consider all of the costs of an operation's beverage products, labor, and other expenses along with desired profits.

3. **Prices must be considered fair:** Because buyer perceptions of price affect their purchase decisions, it is essential that customers believe they receive good value for the money they spend. Buyers seek value in their purchases. They do not feel responsible for ensuring the profitability of a beverage facility. That is the job of managers, and it is achieved through proper pricing.

Managers must consider three key factors when determining the prices they will charge for the products they sell: their competition, the economic conditions, and pricing-related laws.

REAL MANAGER

IT'S NOT JUST PRICE

I took over an operation in Los Angeles. The prices were moderate, but a large customer survey revealed that many guests thought the prices were too high. Over the course of the first 4 to 6 weeks, I upgraded entertainment, staff dynamics, products, and other operational elements of the business. On about week 10, the bar/nightclub was full and doing far better, so I increased prices significantly (about 25 percent) in three steps over a several week period. After about 16 weeks, with the same basic facility, but upgraded experience dynamics and 25 percent higher prices, I completed a second guest survey. The responses included virtually *no* comments about pricing.

So, when people tell you that prices are too high, they are really saying that your experience is not worth your price. Guests do not leave a great restaurant or bar experience and say it was "expensive." Fine-dining and upper-positioned operations prove that every day. Guests leave only marginal or disappointing experiences and say it was expensive. Perceived value beats absolute value every time.

Competition

Managers need to be aware of the prices charged by an operation's competitors. Before establishing their own prices, it is a good idea for managers to research what their direct competitors charge for their products. Managers generally want to be within a range of their competitors: not too high, but not at the lowest end of the pricing scale either.

Economic Conditions

Economic conditions impact how often customers frequent any hospitality operation. Managers should consider several economic-related questions prior to determining product selling prices:

- How is the quality of life in the market area?
- Is the area growing or declining in population?
- How are people spending their discretionary income: the money available to spend after their expenses are paid?

If the economy is not doing well, people may be less inclined to go out, especially if an operation's prices are perceived to be too high.

Pricing-Related Laws

In most states, managers of beverage operations are required to follow very detailed pricing laws. Laws vary by state but must be well known by managers. In addition to following the state and local laws, managers must ensure that prices charged for drinks are known or available to customers in advance of their purchases. Prices must be presented fairly. The question of how to ensure prices are presented "fairly" is an important one that is impacted by customer perceptions of price.

Certainly, it is fair for managers to use their knowledge of customer buying habits to predict how their customers will react to different pricing strategies. For example, some managers set menu prices to end in $0.95 or $0.99. These managers know, for example, that customers do not perceive much difference between a price of $5.50 and $5.99 for a drink item, but would perceive the difference between $5.75 and $6.24. In both of these examples, one price is 49 cents higher than the other. In addition, hidden charges of any kind will always be met with resistance and should not be a part of a manager's pricing strategy. Hidden prices are legally and ethically wrong.

Drink Pricing

Proper pricing involves setting prices that help the operation meet its financial goals while providing value to customers. Pricing is too important to be left to guesswork. The best managers use objective methods when

THINK ABOUT IT . . .

Like fashion, the popularity of beverages changes over time. What drinks are popular now that were less so a few years ago? Should managers charge more for more popular drinks? Why or why not?

calculating beverage prices. There are many approaches managers can use to determine drink prices. However, most managers primarily use one of two basic methods: the beverage cost percentage pricing method, and the contribution margin pricing method.

BEVERAGE COST PERCENTAGE PRICING

Beverage cost is the total cost of the beverage products used to make the drinks an operation sells. This cost is one of the major expenses in every beverage operation. Beverage costs are incurred in a number of ways:

- **Cost of goods sold (COGS): Beverages:** this is literally the cost of the beverages served to guests and includes any costs related to overpouring (see chapter 6).

Exhibit 10.5

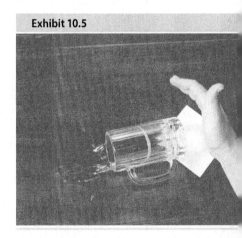

- **Cost of preparation mistakes:** In every beverage operation, mistakes result in discarded drinks. Effective managers minimize mistakes, but some mistakes are unavoidable (*Exhibit 10.5*).

- **Cost of beverages due to theft:** This is the cost of beverages stolen by employees, customers, or suppliers. Suppliers steal beverages when, for example, they charge and receive payment for products that were not delivered.

- **Cost of beverages wasted due to spoilage:** This is the cost of beverages that had to be discarded due to improper storage or excessive age.

The sum of all these costs result in the overall COGS: Beverages. Many beverage operations set pricing to achieve a certain beverage cost percentage. The beverage cost percentage shows the percentage of the operation's total revenue used to purchase beverages.

The beverage cost percentage pricing method is very popular. The method actually goes by several names, including the *simple markup method* and the *factor method*. The various names used to identify the pricing method may make it seem confusing. However, it is actually the simplest of all pricing methods. The prices are based solely on the cost of the products used to make the drinks.

The beverage cost percentage is the cost of goods sold divided by the revenue generated from the sale of the beverage. For example, assume a beverage costs $2 to make and it sells for $6. The beverage cost percentage would be calculated as follows:

$2	÷	$6	=	33%
Cost of goods sold: Beverages		**Revenue generated by beverage**		**Beverage cost percentage**

Managers can also start with a specific beverage cost percentage in mind to determine the price of a drink. For example, assume a manager wishes to achieve 25 percent beverage cost on a specific beer product. Assume further that the beer to be sold cost the operation $1. The formula for calculating the drink price would be as follows:

$$\text{Cost of goods sold: Beverages} \div \text{Target beverage cost percentage} = \text{Suggested selling price}$$

In this case, the manager would calculate the selling price for the specific beer product as follows:

$$\$1 \div 0.25 = \$4$$

By applying basic algebra, the use of the formula means that if any two of the numbers in the formula are known by a manager, the third number can easily be calculated. Thus, if beverage cost and selling price are known, the formula to compute *beverage cost percentage* is as was shown previously:

$$\text{Cost of goods sold: Beverages} \div \text{Revenue generated by beverage} = \text{Beverage cost percentage}$$

If targeted beverage cost percentage and desired selling price are known, the formula to compute *beverage cost* is as follows:

$$\text{Selling price} \times \text{Target beverage cost percentage} = \text{Cost of goods sold: Beverages}$$

In the previous example, if the manager wanted to sell an item for $4, and knew that the targeted beverage cost was 25 percent, then the allowable beverage cost would be calculated as follows:

$$\$4 \times 0.25 = \$1$$

After mastering the basic formulas, the beverage cost percentage pricing method is simple to use. However, the selling price that results from using this method is often simply a starting point. To illustrate, assume an item cost $1.10 to make. The manager has a 30 percent target food cost. Using the beverage cost percentage formula yields this selling price:

$$\begin{array}{ccc} \$1.10 & \div & 0.30 & \div & \$3.67 \\ \text{Cost of goods} & & \text{Target beverage} & & \text{Suggested} \\ \text{sold: Beverages} & & \text{cost percentage} & & \text{selling price} \end{array}$$

In this case, the managers would likely round the selling price to $3.75, $3.95, or even to $4.00 to take advantage of consumer pricing perceptions and to ease the complexity of remembering prices for servers.

Manager's Memo

The beverage cost percentage method is often referred to as the "markup" or "factor" method because managers can use a factor as a shortcut way to calculate selling prices.

Dividing any targeted beverage cost percentage into 1.00 yields a factor that can be multiplied by an item's beverage cost to yield its selling price. The factor table shows the factors that result for several popular beverage cost percentage targets.

Target Beverage Cost %	Factor
15	6.67
20	5.00
25	4.00
28	3.57
30	3.33
32	3.12
30	3.00
34	2.94
36	2.77
40	2.50

Assume that the beverage cost of the item is $3.00 and the targeted beverage cost percentage is 30 percent. Using the factor from the table, the selling price would be calculated as follows:

$$\begin{array}{ccc} \$3.00 & \times & 3.33 & = & \$9.99 \\ \text{Cost of beverage} & & \text{Factor} & & \text{Selling price} \end{array}$$

A manager's targeted beverage cost percentage may be established per beverage type. For instance, there may be a set percentage for beer, another for wine, and yet another for spirits. Alternatively, managers may seek to achieve the same or a very similar percentage in each beverage category. In all cases, however, the manager establishing an operation's drink prices must consider the total cost of beverages required to produce each drink before determining the drink's selling price.

The beverage cost percentage pricing method requires precise information about the cost of the item being priced. Two things must be in place to calculate the cost. First, drink production staff members must use standardized recipes. When they do, the manager will know what ingredients were used and the amounts. Second, the manager must know the current cost of all ingredients. Then the amount of each ingredient used must be calculated to determine the cost of the ingredients used.

When determining drink costs, it is also important to include the cost of garnishes served with the drink. For that reason, managers always include garnishes on standardized drink recipes. Doing so allows these costs to be easily calculated, along with the cost of the alcoholic beverages included in the drink (*Exhibit 10.6*).

MANAGER'S MATH

A manager is calculating proposed beverage prices for three new drinks. Using the information shown, calculate the selling price the manager should charge for each new item. Then use the information to answer the questions that follow.

Item	Beverage Cost	Target Beverage Cost Percentage	Selling Price
Vodka and vanilla bean	$1.75	30%	
House Tuscan red wine	1.00	28	
Jumbo draft beer	0.75	20	

1. What is the selling price for the vodka and vanilla bean drink?

2. What is the selling price for house Tuscan red wine?

3. What is the selling price for the jumbo draft beer?

4. If you were the manager, would you adjust these prices (up or down) prior to finalizing them? Why or why not?

(Answers: 1. $5.83; 2. $3.57; 3. $3.75)

CONTRIBUTION MARGIN PRICING

Contribution margin (CM) is what is left over after the beverage cost of a drink is subtracted from the drink's selling price. That amount is what each item contributes to paying for labor, other operating expenses, and profit. The CM figure, once known, is then added to the cost of each item to determine that item's price.

The CM pricing method is also easy to use if managers know or can estimate several variables:

- The number of customers they will serve in a budget or time period
- Their non-beverage operating costs
- Their desired profit

To illustrate, assume that a manager has created a budget that indicates the operation will serve 200,000 drinks in the coming year and that all nonfood costs, including labor and all other operating expenses, will be $824,000. The

Exhibit 10.6

operation's target profit goal is $112,000. To use CM pricing, managers would follow these two steps:

Step 1: Calculate the average CM per drink:

($824,000 + $112,000)	÷	200,000	=	$4.68
(Non-beverage costs + Profit)		Number of drinks served		Average CM per customer

Step 2: Determine the selling price for the item by adding the beverage cost to the CM.

For example, the base selling price for a drink with a $1.00 beverage cost would be as follows:

$1.00	+	$4.68	=	$5.68
Beverage cost		Contribution margin		Selling price

CM menu pricing is easy to use because the operation's operating budget or revenue forecast generally contains all the necessary information. CM is practical when the nonbeverage costs required to serve each customer are basically the same except for different product costs.

Managers who use the CM pricing method consider the contribution margin per drink as being just as important or even more important than beverage cost in the pricing decision. This pricing method reduces the range of selling prices because the only difference in selling price is the cost of beverages provided to the customer.

WINE PRICING

The pricing of wine in establishments has been hotly debated for years, and the debate continues. On one side of the argument are managers, wine producers, and wine distributors who believe that operators hurt wine sales and overall establishment profitability by marking up the price of wines excessively.

These professionals point out that a guest who can buy a bottle of popular wine in a grocery store for $12 may hesitate to pay $40 for that same bottle of wine in an establishment. To sell more wines, they contend, restaurateurs should reduce the markups on their wines to no more than two times the cost of the wine, and even less for very expensive wines.

On the other side of the argument are the establishment operators who have traditionally marked up the price of the raw food and beverage ingredients they purchase by a factor of three, four, or even five times the cost. That is, a chicken breast purchased for $2 may be the main ingredient in a dish that sells for $6, $8, or $10, depending on the markup factor used.

These managers contend that they should be able to apply the same pricing factors to wine. For example, assume the restaurateur purchased a wine for $10 per bottle. Using a three times markup, the wine would sell for $30.

BY THE CUSTOMER/ FOR THE CUSTOMER

A large number of establishment review–related comments posted on social network sites refer to an operation's selling prices. Some of these comments are very direct:

The prices charged are too high!

The prices charged at this place are really reasonable!

Other comments are less direct, but still relate to pricing:

We got a lot for our money at this place!

They charge too much for what you get!

Pricing is always important, and managers monitoring social media sites should carefully watch for comments related to pricing. These comments can provide valuable clues about how an operation's prices are perceived by its guests.

Some managers point out that if wines are priced too low it is more profitable to sell alternative alcoholic beverages such a cocktails or beer (*Exhibit 10.7*). These other products sometimes generate markups of three, four, or even five times their cost. If wines were marked up only two times their product costs, a $10 wine would sell for $20. In this example, if guests purchased the wine rather than beer or spirits, the low markup would reduce overall profits.

Managers on either side of this issue make valid points. In most cases, excessive markups on wine will result in decreased sales. Wine, however, must be a profitable item or establishments will not sell it. Lost in the argument, perhaps, is the fact that some customers perceive that meals are more elegant, more memorable, and more festive when wine is included.

Exhibit 10.7

Total revenue is the result of guests who spend money each time they come to the establishment. When wines complement meals and are sold at a fair price, repeat business often results. Repeat business usually means an increase in profits. Just as it is difficult to state what managers should charge for a steak listed on the menu, it is similarly difficult to declare how much should be charged for a specific wine or even how its selling price should be determined.

Managers should always use a rational approach to wine pricing. Such an approach results in the manager following some reasonable guidelines regarding wine by-the-bottle markups and prices:

- **Price wines in keeping with the overall price structure of the menu:** Guests who visit moderately priced operations will expect moderately priced wines. If an establishment is very elegant and higher priced, it makes sense for the wines offered to reflect that. Just as most food menus offer a range of entrée prices that define how expensive the establishment is, the same is true of the wine list. Make sure that the prices of the wine list and of the food menu are in harmony.

- **The wine list should include some inexpensive wines:** The additional cost incurred to serve wine to guests already dining in an operation is minimal. If the operation wants to achieve a reputation as one where wine is a natural part of the dining experience, some inexpensive wines should be offered to encourage even the most cost-conscious diners to try them.

- **Offer something for those who want very good quality:** All of the wines selected for the wine list should be good; however, in addition to well brands many bars stock premium and super premium products for those who desire them. In a similar manner, wine drinkers who want the "best of the house" should be able to purchase it. This should be reflected in the wine's price.

- **Consider the guests' alternatives when pricing:** Wine is one of several choices guests have when electing to purchase alcoholic beverages as part of their meal. Consider the couple that desires a very nice dining experience. Assume this couple will consume two drinks each during their visit. Their alternatives are many. They could, for example, order before-dinner cocktails and after-dinner drinks. The total cost to this couple of their alcoholic beverage choices will be the price of the four drinks. Alternatively, assume they elect to buy a 750-milliliter bottle of wine that will yield four large glasses. It makes sense that the price of the wine must have some relationship to the costs of these guests' other beverage alternatives. If the wine is the same or lower in cost than the four-drink alternative, it will likely sell better than if it is perceived as much more expensive than the four-drink alternative. Managers must evaluate the prices charged for all alcoholic beverages and price the wine list accordingly.

- **Evaluate contribution margin as well as cost percentage:** At the heart of the wine list pricing debate is the issue of the importance of contribution margin relative to the importance of low product cost percentages. In the case of wine pricing, the issue is less confusing than in other areas of restaurant and foodservice pricing. Contribution margin is the wine's selling price minus its product cost. Contribution, not its cost percentage (or product cost divided by selling price), must dictate the wine-pricing decision. It is the profit per bottle that is important rather than the wine's cost to selling price ratio.

If the manager elects to use markup factors to price wines, *Exhibit 10.8* suggests commonly used markup factors to apply by wine type.

Exhibit 10.8

SUGGESTIONS FOR MARKUP FACTORS BY WINE TYPE

Wine Type	Markup Factor
Inexpensive bulk wines (e.g., box, carafe, and house wines)	4–5 times cost
Inexpensive bottled wines	3 times cost
Moderately expensive bottled wines	2 times cost
Highest-priced bottled wines	Less than 2 times cost

Remember, marketing is a means of communicating with guests. Marketing messages are designed to encourage guests to visit the operation. Those managers who design and deliver their marketing messages, however, must ensure they do so in a responsible way. While each beverage operation is different, there are basic principles of responsible beverage marketing with which most all managers would agree:

- The marketing message is legal, honest, and truthful.
- The message is prepared with an appropriate sense of social responsibility.
- The message is consistent with sound business practices.
- The message does not offend the local community's generally prevailing standards of taste.
- The message encourages responsible drinking.
- The message does *not* encourage irresponsible drinking.

ON-PREMISE SELLING

It is important to encourage guests to come to an establishment for the first time and to provide them with an enjoyable experience at the establishment. Part of this experience is the communication between the guests and the operation. This communication begins when the guests arrive and continues through their entire visit. Describing the operation and the products and services offered for sale is a major component of this communication effort. There are a collection of internal tools managers use to communicate what they have to offer to guests:

- Exterior signage
- Interior signage
- Table tents
- Sound-system announcements
- Menus
- Service staff recommendations
- Atmosphere
- Beverage promotions
- Vendor resources

Exterior Signage

Guests arriving at an establishment make their first judgment about its quality when they see its exterior signage. The on-premise signage conveys an indication of the type of experience guests that will encounter at the establishment. On-premise signage generally identifies the facility's name and type of operation. The specific words chosen for use on exterior signage is important.

THINK ABOUT IT . . .

Have you ever received a marketing message that you felt was less than honest or accurate? How did you feel about the organization that provided the message? As a manager, what steps might you take to ensure honesty in your operation's marketing messages?

The operation may be a club, pub, restaurant, brewery, lounge, sports bar, tavern, or some other descriptive term that gives the guest an indication of the establishment's character. Each of these words has a slightly different meaning. A guest would more likely expect that dancing might be available at John Flower's Nightclub. They might not expect this same entertainment at John Flower's Tavern.

In addition to the words used on the exterior sign, its appearance is also important. For example, if the sign is lighted, it is essential that all bulbs be in working order. If it is a painted sign, it is important that the sign look fresh and clean. The name of the facility should be easily remembered, and the sign should be large enough to catch the eye of a potential guest.

Interior Signage

Interior signage can also be used to advertise drink specials, happy hours, available entertainment, or other special features the establishment is promoting at the time. Interior signage is an extremely effective way to help build sales volume. In addition to reading tables tents, the advertising materials placed directly on the table, and the operation's drink menus, guests will visually scan the walls of the facility. It is possible to catch the guest's eye and continue the communication process by displaying interior signage that is both attractive and interesting. Beverage vendors frequently provide such signage for free or at reduced cost. These signs typically advertise a particular brand of product and help contribute to the overall atmosphere of the operation.

Managers can also create interior signage. These signs can take the form of chalkboards; light boards that, when written on with special pens, cause the lettering to glow; or digital display boards used to promote products or services offered by the operation. Many operators use interior signage to advertise daily or weekly drink specials.

Interior signage can be an extremely cost-effective way to communicate with guests once they are in the facility. Managers can easily update interior signage, and the signage adds to the overall atmosphere of the operation. However, be sure that signs fit the establishment. Signs, for example, that advertise beer products are appropriate in a casual club. They would not be appropriate in the lounge of the fine-dining establishment. In addition, too many signs can cause a cluttered look and should be avoided.

Table Tents

Table tents are also effective ways to continue the communication process and to encourage impulse buying. A table tent is a print advertisement that sits on guest tables.

Many beverage vendors supply attractive four-color signs that can be placed on the tabletop to advertise their products. While these table tents are economical, some managers believe that they are less effective than table tents unique to a facility, since customers may see the same liquor distributor's table tents in several facilities. It is always a good idea to personalize the table tent with the name of the establishment. Of course, operators may elect to create their own table tent items to promote special events or special products. Table tents can also be created to inform the guest of interesting facts about the facility and its history, décor, or special location.

Table tents are effective marketing tools, but too many table tents make a table look cluttered and can obscure the intended message. In addition, table tents must be kept clean. Graffiti or food and beverage stains detract from the messages and lower the image of the facility. Tabletop advertising items should be changed regularly to alert customers to new products and services.

Sound-System Announcements

Some beverage facilities have a speaker or sound system for communication with guests. Periodically, the sound system can be used to announce drink specials or upcoming events that encourage guests to purchase products or return at a later date. This communication effort can be overused and can even become annoying if used in excess. The ability to make on-the-spot announcements, however, can be quite useful in increasing beverage revenue. Examples include announcing sports results, particular groups that may have arrived at the establishment, birthdays, or other information that may be important to guests.

Menus

Beverage menus are among the most effective ways operators can communicate with guests. Many operations create separate menus for food and beverage products. Other managers find it more appropriate to have menus that combine food and beverage offerings. Regardless of the choice the manager makes, the menu is an excellent opportunity to build impulse sales or to communicate special sales and services the facility has to offer.

With the advent of computerized desktop publishing and inexpensive on-site color printing, many managers can create their own beverage menus for a very low cost. They are also able to change their menus more frequently than they could in the past. In addition, menu clip-ons, which are smaller menu segments clipped on to more permanent menus, can prove very effective in influencing impulse buying. Menus should be clean and not worn. Like table tents, they should be free of writing or food and beverage stains because menus give the guest an indication of the overall quality of the facility.

OPEN FOR BUSINESS — RESTAURANT TECHNOLOGY

Today's availability of advanced software and high-quality color printers means that managers can easily produce their own table tents on premise. Doing so allows for reduced costs and customization of messages.

It is important, however, to ensure that the writing, spelling, and grammar appearing on a table tent is high quality and accurate. Poorly written, misspelled, or improperly stated messages reflect badly on an operation. As a result, managers must select carefully to ensure they choose software that makes it easy to detect, edit, and correct these types of critical messaging errors.

Service Staff Recommendations

Quality service may be the most important marketing technique available to the operator. Successful managers have employees who are pleasant, outgoing, and enjoy working with people. All employees should be trained in effective selling techniques. Effective selling begins with thorough product knowledge. Employees should know prices and ingredients of cocktails and specialty drinks, and the differences among wines and beers.

Consider the following example. A customer enters a beverage facility, sits at the bar and says, "I'll have a vodka tonic." The bartender replies, "Would you like that made with (*name of call brand vodka*)?" In most cases the customer will agree and the facility will have sold a higher priced, more profitable drink. This example of suggestive selling demonstrates several key points regarding staff recommendations:

- The bartender had the product knowledge required to know the call brands of vodka.
- The bartender was trained to sell responsibly.
- The bartender was comfortable using people skills to engage the guest in conversation.
- The bartender took the time to seek out the guest's needs.

Employees need to know how to communicate with customers. Friendly greetings make customers feel welcome, and encourage their patronage. When taking beverage orders, servers should recommend specialty drinks and answer any questions guests may have. When customers are leaving the facility, employees should thank them—by name if possible—for their visit.

Atmosphere

The bar's general decor and the products customers see are extremely important to an operation's ability to sell drinks to guests. Displays should "show off" the operation's products and let customers know what products are available. Labels should always face outward. Bottles should be organized and neat. Some operations categorize their beverage inventory by price. They keep the more expensive brands on the right-hand side of the bar, since the guest's eye normally travels in that direction.

If wines are sold, wine lists should be available, interesting, and appealing to guests. An establishment's demographics are influenced, in part, by its atmosphere and image. A quiet, romantic environment will attract different customers than a loud, bright sports bar. Naturally, all establishments should be clean, well lit, and comfortable.

Staff uniforms also contribute to the atmosphere of an operation. Many bars that try to appeal to the younger crowd have uniforms that are very un-uniform, such as same-color polo shirts and pants that look like outfits

Exhibit 10.9

patrons might wear. This tactic is designed to make patrons feel comfortable with the staff. Guests may feel that staff members are "one of them," especially if there is a similarity in age. In contrast, attractive, distinctive staff uniforms that fit the image of the facility are a good way to help guests easily know who the staff members are (*Exhibit 10.9*).

Beverage Promotions

Sales promotions are special incentives for customers to patronize a beverage operation. There are many types of sales promotions, and different tools or materials can be used. All are designed to give customers an extra "boost" to get them into a facility or to purchase certain items. Sales promotions are useful only when customers know about them, so they are often the focus of an establishment's external and internal advertising.

The most important task facing managers who design and implement on-premise selling promotions is to ensure beverages are always sold responsibly. For example, an operation may decide to feature a draft beer artificially colored green during a St. Patrick's Day special event. This can be a fun way to encourage draft beer sales during the event. The *amount* of beer sold to a customer during such a promotion, however, should not be different than from any other time. Similarly, a special cocktail may be featured in an on-premise drink promotion. The special drink, however, should be served to guests just as carefully and as responsibly as any other drink that is not being specially promoted.

The marketing of alcoholic beverages within restaurants has undergone significant change in the past decade. Promotions such as "buy one and get one free" or "pay one price" to receive unlimited alcoholic beverages are used less frequently than they used to be. These and similar approaches to marketing alcohol are often viewed as encouraging irresponsible drinking.

While most managers understand that advertising in a manner that encourages irresponsible drinking is unwise, they also know that most drinkers are responsible and often like to try new, different, and sometimes higher-priced beverages. As a result, the effective in-house promotion of *responsible* alcohol consumption can lead to significantly increased check averages and profits.

When developing advertisements and promotions related to alcohol, managers should consider several key issues:

- Does the advertising message promote the attractiveness of the business as well as the appeal of the beverage? The best alcoholic beverage ads include mention of the setting, such as a comfortable dining area and appealing cocktail lounge.

- Is the focus of the message related to the quantity of alcohol to be served? Promoting excessive alcohol consumption can result in negative consequences for the business in terms of image and potential legal liability should a guest overindulge.

- Is the focus of the ad related to the low price of alcohol to be served? This is a delicate area. Certainly, happy hour specials, specialty drinks, and new beverage product introductions may suggest that price should be a featured part of the message. Managers, however, should approach low-price beverage advertising cautiously as these ads have the potential to result in a negative consequence, much like advertisements relying on quantity.

- Could the ad be perceived as encouraging alcohol consumption by those under the legal drinking age? These must be avoided in all cases.

- Is the ad in compliance with relevant state and local liquor licensing regulations? A thorough knowledge of applicable laws and regulations is necessary and they must not be violated.

Many establishments feature selected beverages with special menus or complimentary *hors d'oeuvres*. Many managers plan beverage promotions that focus on a particular event or time of year such as Mardi Gras, or a season, such as Oktoberfest. It is hard to overestimate the importance of variety in keeping the beverage operation's revenue levels high.

One of the most misunderstood concepts within the beverage business is consumer loyalty. Beverage patrons often seek the comfort level associated with a familiar operation, yet even these guests seek variety and stimulation in their experience. This excitement can come from new products or services offered in the same comfortable environment they have come to enjoy. Beverage specials are an excellent way to communicate the newness and excitement that creative beverage operators can bring to their establishments.

Vendor Resources

Vendors can be an excellent source of valuable promotional information and materials. Vendors are often among the first to know about innovative approaches and popular new beverage products. A good vendor can provide information about consumer behavior, as well as insight into changing market conditions that may affect pricing. If, for example, demand for Merlot grapes outpaces supply, prices for that type of wine will likely increase. Vendors will know about these price movements long before most managers, and they can be of help in adjusting buying patterns accordingly.

An ideal vendor should have great product knowledge, a true interest in the success of the beverage operation, and the time to put the two of these together. Any vendor worth buying from must bring more to the table than low price and consistent delivery schedules. Service, including information about what is popular, should be a standard part of any vendor's relationship with an effective beverage manager.

THE FUTURE OF BEVERAGE MANAGEMENT

The upcoming years will likely be challenging ones for managers of beverage operations. Managers will be increasingly faced with the prospect of both socially and legally sanctioned moderation in alcoholic beverage consumption. Even if this trend stops, it will leave a lasting impact on the beverage industry. Operations that serve alcohol responsibly will thrive in the face of these future challenges.

Despite past challenges, the consumption of alcoholic beverages has long been a source of great joy to humankind. There is no question that this will continue. For the professional beverage operator, this means that the opportunity to play an important role in many of life's significant events is ensured. Whether it is a wedding reception, an anniversary party, a special sporting event, or just relaxing with friends, the responsible consumption of alcoholic beverages will continue to be an important part in the lives of many.

Notwithstanding the many challenges facing the beverage operator, the long-term viability of beverage operations is ensured. Profitable beverage operations will continue to be the result of recognizing several consistent facts about beverage operation guests:

- Guests will continue to reward those operations that provide high value.
- Guests will continue to frequent operations they feel provide something new and exciting.
- Guests will continue to seek out those operations that provide high levels of quality service.

- Guests will continue to drink more responsibly and with greater care.

- Guests will reward, with loyalty, those beverage managers who put the interests of guests and society first as they seek profitability.

- Guests will seek out and return to operations that are staffed with friendly, well-trained employees.

- Guests will prefer beverage operations managed by individuals who love their work so much that it shows.

For those managers who understand all of these important truths, the future of their professional success and the success of their operations is bright indeed.

SUMMARY

1. **Describe the manager's primary goal in marketing a beverage operation.**

   A manager's primary marketing-related goal is to continually grow the operation's customer base. Identifying and capturing the business of a sufficient number of guests is the key to operational profitability and long-term financial success. If too few customers are served, the business will inevitably cease to exist. When a large customer base is obtained, profit goals can be met, service levels can be maintained, and the business can prosper.

2. **Explain the importance of identifying an operation's target market.**

   Because different beverage operations appeal to different people, managers must accurately identify potential customers. Managers group those customers who are most likely to visit their operations into categories, or target markets. Target markets are those potential customers whose specific needs and wants an operation seeks to meet. Managers segment target markets by demographics and psychographics. By targeting specific markets, managers can make the most effective use of selling and promotional efforts.

3. **State the purposes of a marketing plan, marketing budget, and marketing schedule.**

   A marketing plan is a formal statement detailing how an operation will achieve its marketing goals. A marketing plan details the operation's marketing activities and identifies who will do them. It addresses when the activities will take place and how much money is needed to complete them. Finally, it addresses how the plan's results will be measured. Because financial resources are limited, a manager's marketing plan must be based on a budget. The budget ensures that the funds set aside for marketing will be sufficient to fully fund all activities presented in the plan. The marketing schedule is the part of the marketing plan that contains three key pieces of information about an operation's specific marketing activities: What is to be done? When will it be done? and Who will do it?

4. **Describe the two primary drink-pricing methods used by beverage managers.**

The two basic methods used to establish drink prices are the beverage cost percentage and the contribution margin (CM) methods. When using the beverage cost percentage method, managers set their drink prices based on the product cost of the drinks sold. These product costs are expressed as a percentage of the drink's total selling price. In the contribution margin method, a fixed amount required to recover the non-beverage costs of producing the drink and a predetermined profit amount per drink are added to the drink's product cost to arrive at the drink's selling price.

5. **Identify on-premise beverage selling opportunities available to managers.**

A wide variety of on-premise selling opportunities are available to managers of beverage establishments. These alternatives include exterior signage, interior signage, and table tents. If available and used sparingly, an in-house sound system can be an effective selling tool. Menus and service staff recommendations also may influence sales. An operation's atmosphere and its special promotional activities are additional on-premise components that directly impact sales. Finally, beverage suppliers can be an excellent source of on-premise selling tools such as table tents and signs. Just as important, suppliers can provide managers with valuable selling advice based on their knowledge of new products and consumer buying trends.

APPLICATION EXERCISE

Gene operates the D-Town Grill. Last month Gene calculated the following cost of goods sold (COGS) separately for the beer, wine, and spirits sold in his operation. Using his POS system, Gene determined the total sales revenue he achieved in each of these same three categories. Complete the form and answer the questions that follow.

Product	COGS (Beverages)	Beverage Revenue	Beverage Cost Percentage
Beer	$1,500	$ 4,500	
Wine	950	2,375	
Spirits	2,100	10,500	
Total			

1. What were the total COGS for the month?
2. What was the total beverage revenue for the month?
3. What was the beer beverage cost percentage for the month?
4. What was the wine beverage cost percentage for the month?
5. What was the spirit beverage cost percentage for the month?
6. What was the total beverage cost percentage for the month?

REVIEW YOUR LEARNING

Select the best answer for each question.

1. **What is the primary function of marketing?**
   A. Explaining and showing how a business meets customers' needs
   B. Selling new products and services to many new customers
   C. Selling products and services at their maximum prices
   D. Advertising what a business has available for sale

2. **What is the most critical characteristic of a formal marketing plan?**
   A. That it is written
   B. That it is revised weekly
   C. That it includes a large budget
   D. That it is rewritten each month

3. **What is an example of a customer psychographic?**
   A. Age
   B. Gender
   C. Lifestyle
   D. Race

4. **What is an example of a customer demographic?**
   A. Weight
   B. Age
   C. Height
   D. Lifestyle

5. **Peggy has decided her marketing budget will be 5% of next year's forecasted revenue. What will happen if Peggy fails to achieve her revenue forecast?**
   A. Her marketing budget will remain the same.
   B. Her marketing budget will be less than she planned.
   C. Her marketing budget will go down if product costs go up.
   D. Her marketing budget will go down if product costs go down.

6. **What would be the total for a marketing budget if it were set at 4% of a projected $150,000 in revenue?**
   A. $3,750
   B. $6,000
   C. $37,500
   D. $60,000

7. **A beverage operation created a drink with a standardize recipe cost of $2.25. It wants to achieve a 25% beverage cost percentage on this drink's selling price. What should be the selling price of the drink?**
   A. $8.25
   B. $9.00
   C. $9.25
   D. $10.00

8. **What is the primary disadvantage of using the beverage cost percentage method when pricing expensive bottled wines?**
   A. The method is too complicated to calculate easily.
   B. The price may be viewed as too low to provide quality.
   C. Guests may think the price does not provide value.
   D. Too little profit may be achieved with each bottle's sale.

9. **When do a beverage operation's on-premise selling opportunities begin?**
   A. On the guest's way to the facility
   B. When the guest arrives at the facility
   C. When the guest enters the facility
   D. When the guest's first beverage order is placed

10. **What is the most important task facing managers who design and implement on-premise selling promotions?**
   A. To maximize sales
   B. To maximize profits
   C. To sell beverages responsibly
   D. To sell designated beverage brands

FIELD **PROJECT**

You have just been chosen as the bar manager for one of the largest fine-dining establishments in your favorite city. The operation will be opening soon and you have been given the responsibility for designing and implementing the entire beverage management program.

To help you get started, answer the following questions. Use your knowledge and the Internet to research and gather any information you need to set up an outstanding beverage program.

1. What is the name of the state agency that will regulate the sales of alcoholic beverages?

2. What classification of alcoholic beverage sales license will you be operating under?

3. What are the state or local regulations regarding the following:
   A. The time of day at which you can begin to sell alcoholic beverages
   B. The time of day at which you must stop selling alcoholic beverages
   C. Sunday alcohol sales
   D. Alcohol sales on holidays
   E. Alcohol sales on election days

4. What are the qualifications or mandatory training requirements for the following:
   A. Managers
   B. Bartenders
   C. Servers

5. Create a one-hour bartender or server training program for the topic Understanding BAC. Indicate these items for this program:
   A. An outline of the content to be taught
   B. The method you will use for teaching
   C. The manner in which you will test trainees for mastery of the topic
   D. A feedback document for use in gaining employee input into how the training program could be improved in the future

E. A form for use in each employee's file documenting his or her successful completion of the training program

6. Indicate how you will consider these *customer-related* factors:
   A. The number of beers you will offer
   B. The number of draft beers you will offer

7. Indicate how you will consider these *facility-related* factors:
   A. The number of beers you will offer
   B. The number of draft beers you will offer

8. You are meeting with the establishment's owner to discuss the best way to present the wines you have chosen to the operation's dining guests.
   A. Which order of wine presentation will be your first choice? Why?
   B. Which order of wine presentation would be your least favorite? Why?

9. Consider the following five drink recipes. Calculate the number of standard drinks contained in each recipe. Assume that all spirits used in the recipe are 80 proof:

COLORADO BULLDOG
Ice
1 1/2 oz vodka
1/2 oz coffee liqueur
1 oz cream
Cola to fill glass

_____ Standard drinks

MANHATTAN

Ice
2 oz rye whiskey
1/2 oz dry vermouth
2–3 dashes bitters
Maraschino cherry (garnish)
_____ Standard drinks

JUMBO CHOCOLATE MARTINI

Ice (shaker/strained)
1 oz chocolate liqueur
1 oz crème de cacao
1 oz vodka
2 oz half-and-half
Cocoa powder (as a rim garnish)
_____ Standard drinks

CAFÉ ROYALE

1 oz bourbon
1/2 oz simple syrup
4 oz hot coffee (Irish coffee mug)
Whipped cream (for topping)
_____ Standard drinks

GRASSHOPPER

3/4 oz crème de menthe
3/4 oz crème de cacao
1 oz cream
Blend or shake into cocktail glass (chilled)
_____ Standard drinks

10. As the operation's manager you will need to hire new bartenders. Develop a list of 10 pre-employment questions you think would be most important to ask your prospective bartenders before they were hired. You have two options for research, depending on your age:

   A. *If you are at least 21 years of age,* visit a local beverage operation that offers at-the-bar service and ask the "bartender" who serves you what questions he or she would ask a prospective bartender if responsible for hiring new ones.

   B. *If you are under 21 years of age,* visit a local restaurant or foodservice operation and ask if the manager will share with you key questions he or she asks prospective employees who will be hired to prepare food items, rather than beverage items. Use the information you gain to help you complete this part of the field project.

11. Assume the operation is in the state where you now live.

   A. *If you are at least 21 years of age,* visit a local beverage operation and ask if all beverage products must be purchased from the state, which is the case in a control state. If it is a license state, determine the number of different beverage suppliers available. Which are used by the operation you are visiting? Why?

   B. *If you are under 21 years of age,* visit the local ABC or go online to its Web site to determine if the state where you now live is a control state or a license state. Consider how the answer to that question will affect your beverage purchasing policies.

12. Visit two bars or establishments that serve alcohol and ask the manager his or her opinion about using mystery shoppers to monitor the employee's adherence to operating standards. Then make a decision on whether you will or will not choose to use a mystery shopper service to monitor your employee's adherence to the policies and procedures you will establish for your operation. Write a business memo of no more than one page explaining your decision.

13. Visit three bars or establishments that serve alcohol and ask the manager who establishes the drink prices charged to customers. Also ask the following:

   A. Are prices established using a beverage cost percentage or a contribution margin pricing philosophy?

   B. Are beer prices allowed to vary for special promotions?

   C. Are wine prices allowed to vary for special promotions?

   D. Are spirit prices allowed to vary for special promotions?

   E. What are the two most popular and successful beverage-related promotions the manager has implemented in the past 12 months?

APPENDIX

This appendix illustrates recipes from 25 common and classic mixed alcoholic beverages. Each recipe identifies key components of the drink, such as spirit type used, drink name, specific ingredients required, quantity of required ingredients, preparation method, glassware to be used, garnish to be used, and drink strength measured in standard drinks. For the purpose of this appendix, assume that all spirits are 80 proof. Recall from previous chapters that one standard drink equals 1 1/2 or 1.5 ounces of an 80-proof spirit. As an example, a mixed drink requiring 2 1/4 or 2.25 ounces of an 80-proof spirit equals 1.5 standard drinks.

STANDARDIZED DRINK RECIPE
Spirit Category: Brandy

Name	Quantity and Ingredients	Preparation	
Brandy Alexander	1 3/4 oz brandy 1 1/4 oz dark crème de cacao 1 oz half-and-half 1/4 tsp nutmeg, grated (garnish)	Combine the brandy, crème de cacao, and half-and-half in a cocktail shaker filled halfway with ice cubes. Shake well. Strain into a martini glass. Garnish with the nutmeg. *This recipe equals 2 standard drinks.	
Hot Toddy	1 tbsp honey 1 1/2 oz brandy 1 1/2 tsp lemon juice 1 tea bag 1 c boiling water Cinnamon stick (garnish)	Coat the bottom of an Irish coffee glass with the honey; add the brandy and lemon juice. Place the tea bag in boiling water. Pour hot tea into the glass and stir. Garnish with a cinnamon stick. *This recipe equals 1 standard drink.	
Metropolitan	1 1/2 oz brandy 1 oz sweet vermouth 1/2 tsp simple syrup 2 dashes aromatic bitters	Pour all the ingredients into a cocktail shaker filled with ice cubes. Shake well. Strain into a chilled martini glass. *This recipe equals 1 standard drink.	

STANDARDIZED DRINK RECIPE
Spirit Category: Combinations

Name	Quantity and Ingredients	Preparation	
Long Beach Iced Tea	1/2 oz vodka 1/2 oz gin 1/2 oz light rum 1/2 oz tequila 1/2 oz orange liqueur 1 oz cranberry juice 6 oz lemon lime soda Lemon twist (garnish)	Combine all ingredients in a Collins glass filled with ice cubes. Top with lemon lime soda. Garnish with a lemon twist. *This recipe equals 1.67 standard drinks.	
Long Island Iced Tea	1/2 oz vodka 1/2 oz gin 1/2 oz rum 1/2 oz tequila 1/2 oz orange liqueur 1 oz sweet and sour mix 6 oz cola Lemon twist (garnish)	In a cocktail shaker filled halfway with ice cubes, combine the vodka, gin, rum, tequila, sweet and sour mix, and orange liqueur. Shake well. Pour into a Collins glass filled almost all the way with ice. Top with cola. Garnish with a lemon twist. *This recipe equals 1.67 standard drinks.	

STANDARDIZED DRINK RECIPE
Spirit Category: Gin

Name	Quantity and Ingredients	Preparation	
Gimlet	2 oz gin 1 1/2 oz fresh lime juice 1 oz sugar syrup Large mint sprig (garnish)	Combine all ingredients in a cocktail shaker filled with ice cubes. Shake well. Strain into a chilled martini glass. Garnish with a mint sprig. *This recipe equals 1.33 standard drinks.	
Gin and Tonic	2 oz gin 6 oz tonic water Lime wedge (garnish)	Pour the gin and tonic water into a highball glass filled almost all the way with ice cubes. Stir well. Garnish with a lime wedge. *This recipe equals 1.33 standard drinks.	
Martini	2 oz gin 1/4 oz dry vermouth Olive or lemon twist (garnish)	Combine all the ingredients in a cocktail shaker filled with ice. Shake well. Strain into a chilled martini glass. Garnish with an olive or lemon twist. *Use less vermouth for drier martinis. This recipe equals 1.33 standard drinks.	
Tom Collins	2 oz gin 2 oz lemon juice 1 tsp sugar, granulated 1/4 c cold club soda Lemon slice (garnish) Maraschino cherry (garnish)	Combine the gin, lemon juice, and sugar in a cocktail shaker filled halfway with ice cubes. Shake well, until the outside of the container is frosty, about 15 seconds. Strain into a Collins glass full of ice. Top with club soda. Garnish with a lemon slice and maraschino cherry. *This recipe equals 1.33 standard drinks.	

STANDARDIZED DRINK RECIPE
Spirit Category: Liqueurs

Name	Quantity and Ingredients	Preparation	
Fuzzy Navel	1 1/2 oz peach schnapps 6 oz orange juice	Pour all the ingredients into a rocks or highball glass filled with ice cubes. Stir well. *This recipe equals 1 standard drink.	
Caramel Apple	1 oz vodka 1 oz sour apple schnapps 1 oz butterscotch schnapps	Pour all the ingredients into a cocktail shaker filled with ice cubes. Shake until ice cold. Pour into a rocks glass with ice. *This recipe equals 2 standard drinks.	

STANDARDIZED DRINK RECIPE
Spirit Category: Rum

Name	Quantity and Ingredients	Preparation
Daiquiri	2 oz light rum 1/2 oz lime juice 1/4 oz simple syrup	Pour the light rum, lime juice, and simple syrup into a cocktail shaker filled with ice cubes. Shake well. Strain into a chilled rocks glass. *This recipe equals 1.33 standard drinks.
Mai Tai	1 oz light rum 1/2 oz crème de almond 1/2 oz orange liqueur Sweet and sour mix Pineapple juice 1/2 oz dark rum Lime wedge (garnish)	Pour the light rum, crème de almond, and orange liqueur into a Collins glass filled with ice cubes. Add equal parts of sweet and sour mix and pineapple juice. Top with dark rum. Garnish with a lime wedge. *This recipe equals 1.67 standard drinks.
Mojito	10 mint leaves 1/2 lime (cut into 4 wedges) 2 tbsp sugar, granulated 1 1/2 oz white rum 1/2 c club soda	In a Collins glass, muddle the mint leaves and 3 lime wedges, then add the sugar. Fill the glass almost to the top with ice cubes. Pour the rum over the ice. Fill the glass with club soda. Stir well. Garnish with a lime wedge. *This recipe equals 1 standard drink.
Piña Colada	1 1/2 oz light rum 1 1/2 oz coconut rum 2 oz pineapple juice 1 oz milk Maraschino cherry (garnish) Pineapple chunk (garnish)	Pour all the ingredients into a shaker filled with ice cubes. Shake well. Pour into a rocks or highball glass. Garnish with a maraschino cherry and pineapple chunk. *This recipe equals 2 standard drinks.

STANDARDIZED DRINK RECIPE
Spirit Category: Tequila

Name	Quantity and Ingredients	Preparation
Margarita	Salt (to rim the glass) 2 oz tequila 1 oz orange liqueur 1/2 oz lime juice Lime wedge (garnish)	Salt the rim of a margarita, rocks, or martini glass. Combine all the ingredients in a cocktail shaker filled with ice cubes and strain into the glass. Garnish with a lime wedge. *This recipe equals 2 standard drinks.
Tequila Sunrise	1 1/2 oz tequila 4 oz orange juice 1/2 oz (approx) grenadine syrup	Fill a highball glass with ice cubes. Pour the tequila into the glass of ice and then add the orange juice. Generously pour the grenadine syrup onto the side of the tilted glass to create a sunrise effect. *This recipe equals 1 standard drink.

STANDARDIZED DRINK RECIPE
Spirit Category: Whiskies

Name	Quantity and Ingredients	Preparation	
Mint Julep	1/2 c mint leaves 1 tsp sugar, granulated 2 tsp water 2 1/2 oz bourbon whiskey 4 fresh mint sprigs (garnish)	Muddle the 1/2 cup of mint leaves, sugar, and water in a Collins glass. Fill the glass with crushed ice and add whiskey. Top with more ice and garnish with a mint sprig. *This recipe equals 1.67 standard drinks.	
Washington Apple	1 1/2 oz whiskey 1 oz sour apple schnapps 1 oz cranberry juice Apple slice (garnish)	Pour the ingredients into a cocktail shaker filled with ice cubes. Shake well. Strain into a chilled highball glass. Garnish with an apple slice. *This recipe equals 1.67 standard drinks.	
Whiskey Sour	2 oz rye whiskey 1 oz lemon juice 1 dash simple syrup Orange slice (garnish) Maraschino cherry (garnish)	Combine all the ingredients in a cocktail shaker filled with crushed ice. Strain into a chilled rocks glass. Garnish with an orange slice and maraschino cherry. *This recipe equals 1.33 standard drinks.	

STANDARDIZED DRINK RECIPE
Spirit Category: Vodka

Name	Quantity and Ingredients	Preparation	
Bloody Mary	1 1/2 oz vodka 1/2 c tomato juice 2 tsp fresh lemon juice 1/8 tsp Worcestershire sauce 1/8 tsp Louisiana-style hot sauce 1/8 tsp celery salt 1/8 tsp black pepper 1/8 tsp horseradish Celery stick (garnish)	Combine all the ingredients in a cocktail shaker. Shake well. Strain into a highball glass filled with ice cubes. Garnish with a celery stick. *This recipe equals 1 standard drink.	
Cosmopolitan	1 oz vodka 1/2 oz orange liqueur 1/2 oz lime juice 1 oz cranberry juice Lime wedge (garnish)	Combine all the ingredients in a cocktail shaker filled with ice cubes. Shake well. Strain into a martini or rocks glass. Garnish with a lime wedge. *This recipe equals 1 standard drink.	
Kamikaze	1 oz orange liqueur 1 oz vodka 1 oz lime juice Lime wedge (garnish)	Combine all the ingredients in a cocktail shaker filled with ice cubes. Shake well. Strain into a rocks glass. Garnish with a lime wedge and a stir stick. *This recipe equals 1.33 standard drinks.	
Screwdriver	1 1/2 oz vodka 6 oz orange juice Orange slice (garnish)	Add the vodka to a highball glass filled with ice cubes. Top with the orange juice. Garnish with an orange slice. *This recipe equals 1 standard drink.	
White Russian	2 oz vodka 1 oz coffee liqueur 3/4 oz light cream or milk	Pour the vodka and coffee liqueur into a rocks glass over ice cubes. Fill with the light cream or milk. *This recipe equals 2 standard drinks.	

GLOSSARY

Action plan A series of steps that can be taken to resolve a problem.

Actual damages Real, identifiable losses that are the direct result of wrongful acts.

Adjuncts Additional cereal grains added to beer to add flavor or reduce brewing costs.

Alcoholic beverage Any drinkable liquid that contains ethyl alcohol.

Alcoholic Beverage Control (ABC) A state agency that is responsible for granting licenses and regulating the sale of alcohol.

Ale A beer made with top-fermenting yeast; characterized by a more complex flavor than lager.

Aromatized wine Wine flavored with something other than the grapes used for its production, such as herbs, roots, flowers, and barks.

Assisted drink production system A system in which bartenders use metered pour spouts to help control beverage quantity in the drinks they produce.

Automated drink production system A system in which all or nearly all of a drink's production is performed by machine.

Average inventory The value, or amount, of products in inventory at the beginning of the period plus the amount of inventory at the end of the period, divided by two.

Beer A beverage fermented from cereals and malts and usually flavored with hops.

Beer-clean glass A glass that is cleaned and prepared especially for draft beer.

Beginning inventory The value of all beverage products available for sale at the start of an accounting period.

Beverage-control system The computer hardware and software used to manage an operation's automated drink sales.

Beverage cost percentage The proportion of beverage revenue spent on the products that generate that revenue.

Bin number A number that tells the location in a wine cellar where a specific wine is being held for service.

Blender drink A drink that is mixed with the use of an electric blender.

Blood alcohol content (BAC) The amount of alcohol contained in the blood of a drinker.

Blue laws Laws that restrict or prohibit the sale of alcohol on Sundays.

Blush wine A very light red wine.

Bonds A guarantee of the ability to pay in case of a liability.

Bouquet The aroma of a wine.

Brandy A distilled spirit made from a fermented mash of fruit, bottled at 80 proof or more.

Breached (duty of care) Violated.

Call brand (spirit) A specific brand of liquor requested by a guest.

Call-in (employee) The industry term used to describe an employee who, on a scheduled work day, notifies a manager that he or she will not be working.

Capital The amount of the owner's money invested in the business that could be used for other purposes.

Carafe A glass container used to serve wine or water.

Cash bank The amount of money issued to bartenders and servers for use during their shift.

Cash flow The amount of money needed to pay bills when due.

Cellar temperature Temperature between 65°F and 70°F (18°C and 21°C).

Centralized storage area An area that is used to store all alcoholic beverages from the time they are received until they are issued to the bar.

Certification (professional) The confirmation that a person possesses certain skills, knowledge, or characteristics. In most cases, this is supplied by some form of external review, education, or assessment.

Civil lawsuit A lawsuit in which the plaintiff is an individual or company.

Closing (a tab) Recording sales as "final" when guests pay for their charges; all revenue from the sale is then deposited in the proper cash bank.

Coaching Informal training in which managers emphasize when employees are working correctly (positive coaching) and discourage employees from working incorrectly (negative coaching).

Cocktail A spirit that is combined with other drink ingredients or flavorings to create a mixed drink.

Competencies Standards of knowledge; skills and abilities required for successful job performance.

Contribution margin (CM) What is left over after the beverage cost of a drink is subtracted from the drink's selling price.

Control state In control, or monopoly, states the state is the sole supplier of liquor.

Cordial A spirit that has sweet flavorings steeped in it like tea; also known as a **liqueur**.

Cost of goods sold (COGS) The cost to purchase the products that generate revenue within a specific time period.

Cost-effective (training) Resulting in time and money savings that are greater than what the product or service costs.

Coupler A mechanism that allows beer to flow out of the keg.

Craft brewery A brewery that focuses on smaller batches of higher-quality beers, generally using traditional brewing methods.

Criminal proceeding A lawsuit in which the plaintiff is a governmental entity and the allegation is that a law has been broken by the defendant.

Customer count The number of guests served in a specific time period.

Décor The style of furnishings and decorative items that give an operation its character.

Defendant In a lawsuit, the party that is required to respond to the charge of the plaintiff.

Demographics Statistical characteristics of the population, such as age, gender, race, education, and income level.

Depressant A drug that decreases the body's activities and acts as a tranquilizer; its misuse can cause coma or even death.

Discretionary income The money available to spend after consumers' expenses are paid.

Distillation (or distilling) The process of removing water from a liquid that contains alcohol.

Dram shop legislation Legislation that holds operators responsible for the acts of their intoxicated customers.

Drink recipe evaluation A formal process in which a taste test panel may be used to assess whether a standardized drink recipe yields an acceptable product.

Drink tab A guest's running total of charges for drinks that have been served but not yet paid for.

Drug Any substance that, when absorbed into the body, alters normal bodily function.

Dry (wine) Wine with a sugar content of less than 0.8 percent.

Duty of care A legal concept that requires managers to use reasonable care when performing any act that could harm others.

Ending inventory The value of the beverage inventory at the end of the accounting period.

Fermentation A chemical reaction that splits a molecule of sugar into equal parts of ethyl alcohol and carbon dioxide.

First in, first out (FIFO) An inventory method that assumes that products are withdrawn from inventory in the order in which they are received and entered into storage. The value of inventory becomes the cost of the most recently purchased products.

Foodborne illness An illness resulting from the consumption of contaminated food, pathogenic (disease-causing) bacteria, viruses, or parasites that contaminate food.

Forced carbonation Adding carbonation back to the nearly finished beer, if the beer is not naturally carbonated.

Foreseeable (harm) Able to be reasonably anticipated or predicted.

Fortified wine Wine that has had a spirit added to it to increase its alcohol content.

Free pour To pour alcohol without using a portioning tool.

Garnishes Pieces of fruit or vegetables, salt, spices, or other ingredients added to a mixed drink.

Gin A spirit flavored with juniper berries.

Gross negligence A total disregard for the welfare of others.

Guest A customer who seeks to lawfully obtain food or beverages from a hospitality business.

Half-barrel A keg that contains 15.5 gallons of beer.

Head The frothy foam that forms on top of liquid beer when it is poured into a glass.

Highball The broad name given to the family of mixed drinks that are composed of a spirit and a larger proportion of a nonalcoholic mixer.

Hops The female flower clusters of *Humulus lupulus*, which are used to flavor beer and give it its characteristic bitterness.

House brand (spirit) The brand of liquor that is served by the operation when the guest does not indicate a preference for a specific brand; also referred to as a **well brand**.

House wine A wine designed to be sold at a low cost and often in a single serving.

Incident report The form used to document what happened and what was done in response when a critical incident related to alcoholic beverage service occurs.

Income statement The financial document that summarizes the operation's profitability for a specific period of time.

Infusion The process by which a flavoring ingredient is left in contact with vodka in a sealed container until the ingredient imparts (infuses) its flavor into the vodka.

Intoxication The physiological state that occurs when a person has a high level of alcohol in his or her blood, also known as *drunkenness* or *inebriation*.

Inventory turnover rate A measure of the frequency with which beverages are ordered and sold.

Jigger A small shot glass–type tool used to accurately measure the amount of alcohol served in drinks, to ensure portion control.

Keg A small barrel used to store beer.

Krausening Adding natural carbonation to beer that results from renewed fermentation.

Labor cost percentage A measure of productivity that expresses labor costs as a percentage of revenue achieved.

Lager A beer with an approximately 4 to 5 percent alcohol content, made with bottom-fermenting yeasts; characterized by a cleaner flavor than ale.

Last call The statement used to notify guests that alcohol service is about to end.

Last in, first out (LIFO) An inventory method that assumes that products most recently purchased are used first. The value of inventory is represented by the unit cost of items in inventory the longest.

Lead time The estimated number of purchase units used between the order and delivery dates.

Legally impaired A blood alcohol content (BAC) of 0.08 or more; it is illegal in all states to operate a motor vehicle at this level.

Liable Legally responsible for the consequences of an action or failure to act.

License state In license states, the state frequently licenses wholesalers, distributors, and sometimes manufacturers to sell alcoholic beverages.

Licensee The entity holding the liquor license.

Lifestyle The patterns in which people live and spend their time and money.

Liqueur A liquor that is bottled with added sugar and added flavorings steeped in it like tea; also known as a **cordial**.

Liquor A distilled alcoholic beverage that contains at least 20 percent alcohol, also referred to as a **spirit**.

Liquor license A document issued by a state that allows for the sale or service of alcoholic beverages.

Malt Cereal grains used as a starch source in beer production; they are first germinated and then dried in a process known as *malting*.

Manual drink production system A system in which skilled bartenders make each drink themselves.

Marketing The formal process of telling and showing customers how their needs and wants will be met by an operation.

Marketing plan A detailed listing of specific activities designed to reach the revenue goals of a beverage operation.

Marketing schedule A schedule that contains three key pieces of information about an operation's marketing activities: what is to be done, when it will be done, and who will do it.

Menu clip-on A smaller menu segment clipped on to a more permanent menu, which can be changed frequently.

Mixed drink A spirit that is combined with one or more other beverages.

Mixers Carbonated beverages, flavorings, fruit and vegetable juices, or dairy products that are ingredients in most mixed cocktails.

Mixology The making of mixed drinks.

Neat A spirit that is served by itself and at room temperature.

Negligent Not exercising reasonable care.

Non-alcoholic (NA) beers Beers that contain less than 0.5 percent alcohol.

No-show (employee) The industry term used to describe an employee who, on a scheduled workday, does not notify a manager that he or she will not be working, and then does not report for the assigned shift.

Oenology The science and study of all aspects of wine and wine making.

On-the-job training Training that occurs when the manager or another trainer teaches job skills and knowledge to one trainee at a time, usually at the work site.

On the rocks A spirit that is served over ice.

Operating budget A financial plan that estimates revenues and expenses for a specific time period.

Order point The estimated number of purchase units used between the order and delivery dates, or lead time, plus the number of units required to maintain the safety level.

Overpour To use more alcohol than allowed by the recipe.

Par stock The amount of a product that should be readily available to bartenders at all times.

Pasteurization Heating to 140°F to 150°F (60°C to 66°C) for a short time period to kill any bacteria and remaining live yeast cells in the beer.

Perpetual inventory A continuous count of the number of items in inventory.

Physical inventory A system in which managers count and record the amounts of each product in storage.

Plaintiff In a lawsuit, the party that claims to have suffered a loss as the result of something the defendant did.

Point of sale (POS) system A system that records and stores a bar's sales, product usage, and other important operating information.

Prohibition The period in U.S. history from 1920 to 1933 following the passage of the Eighteenth Amendment, when the production and consumption of alcoholic beverages was illegal.

Promotion A special incentive for customers to patronize a beverage operation.

Proof The percentage of alcohol in a beverage; the proof of an alcoholic beverage is two times its alcohol content.

Psychographics Market segmentation based on differences in customers' social class, beliefs, attitudes, and other lifestyle factors.

Public accommodation A business that provides eating, sleeping, or entertainment services to the general public.

Public areas The areas within normal view of an establishment's guests.

Public bar The bar over which bartenders directly serve guests.

Public intoxication A state in which an individual who has consumed alcoholic beverages is a danger to himself or herself or others.

Public space Any area in a facility to which guests are routinely permitted access.

Punitive damages Damages awarded in excess of the actual losses suffered by the injured party.

Reasonable care The degree of caution and concern for the safety of others that an ordinarily reasonable, prudent, and rational person would use in the circumstances.

Regulator A gauge attached between the tank of gas and the coupler, which allows the right amount of gas to be released when the beer faucet is opened.

Rosé wine A light red wine whose color is produced by short contact with grape skins.

Rotation The process used to ensure the use of oldest products first by placing all incoming products behind or under those items already in inventory.

Rum A spirit distilled from a fermented sugarcane product, such as molasses; it is perhaps the oldest distilled beverage.

Safety level A minimum inventory level below which inventory should not fall to allow for greater than anticipated sales or longer than anticipated delivery times.

Saké A Japanese brew made from rice, with an alcohol content of 15 to 20 percent.

Sales forecast An estimate of what an operation will sell in a specific future time period.

Sales history A record of drink sales in a given time period.

Semi-dry wine A wine with a 0.8 to 2.2 percent sugar content.

Service bar The area at which service staff pick up drinks to deliver to customers.

ServSafe Alcohol The name of the responsible alcohol server program developed by the National Restaurant Association (NRA).

Shaken cocktail A mixed drink made by using a shaking motion to combine the ingredients.

Shelf life The amount of time a product can be stored under normal conditions and retain its quality.

Shopper Personnel hired to secretly evaluate an operation to make sure procedures are being followed.

Sommelier A service employee with extensive knowledge about wine, including its storage and wine and food pairings.

Sparkling wine Wine that has bubbles caused by the presence of carbon dioxide.

Specialty drink A unique drink developed by an operation to respond to consumer trends or to assist in promoting the image of the operation.

Spirit A distilled alcoholic beverage that contains at least 20 percent alcohol, also referred to as a **liquor**.

Standard drink (spirit) A drink that contains 1.5 fluid ounces (44 milliliters) of a 40 percent (80-proof) spirit.

Standardized recipe Instructions for preparing a food or beverage item that includes the type and amount of ingredients and how they are combined, as well as information about garnishing and serving.

Standard of care The reasonably accepted levels of performance that qualified managers use in fulfilling their duties of care.

Still The device used to distill an alcoholic beverage.

Still wine A nonsparkling wine.

Stirred cocktail A cocktail of two different types: **straight up** is made in a shaker with ice and transferred to a glass without the ice; **on the rocks** is mixed in the service glass with ice, or stirred in a shaker and then transferred to an ice-filled glass.

Straight (drink) A spirit consumed by itself; it may be served chilled, over ice, or at room temperature.

Straight up A spirit that is shaken or stirred with ice, then strained from the ice and served by itself; sometimes used by guests to mean the same as **neat**.

Sweet (wine) A wine with a sugar content of more than 2.2 percent.

Table tent A print advertisement that sits on guest tables.

Target market A market made up of those potential customers whose specific needs and wants an operation seeks to meet.

Tequila A spirit made from the blue agave plant in the area surrounding the Mexican city of Tequila, most often made to achieve a 38 to 40 percent alcohol content (76 to 80 proof).

Third-party liability Liability for damages to an injured third party (who was not involved in the transaction of buying or selling alcohol), which is borne by the first party (the person who consumed the alcohol) and the second party (the person or establishment that served the alcohol).

Transfers Adjustments to initial inventory values that result in increases or decreases in beverage expense to match product costs with the revenue generated by the product's sale.

Unadjusted cost of goods sold The amount of beginning inventory, plus the value of all purchases, minus the amount of ending inventory.

Underpour To use less alcohol than required by the recipe.

Vintage The year in which grapes used to make the wine were grown.

Vodka An odorless and tasteless spirit distilled from fermented grain mash at high proof. In the United States, vodka must contain a minimum alcohol content of 40 percent (80 proof).

Well brand (spirit) The brand of liquor that is served by the operation when the guest does not indicate a preference for a specific brand; also referred to as a **house brand**.

Whiskey (or whisky) A family of brown, or colored, spirits distilled from grain beverages and aged in wood.

Wine An alcoholic beverage produced from fermented fruit, especially grapes.

Wine list A wine menu that informs customers about the wines for sale in an establishment.

Wine steward An employee who assists guests in selecting wines.

Wort A sweet liquid drained from mash and fermented to make beer or whiskey.

INDEX